IARIA

CYBER 2016

The First International Conference on Cyber-Technologies and Cyber-Systems

October 9 - 13, 2016

Venice, Italy

CYBER 2016 Editors

Thomas Klemas, SimSpace Corporation, Boston, USA

Rainer Falk, Siemens AG, Germany

Printed from e-media with permission by:

Curran Associates, Inc.
57 Morehouse Lane
Red Hook, NY 12571

Some format issues inherent in the e-media version may also appear in this print version.

Printed by Curran Associates, Inc. (2016)

International Academy, Research, and Industry Association (IARIA)
412 Derby Way
Wilmington, DE 19810

Phone: (408) 893-6407
Fax: (408) 527-6351

petre@iaria.org

Additional copies of this publication are available from:

Curran Associates, Inc.
57 Morehouse Lane
Red Hook, NY 12571 USA
Phone: 845-758-0400
Fax: 845-758-2633
Email: curran@proceedings.com
Web: www.proceedings.com

TABLE OF CONTENTS

CYBER 1 / CYMADA: CYBER SECURITY ASSESSMENT, RISK MANAGEMENT, TRAINING TECHNOLOGIES AND DATA ANALYTICS

Network Complexity Models for Automated Cyber Range Security Capability Evaluations 1
Thomas Klemas, Lee Rossey
Advanced Swarm Imaging for Three-Dimensional Mapping 7
Martin L. Duncan, Paul D. Weil, Thomas J. Klemas
Cyber Assessor: Assessment Framework to Characterize Cyber Aptitudes 11
Thomas Klemas, Greg Gimler, John Nelson

CYBER 2: CYBER CRIME

Intelligent Data Leak Detection Through Behavioural Analysis 17
Ricardo Costeira, Henrique Santos
Quantifiable Measurement Scheme for Mobile Code Vulnerability Based on Machine-Learned API Features 27
Hyunki Kim, Joonsang Yoo, Jeong Hyun Yi
Single Sign-On Webservice with Adaptable Multi Factor Authentication 29
Sandra Kübler, Christian Rinjes, Anton Wiens, Michael Massoth
Forensic Analysis of the Recovery of Wickr's Ephemeral Data on Android Platforms 35
Thomas Edward Allen Barton, M A Hannan Bin Azhar

CYBER 3: CYBER RESILIENCE

Designing An IEC 61850 Based Power Distribution Substation Simulation/Emulation Testbed for Cyber-Physical Security Studies 41
Eniye Tebekaemi, Duminda Wijesekera
Exchanging Database Writes with Modern Crypto 50
Andreas Happe, Thomas Loruenser
Experiment of Sensor Fault Tolerance Algorithm combined with Cyber System for Coil Tilter on the Smart Hybrid Powerpack 54
Jaegwang Lee, Janggeol Nam, Buchun Song, Hyeonwoo Kim, Iksu Choi, Hunmo Kim
An Approach for Protecting Privacy in the IoT 60
George O. M. Yee

CYBER 4: CYBER SECURITY

Consideration of Security Threats for Identification System in Internet of Things 67
Daewon Kim, Jeongnyeo Kim, Yongsung Jeon
Advanced Device Authentication: Bringing Multi-Factor Authentication and Continuous Authentication to the Internet of Things 69
Rainer Falk, Steffen Fries
Author Index

CYBER 2016

Forward

The First International Conference on Advances in Cyber-Technologies and Cyber-Systems (CYBER 2016), held between October 9 and 13, 2016 in Venice, Italy, was an inaugural event covering many aspects related to cyber-systems and cyber-technologies considering the issues mentioned above and potential solutions. It was also intended to illustrate appropriate current academic and industry cyber-system projects, prototypes, and deployed products and services.

The increased size and complexity of the communications and the networking infrastructures are making it difficult the investigation of the resiliency, security assessment, safety and crimes. Mobility, anonymity, counterfeiting, are characteristics that add more complexity in Internet of Things and Cloud-based solutions. Cyber-physical systems exhibit a strong link between the computational and physical elements. Techniques for cyber resilience, cyber security, protecting the cyber infrastructure, cyber forensic and cyber crimes have been developed and deployed. Some of new solutions are nature-inspired and social-inspired leading to self-secure and self-defending systems. Despite the achievements, security and privacy, disaster management, social forensics, and anomalies/crimes detection are challenges within cyber-systems.

The event was very competitive in its selection process and very well perceived by the international scientific and industrial communities. As such, it has attracted excellent contributions and active participation from all over the world. We were very pleased to receive a large amount of top quality contributions.

The conference had the following tracks:

- Cyber Security Assessment, Risk Management, Training
- Cyber Crime
- Cyber Resilience
- Cyber Security

We take here the opportunity to warmly thank all the members of the CYBER 2016 technical program committee, as well as the numerous reviewers. The creation of such a high quality conference program would not have been possible without their involvement. We also kindly thank all the authors that dedicated much of their time and effort to contribute to CYBER 2016. We truly believe that, thanks to all these efforts, the final conference program consisted of top quality contributions.

Also, this event could not have been a reality without the support of many individuals, organizations and sponsors. We also gratefully thank the members of the CYBER 2016 organizing committee for their help in handling the logistics and for their work that made this professional meeting a success.

We hope CYBER 2016 was a successful international forum for the exchange of ideas and results between academia and industry and to promote further progress in the area of cyber technologies and cyber systems.

We also hope that Venice, Italy, provided a pleasant environment during the conference and everyone saved some time to enjoy the unique charm of the city.

CYBER Advisory Committee

Carla Merkle Westphall, Federal University of Santa Catarina - Florianópolis, Brazil
Mohamed Eltoweissy, Virginia Military Institute and Virginia Tech, USA
Syed Naqvi, Birmingham City University, UK
Thomas Klemas, Sensemaking-PACOM Fellowship & AIRS, Swansea University/Hawaii Pacific University, UK/USA
Rainer Falk, Siemens AG, Germany
Yao Yiping, National University of Defence Technology - Hunan, China
Steve Chan, Sensemaking-PACOM Fellowship & AIRS, Swansea University/Hawaii Pacific University, UK/USA
Jiankun Hu, UNSW-Camberra, Australian Defence Force Academy/Australian Centre for Cyber Security, Australia

CYBER 2016

Committee

CYBER Advisory Committee

Carla Merkle Westphall, Federal University of Santa Catarina - Florianópolis, Brazil
Mohamed Eltoweissy, Virginia Military Institute and Virginia Tech, USA
Syed Naqvi, Birmingham City University, UK
Thomas Klemas, Sensemaking-PACOM Fellowship & AIRS, Swansea University/Hawaii Pacific University, UK/USA
Rainer Falk, Siemens AG, Germany
Yao Yiping, National University of Defence Technology - Hunan, China
Steve Chan, Sensemaking-PACOM Fellowship & AIRS, Swansea University/Hawaii Pacific University, UK/USA
Jiankun Hu, UNSW-Camberra, Australian Defence Force Academy/Australian Centre for Cyber Security, Australia

CYBER 2016 Technical Program Committee

Sherif Abdelwahed, Mississippi State University (MSU) - Distributed Analytics and Security Institute (DASI), USA
Mohamad Badra, Zayed University, UAE
Juan Carlos Bennett, SSC Pacific, USA
Paul Bogdan, University of Southern California, USA
Kevin Borgolte, UC Santa Barbara, USA
Stefano Calzavara, Università Ca' Foscari Venezia, Italy
Steve Chan, Sensemaking-PACOM Fellowship & AIRS, Swansea University/Hawaii Pacific University, UK/USA
Albert M. K. Cheng, University of Houston, USA
Maxim Chernyshev, Security Research Institute - Edith Cowan University, Perth, Australia
Jean Degabriele, Royal Holloway, University of London, UK
Mohamed Eltoweissy, Virginia Military Institute and Virginia Tech, USA
Levent Ertaul, California State University, East Bay, USA
Rainer Falk, Siemens AG, Germany
Francesco Flammini, Ansaldo STS, Italy
Víctor Gayoso Martínez, Spanish National Research Council (CSIC) - Institute of Physical and Information Technologies (ITEFI), Spain
Lorena González-Mazano, University Carlos III of Madrid (UC3M), Spain
Danny Hendler, Ben-Gurion University of the Negev, Israel
Luis Hernandez Encinas, Institute of Physical and Information Technologies (ITEFI) - Spanish National Research Council (CSIC), Spain

Copyright Information

Network Complexity Models for Automated Cyber Range Security Capability Evaluations

Relating Network Complexity to Defensive Difficulty to Enable Comprehensive Evaluation

Thomas J. Klemas and Lee Rossey
SimSpace Corporation
tom@simspace.com

Abstract—**For any organization to maintain a strong cyber security posture, it is important to test readiness and capabilities of cyber security teams and the tools that they use. In order to design and conduct experiments to assess performance of defensive cyber security teams and tools, it is crucial to either ensure the test range accurately represents the real environment in which the defensive teams or tools normally would operate or to ensure that testing is conducted across a suite of test ranges that provides comprehensive coverage of the potential real-life network environments. In this paper, we present a novel network complexity scoring framework that is designed to capture the set of the network attributes that have the principal impact on the performance of defenders and defensive tools and to differentiate networks according to defensive difficulty.**

Keywords – Network; network complexity; network theory, graph theory; degree; connectivity; connectance; centrality; degree centrality; hyper-edge; hypergraph; information theory, eigen decomposition; eigen vector; eigen value; eigen centrality; Bonacich centrality.

I. Introduction

No longer a newly emerging issue, cyber security is a continuing and rapidly growing challenge, facing all organizations, whether small, large, public, or private. Thus, added to conventional risk management, there is an imperative to manage cyber risk by a combination of building and maintaining a strong cyber security readiness posture, as well as other approaches, such as cyber insurance. Cyber security readiness depends on knowledge skills, regular training of cyber security defenders, in addition to the organization's information technology architecture, cyber security policies, enforcement of these policies, defensive technologies, and many other contributing elements of cyber readiness. To train cyber security staff and develop defensive skills, many organizations have initiated regular red-blue challenges, with real or automated "red" cyber adversaries attacking a virtual organization that "blue" cyber defenders are tasked to defend, on cyber ranges that are intended to emulate the organization's real networks. In addition, cyber defensive technology companies validate and demonstrate their tools, similarly, on cyber ranges. In either of these emerging applications, it is critical to develop a notion of the complexity of the network on which the red-blue gaming or performance testing is conducted in order to understand cyber defensive performance.

Many notions of complexity have been explored heretofore and Wikipedia, [11], has a nice overview of several of these, but an immediate observation from examining the Wikipedia page is that there is great variation in the definition across applications. Most specific previous descriptions of complexity and research in modeling network complexity, such as the research presented in [2][3][7], was primarily focused in other application areas either non-specific to or other than cyber security, so that work could not be directly leveraged for our purposes. In addition, a number of the earlier efforts are primarily qualitative in nature, such as [1], and therefore did not align with our objectives for this research. Some previous efforts that were closer to the computer network application area, like [4], either were focused on a different objectives or overly simplified the problem, employing tabular approaches to compute network complexity scores that were too limited to capture subtleties of connectivity between nodes and only allowed a linear type of model, so these methods were insufficient for our purposes. Other methods focused only on a narrow sub-set of aspects of complexity that impact defensive difficulty, ignoring many other important factors, so, again, the limitations of other approaches forced us to explore a new technique to model network complexity. However, despite the various shortcoming enumerated above, many of these antecedent approaches have influenced our efforts.

This paper introduces a hybrid complexity modeling approach that treats the network in a multimodal fashion, encapsulating certain parameter like numbers or operating systems or number of device types hyper edges of a hypergraph, abstracting them as attributes of the associated subnets or the network itself, but maintaining flexibility to model more complicated network properties. Many global network and subnet-specific single-parameter attributes are captured with a tabular method. Concepts of complexity that are distributed in nature, related to connectivity, or describe the balance of a specific property across the network are analyzed using information theoretic and related approaches that better address those concepts. For example, certain aspects of subnet and router topology are better described with information theoretic model and corresponding complexity analysis.

To demonstrate the efficacy and overall utility of our complexity model, we developed numerous networks, some devised on paper and other actual cyber range networks, each emphasizing different network attributes. By analyzing this collection of varied networks, we were able to explore the model behaviors as we vary scoring parameters and confirm that the model parameters and network properties interact in the way that the algorithms were designed. As one of the scored networks, we also examine a virtual, large financial network used for cyber range training of cyber security defenders. For the large financial network case, we developed parsing routines to collect network attribute values from configuration files for the cyber range, demonstrating the potential for automating the complexity computations. This exercise directly supports a future in which the input accumulation, analysis, and complexity scoring can be accomplished by automated tools.

The remainder of this manuscript describes the proposed network complexity model in greater detail and is organized as follows. Section II describes the technical details of our model and how it describes the complexity of a network that pertains to cyber security defensive difficulty. Section III describes the performance and provides results of applying our network complexity model to multiple networks that possess sufficient variety of the values of the attributes that we deemed crucial to network complexity. Section V offers our conclusions. Finally, the acknowledgment and reference sections complete the manuscript.

II. Technical Details

We begin this section by describing the fundamental design of the network complexity model and the notations that we will be using throughout the manuscript. The primary purpose of the network complexity model is to distinguish between different networks in a manner that agrees with intuitive notions of cyber defensive difficulty. As mentioned previously, we have adopted a hybrid approach that includes both tabular and information theoretic components to incorporate contributions from both global single-value attributes and distributed attributes, such as connectivity. Thus, the model is designed with the flexibility to accommodate both linear, weighted combinations of attributes and as well as more complicated functions to describe attribute contributions.

Attributes were selected based on several primary premises. We first considered attributes that describe the scale of the network, including numbers of devices and numbers of accounts. Then, we incorporated attributes that capture complexity in the structure or topology of the network, including organization of subnetworks, router connectivity, multiple security zones, and other similar concepts. Finally, we included attributes that directly impact the level of defensive effort or increase the attack surface.

Table 1, below, enumerates the attributes that comprise our network complexity model. It contains a list of network complexity attributes that contribute to the network complexity algorithm and a rating for the differentiation enabled by that attribute. In addition, table 1 provides a differentiation rating for that attribute's relative contribution to the network complexity algorithm.

TABLE I. NETWORK COMPLEXITY ATTRIBUTES

Attribute	Differentiation
User accounts	1
Machines	1
Operating System	2
Device Types	2
Firewalls	1
Protocols	2
Administrative Domains	2
Key Business Systems	1
External Interfaces	1
Router Connectivity	2
Subnet Size Distribution	1

The differentiation ratings have 2 values, 1 or 2, and indicate the relative differentiation provided by that attribute. Thus, attributes with differentiation rating level 1 contribute to the complexity score in a way that distinguishes between network to a greater degree than level 2 attributes. There are numerous other potential attributes that were deemed of less significance and would provide level 3 or lower of differentiation, and therefore not critical to include in this stage of the network complexity algorithm design.

There is no standard accepted definition of cyber defensive network complexity, so our fundamental goal was simply to design an algorithm that best suits our intended applications, in this case the evaluation of cyber defensive performance of cyber security teams, operators, or tools operating on a network, measured against the complexity of the network. As such, attribute contribution to network cyber complexity was designed to match notions of cyber defensive impact. To accomplish this, multiple iterations of functions were explored to capture the contribution of each attribute. Primarily, three types of functions were utilized to represent complexity attribute contributions. For some attributes, a linear, tabular approach best was able to achieve the desired contribution. In other cases, non-linear functions featuring the product of 2 attributes was most suited to capture the complexity. For yet other attributes, an information theoretic approach is used to map a custom probability function analog to information content, which is used to represent complexity. In most cases, a log scale, either base 2 or 10, is used to transform raw attribute quantities of very different orders of magnitude to similar magnitude ranges and yet retain the desired differentiation.

One of our sub-goals is to assess the structural or topological complexity of a modern day computer network as an element of our overall complexity model. The density of edges or connectivity are concepts that come to mind. They are related to measures of the importance or centrality of the nodes. Centrality measures are commonly used for this purpose, as described in [9] and [5]. Degree centrality, Bonacich centrality, closeness or path centrality, betweenness centrality, eigenvector centrality are well known examples. The degree of nodes in a network is useful to describe connectivity but that may not correspond to defensive complexity. Towards that end, we developed several new concepts for complexity, including hop complexity, subnet complexity, and others.

To measure hop complexity, we adapted an approach utilized in [8]. First, we specify that the hop count corresponds to the number of hops for traffic to traverse the shortest path of the network between a particular vertex and each other vertex in the network. In this complexity sub-model, the aforementioned functional is defined as:

$$g_F(r_i) = \beta^{c_1|S_1(r_i)|+c_2|S_2(r_i)|+\cdots+c_{p_r}|S_{p_r}(r_i)|} \quad (1)$$

The router, r_i, is one of N_r routers in the network. The parameter beta, β,is selected empirically to help differentiate between multiple networks based on hop complexity. The functions $S_m(r_i)$, in the exponent, enumerate the number of routers that can be reached within m hops of router r_i and scale each such hop value tally by a corresponding combining coefficient, c_m. Utilizing the g_f function we can construct a related function p for router r_i as follows:

$$p(r_i) = \frac{g_F(r_i)}{\sum_{j=1}^{N_r} g_F(r_j)} \quad (2)$$

Thus, for beta greater than one, the value will be greater for a router which has more routers that can be reached within a certain hop count, all else remaining the same, and we will use that function p to compute information content [10] of the network, based on the hop complexity, as follows:

$$g_{HC}(\bar{x}) = -\sum_{i=1}^{N_r} p(r_i)log(p(r_i)) \quad (3)$$

We observe that the protocol complexity is a complementary attribute to hop complexity and measures the number of types of traffic traversing the network, so we combine these two attributes in one measure by forming the product. Our intuition suggests that this contribution element is potentially an analog for flow complexity.

The subnet complexity is computed in a similar manner except that the probability function is defined as a simpler and more intuitive ratio of the number of nodes in the subnet divided by the total number of nodes in the network.

$$p(S_i) = \frac{N_{ni}}{N_T} \quad (4)$$

The information content or associated complexity computation is the identical formula as previously used to compute the router connectivity.

$$g_{SNC}(\bar{x}) = -\sum_{i=1}^{N_n} p(S_i)log(p(S_i)) \quad (5)$$

Other attributes contribute to our complexity model through straightforward, tabular functions. For example, this approach is used to capture the complexity associated with the diversity of technology deployed on the network. The distribution of operating systems and device types across the subnets are scaled and summed. A slightly more complicated contribution results from pairs of attributes, such as administrative domains and user accounts, that contribute as a scaled product of the direct values.

Employing the approaches described above, to capture complexity contributions from all the attributes enumerated in table 1, we have developed a network complexity model that provides strong differentiation between networks to enhance scoring of cyber range defensive and offensive testing and war-gaming. In the next section, we will discuss the results of applying the model to a variety of networks of different size, structure, and technological diversity.

III. Results

To explore the ability of the model to distinguish key differences in network structure or other attributes that impact network complexity, we developed more than 10 networks that we modeled and analyzed. The largest network, named the large financial network (LFN) has the largest size, most intricate structure, and generally the high degree of all contributing complexity factors. Following that are three similar networks with 8 routers but differing distributions of machines across subnets and router nodes. Clearly demonstrated throughout the results in this section, the scoring model was designed such that evenly distributed networks contribute the most defensive complexity, whereas the networks with the greatest degree of clustering of machines within fewer subnets pose slightly less defensive complexity. Finally, there are multiple 5 node and 4 node networks arranged with three different connection graphs: all the routers in a line, all the routers connected in a ring, and full connectivity between all the routers. These example networks demonstrate that the networks which require the greatest number of hops for traffic to traverse the network tend to incur a higher score in our cyber defensive complexity model, which matches the design objectives.

In this section, we explore the attribute contributions to the overall cyber network complexity score for each of the test networks. Figure 1 illustrates the hop complexity sub-score generated by our model, measured for each of the test networks.

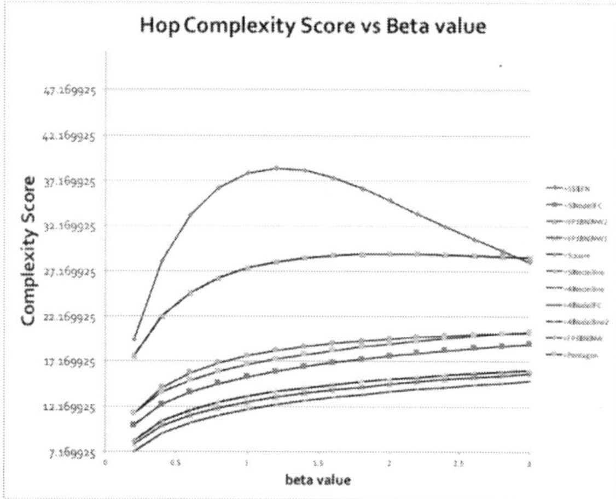

Figure 1: This scatter graph plots the complexity scores, assigned to the selected networks based on the network topology, as measured by hop counts for the various routers, versus the parameter beta. Note that the value 1.2 provides the greatest differentiability.

Since the hop complexity, shown in figure 1, captures topological and structural complexity of the network, captured through a measure of router interconnectivity, we decided to combine hope complexity with the complexity resulting from the number of protocols that must be supported on that very network with the described topology. Thus, figure 2 illustrates the product of hop complexity with protocol complexity

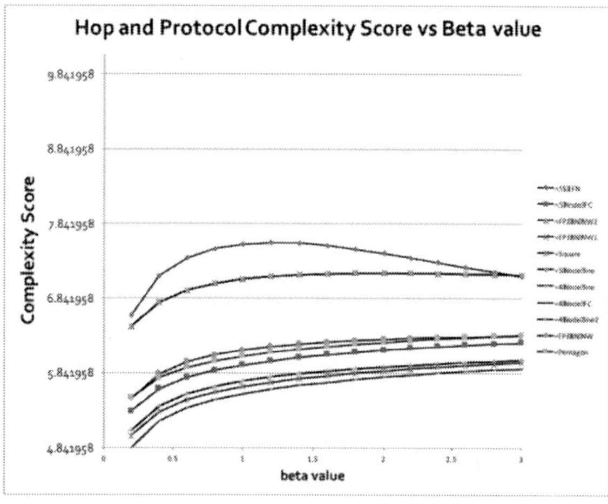

Figure 2: This scatter graph plots the complexity derived from the hop complexity and the protocol traffic traversing the network. It is plotted versus the parameter beta. Note that a beta value of approximately 1.2 provides the maximum differentiability.

As described in the technical details section, the router hop and network protocol derived complexity measures scale with the degree of asymmetry in the distribution of hop complexity across the network routers as well as directly with the number of protocols traversing the network. This relationship is dependent on the parameter beta and as we can see the value 1.2 seems to maximize the differentiability of this complexity measure.

In figures 3 and 4, we can see the influence of the distribution of device types and operating systems in the network. These complexity measures are directly linked to numbers of device types and operating systems, as well as the subnet distribution complexity for these quantities.

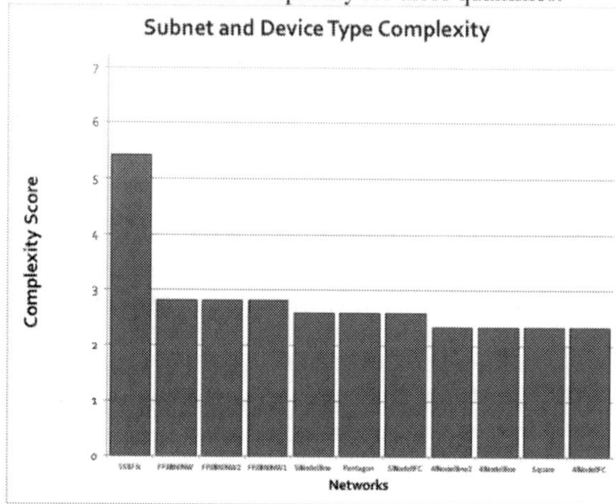

Figure 3: This bar chart shows how subnet and device type complexity impact overall complexity scores for each of the different networks.

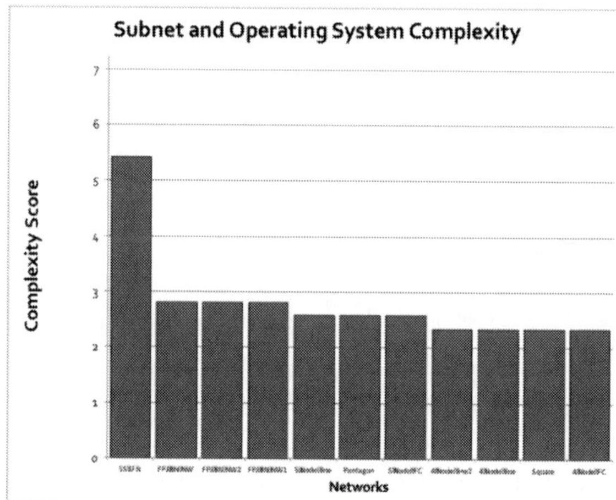

Figure 4: This chart depicts the complexity due to operating systems deployed on the various subnetworks of the network.

The fifth figure presents the complexity associated with firewalls and external interfaces in the network. The subnet complexity sub-score generated by our cyber defensive complexity model is illustrated in figure 6. Notice how the subnet complexity scores scale with the distribution of subnets and machines across the various test networks.

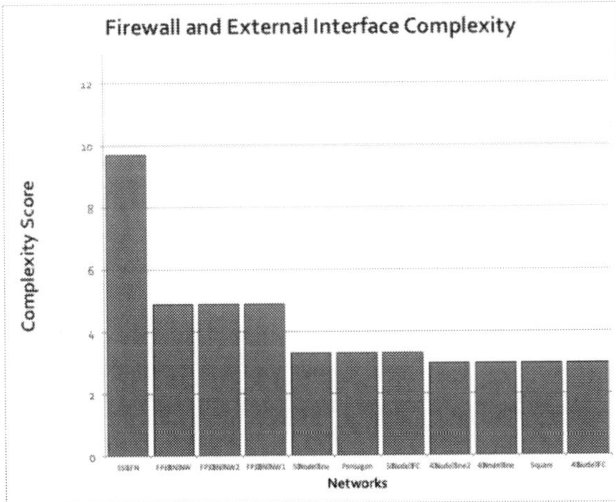

Figure 5: This bar chart shows the complexity derived from firewalls and external interfaces of the overall network.

For example, we see that FPJ 8N NW2 incurs the highest complexity score since it has the most nodes by a significant factor, and those nodes are distributed fairly evenly. Then, FPJ 8N NW1 has the second highest complexity sub-score because it has significantly fewer nodes, but those nodes are arranged evenly. Finally, FPJ 8N NW has the lowest sub-score, because, although it contains the same number of

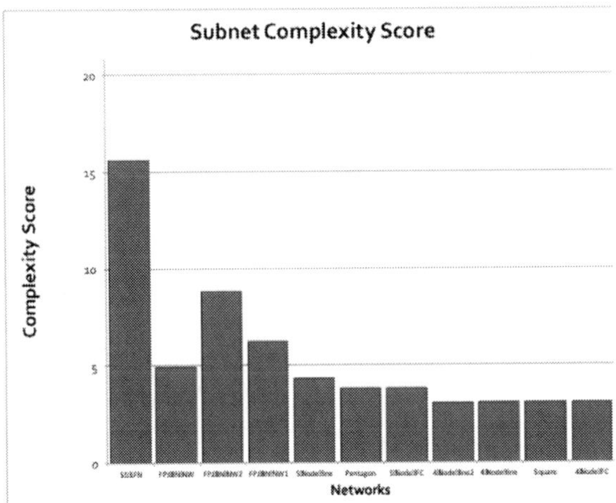

Figure 6: This plot shows scores generated by the subnet functional designed to measure complexity due to topology and machine distribution, based on an information theoretic approach.

nodes as NW1, those nodes are distributed asymmetrically across the subnets of the network, reducing the complexity slightly relative to NW1.

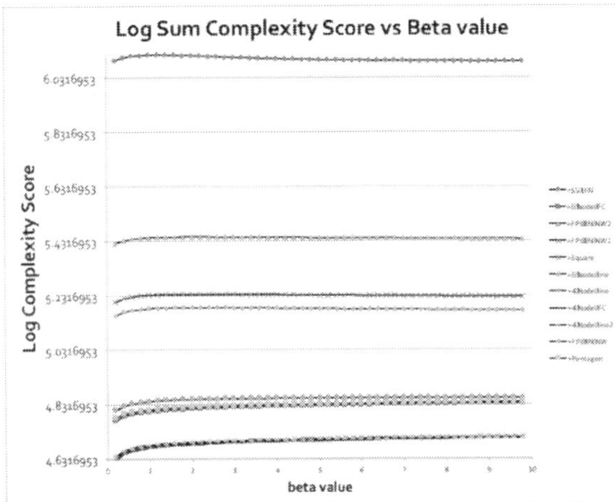

Figure 7: This scatter plot captures the total complexity of the network, summing each of the contributing elements, including hops, protocols, device types, operating systems, administrative domains, user accounts, administrative domains, subnet distribution, and numbers of machines.

Finally, in figure 7, we see a scatter plot showing the overall cyber defensive complexity score computed by superposition of all the complexity model attribute sub-scores. Since the overall scoring model retains the parameter beta, utilized in the hop and protocol complexity sub-model, the overall score is also a function of beta. However, as discussed earlier, a value of approximately 1.2 produced the greatest differentiation between the various test networks. Thus, the overall complexity score would be approximately 6.11 for the LFN network, 5.45 for the FPJ 8N NW2 network, 5.24 for the FPJ 8N NW1 network, 5.19 for the FPJ 8N NW network, 4.85 for the 5 node line network, 4.81 for the 5 node ring network, 4.81 for the 5 node fully connected network, and 4.68 for the 4 node networks.

IV. CONCLUSION

In this research, we have explored the efficacy of using a hybrid approach involving network theory, information theory, and tabular functions to model the cyber defensive complexity of various test networks. The results presented in this paper demonstrate that our model is able to differentiate between a selection of networks with varying attributes. Future work will involve incorporation of new attributes, such as supported applications, inclusion of cloud services, and other features that will enhance the model.

ACKNOWLEDGMENT

The authors would like to thank the SimSpace corporation for presenting us with the opportunity and means to conduct this research and solve this difficult problem and the leadership for sharing insights as to challenges facing the marketplace that we addressed in this research.

References

[1] M. Behringer, "Classifying network complexity", Proceedings of the 2009 workshop on Re-architecting the internet, ACM 978-1-70668-749-3/09/12, pp. 13-18, 2009

[2] D. Bonchev and G. Buck, "Quantitative measures of network complexity," Complexity in Chemistry, Biology, and Ecology, pp. 191-192, 2011.

[3] J. Carlson and J Doyle, "Complexity and robustness", Proceedings of National Academy of Sciences (PNAS), www.pnas.org/cgi/doi/10.1073/pnas.012582499, Vol. 99, Suppl. 1, pp 2538-2545, 2002.

[4] B. Chun, S. Ratnasamy, E. Kohler, "NetComplex: a complexity metric for networked system designs", Proceedings of the 5th USENIX Symposium on Networked Systems Design and Implementation, ISBN: 111-999-5555-22-1, pp. 393-406, 2008.

[5] V. Karyotis, E. Stai, S. Papavassiliou, Evolutionary Dynamics of Complex Communication Networks, CRC Press Taylor & Francis Group, 2014.

[6] T. Klemas and D. Rajchwald, "Evolutionary clustering analysis of multiple edge set networks used for modeling Ivory Coast mobile phone data and sensemaking", Proceedings of Third International Conference on Data Analytics, IARIA, ISBN: 978-1-61208-358-2, pp. 100-104, 2014

[7] M. Mitchell, "Complex systems: network thinking", Elsevier B.V., Artificial Intelligence Vol 170, Iss. 18, pp. 1194-1212, 2006.

[8] T. Moscriboda and R. Wattenhofer, "The Complexity of Connectivity in Wireless Networks", Proceedings of 25th Annual Joint Conference of the IEEE Computer and Communications Societies, INFOCOM, 2006.

[9] M. Newman, Networks, An Introduction. Oxford: Oxford University Press, 2010.

[10] C. Shannon, "A mathematical theory of communication", The Bell Systems Technical Journal, Vol 27, pp. 379–423; 623–656, Oct. 1948.

[11] Wikipedia Community, "Complexity", Wikipedia, https://en.wikipedia.org/wiki/Complexity, 2002.

Advanced Swarm Imaging for Three-Dimensional Mapping

Martin Duncan
University of North Carolina-Wilmington
U.S.A.
E-mail: duncanm@uncw.edu

Paul Weil
Pluribus Technologies, Incorporated
Lafayette, California, U.S.A.
E-mail: dark.illuminations@gmail.com

Thomas Klemas
Sensemaking-PACOM Fellowship
Cambridge, Massachusetts, U.S.A.
E-mail: tklemas@alum.mit.edu

***Abstract*—The richness of detail and ease of usage of three-dimensional mapping has grown by leaps and bounds, but the equipment to create these images is very expensive to purchase and use. Inspired by the Internet-of-Things, Pluribus Technologies has developed a novel imaging approach that combines cybernetics and a plethora of tiny, inexpensive sensors with cloud-based data streaming, Web service and API-based image manipulation software, and cutting-edge Web technologies to enable advanced data visualization and imaging capabilities for numerous applications which previously were cost prohibitive or impossible due to practical limitations of size or space. This system repurposes pre-existing hardware and software components to transmit many streams of low-resolution visual data to a cloud-based server. These streams can be composed into a single detailed 3D image, which can then be viewed, downloaded, or edited collaboratively in real-time 3D on a Web-based client application. Swarm Imaging is achieved through potentially disposable components mounted on an aggregate of mobile units with a modern user interface for the client. Data can then be analyzed from images obtained in physical areas where humans do not wish to, or cannot, venture. Users will benefit from an end result of viewable, manipulable images processed using a high quality Web application client functioning on any device equipped with an A-grade browser. This invention will provide unprecedented terrestrial visualization for purposes of remote data analysis and sensemaking.**

***Keywords: Swarm Imaging; Internet-of-Things; cloud services; digital imaging; mapping; data visualization; high-resolution 3D imaging; Web services; APIs; sensemaking*.**

I. Introduction

When data sets are extremely large, very complex, or the data is changing rapidly, analysis requirements exceed the capacity of most humans. Analysis reaches a complexity and throughput level at which humans are unable to consider the full scope of the data and lack the capacity to keep up, derive insights, and make decisions. In today's world of increasingly smart and interconnected systems, more and more sensors are deployed in civilian, medical, industrial, and military systems. Almost every object used at home or in the workplace contains some form of embedded microchip. The rise of wireless technologies such as Bluetooth and WiFi promotes ever more frequent networking of these devices within programming (automation), monitoring, and remote control. These networks furthermore facilitate software updates, enable interactivity, and enable related objectives. This Internet-of-Things, or IoT, allows much richer and smarter applications in new technology. A well-known example is the Google Nest family of products, allowing such innocuous consumer electronics as a thermostat controller, a smoke/CO alarm, and an indoor/outdoor Web camera to communicate with each other and provide rich aggregate data to home or business owners via Web application. The user monitors and controls the home or office facility on the basis of rich data composited from simple sensors. The trend that all of our possessions can "talk" to each other, from our car to our phone to our wristwatch to our refrigerator, allows for a sort of collective intelligence capable of learning and adapting to users' needs [1].

The emergence of the IoT, as well as increasingly inexpensive 3D printers, has driven the creation of relatively cheap circuit boards for use among a grassroots community of "Makers" who represent a new open-source hardware movement similar to the open source or free software movement that was prominent during the early days of computing. More and more people are building their own devices and robots and programming them using a variety of languages from their personal computers. There are "Maker Faires," or conventions, and people share designs over the Internet, with downloadable specifications and projects analogous to allowing other developers to copy or fork projects on GitHub. President Obama has even created a Federally funded America Makes program. All of this promotes the creation of simple devices and sensors pooling data to deliver much more detailed and robust results. Makers use inexpensive, easily programmable circuit boards and sensors to create their own smart devices [2].

State-of-the art 3D cameras are bulky and expensive, and drones can be used to map a large area in 3D, but they are noisy, cumbersome and hindered by heavy cameras. The method proposed here provides visual data processing that synthesizes the fundamentals of remote imaging, access, and data visualization, implemented in a Web application that facilitates surveillance from multiple angles or manipulation of the image. The Pluribus cybernetic swarm system is intended as a wholly more efficient alternative to 3D cameras, regardless of their attachment to drone vehicles. Furthermore, we anticipate demand for our apparatus in many problem spaces currently underserved by 3D remote imaging technology.

Inspired initially by the theories and practical applications of evolutionary psychologist Steven Pinker [3] and artificial intelligence researcher David H. Freeman [4], the Pluribus Technologies research & development effort has initiated the practical implementation of their ideas by leveraging multiple, advantageous, emerging technologies. The ubiquity of "smart" household items and the demand of Maker Movement hobbyists and developers has driven the creation of miniature circuit boards which can run JavaScript, tiny video and audio sensors, and miniature WiFi transmitters. A need to transmit and aggregate multiple real-time data streams has led to businesses providing these services as a specialty. Three-D imaging industry leader AutoDesk has reimplemented many software products as the cloud-based Forge Platform, a set of Web services, APIs, and SDKs, which allows easy, granular use of their various software features in both the Web browser and the IoT [5].

The ongoing Pluribus R&D utilizes currently available software and hardware components modified minimally for Swarm Imaging objectives. Rather than reinvent the wheel, Pluribus Technologies has assembled many sorts of existing puzzle pieces together in an innovative systems architecture – rather than simply building yet another wheel, the intent is to create an entirely new luxury vehicle from existing parts. Additionally, this approach prioritizes the low price point of Swarm Imaging, and the ability to obtain images from spaces which are impossible or impractical to access with drones and/or 3D cameras, as the key to eventual marketing. The intended data visualization strategy optimizes and synthesizes the best aspects of low-cost cybernetic and sensing hardware components, JavaScript-driven swarm artificial intelligence, inexpensive and fast data streaming services, cloud-based Web services and APIs, and cutting-edge, browser-based Web technologies. This paper presents the pragmatic potential of these technologies employed in concert, and demonstrates a new way to see and make sense of the world.

The remainder of this manuscript is arranged as described herein. Section II describes the technical details of the 3D cloud-based Web services visualization aspect of Swarm Imaging. Section III provides a brief review of prototype specifications and potential applications of Swarm Imaging. Section IV offers our conclusions and anticipation of the benefits of Swarm Imaging. Finally, the acknowledgment and reference sections complete the manuscript.

II. Technical Details

Perhaps the most important consequence of the Maker Movement is the availability of inexpensive circuit boards with pared down versions of the Linux operating system, capable of running NodeJS, a server-side version of JavaScript. This is desirable for two reasons: JavaScript is a Lambda language descended in large part from the Artificial Intelligence (AI) programming language LISP, and JavaScript is the de facto language of the Web. In 2016, most data is transmitted using JSON, a JavaScript-native format, rather than XML. This will simplify the interoperability of the various components of the Pluribus system architecture; a swarm is, in a way of thinking, a distributed AI.

Another consequence of demand from Makers is the availability of microsensors such as tiny cameras and microphones. For example, the Jtron camera for Arduino costs around five US dollars; Adafruit makes an omnidirectional microphone the size of an aphid for less than $1; and Geeetech offers a very advanced motion detector that is about the size of a dime and which sells in the vicinity of $7. Particle makes a WiFi transmitter about the size of a fingernail and at a cost of approximately $10. The Kinoma chip runs JavaScript natively and is also the size of a fingernail, and comes with a simple SDK which can be used to program the chip wirelessly. The small dimensions of these components are the key to their portability, affordability and disposability. The Maker Movement has inspired Pluribus Technologies to an assertive feat of engineering in the service of data analysis. The array of microsensors to be mobilized on our platform is intended to maximize imaging capability. Although the number of sensors may vary, and their mobility may suggest erratic data, this concept is meant to ensure a single, detailed image that may be altered to the degree the user so chooses.

This proliferation of small, simple, and inexpensive off-the-shelf or custom components, combined with easy data streaming, cloud-based 3D editing and rendering Web services, and advanced front-end Web data visualization technology enables data collection from many low-resolution sources positioned around a space. These many streams can subsequently be received and relayed by a Web application running on a tablet device, unified via one of many free or low-cost data streaming and aggregation network services, and delivered to a cloud-based server. On the server, image manipulation Web services can be invoked on these input streams to create a single high-resolution, 3D image, which can then be returned to a Web application running in a browser. The image can then be further viewed and manipulated in the browser by providing Ux controls which invoke image manipulation APIs, permitting real-time collaboration and subsequent output of the file to one of the many popular 3D image formats.

According to Dr. Jingyi Yu of University of Delaware, to obtain photorealistic three-dimensional video images requires 28 sensors [6]. However, to compose a still 3D image from multiple sources could be done with as few as six sensors; the more sensors that can be deployed, the higher the resulting image's resolution and fine detail. The Pluribus camera sensors will be distributed throughout the space in order to provide as many points of view (POVs) as possible within the constraints of a given application. While the cameras will record only what falls within the lens compass, a dynamic image is nevertheless attained as the mobile units' programming orients and drives the collective's movement within the space. Their circuit boards will run JavaScript code that can package the sensor data into data streams, and use a WiFi chip to transmit the streams of data to a JavaScript client Web application running on a tablet device. The client application will relay the streams via a streaming aggregation service to the Pluribus servers, which will run NodeJS software that can call Forge Web services to compose a single 3D image from the streams. The Pluribus Web servers will serve the resulting image to the client application on the tablet, which will invoke APIs, also provided by Forge.

Swarm Imaging will leverage key concepts from neural network approaches to maximize swarm capabilities at a reduced computational cost. The capacity to engage multiple mobile sensors working in concert reduces the cost overall and minimizes the compromise in case of lost or destroyed units. The units will be small enough to be deployed in places not commonly accessible to drone or human entry.

Another novel feature of the Swarm approach is scalability. In case a rough image is all that is required, perhaps only six Pluribus sensor units need be activated. It is true that they could gather more POVs and therefore more detailed images over time; however, battery life would be a limiting factor in this employment. Certainly the more units engaged, the more POVs there will be to stream, and so it will be possible to get increasingly higher resolution images in real time by deploying a larger Swarm to a single location.

The resulting user interface of the Web application will include controls to rotate, edit, share, and export the resulting image file, in real time. The real-time streaming of data should allow for updates to render a progressively more detailed 3D image. From movies to animation, from art to architecture, the plethora of Autodesk products are ubiquitous in use. Forge allows the exporting of files to any Autodesk products' format, so users can leverage their existing software skills to consume and make use of the image as part of their existing workflow. A collaboration feature will allow sharing of the same file in the Pluribus Web application, so multiple users can make edits to the same file concurrently.

III. APPLICATION

There are already companies with offerings in this space, but Pluribus Technologies targets several applications to suit potential users discouraged by the cost and glacier paced image creation of common 3D cameras. An intrepid surveyor would certainly risk sophisticated gear--not to mention life and limb--trying to map a sewer system, for example, but could complete the task somehow. Similarly, drones can carry a 3D camera and map areas outdoors with great precision. These are, however, ill-suited for inspecting for mold or rot between roofing tiles and damage to building foundations.

The Pluribus sensors are estimated to have a production cost and sale price sufficiently low so as to make them potentially disposable. Users can be confident of acquiring a highly effective data analysis apparatus without breaking a budget or being burdened with high maintenance expenses.

Pluribus technology is conceived to leave a light footprint as a terrestrial, mobile system that delivers a flexible imaging/mapping capability. This economical solution should appeal to a variety of users seeking crucial vantage and advantage.

- Architects and designers can use it to create detailed topographical plans to aid their spatial conception, for example determining what set of furnishings will fit best into a room. The room view can be rotated or exported for editing. Most professionals in this area are using Autodesk products already, so swarm imaging will interface well with their workflow.
- City, State, and Federal agencies could use it for infrastructural planning, mapping out old, forgotten sewer systems and subway tunnels. These architects and engineers also overwhelmingly use Autodesk products.
- Real estate sellers could use it to create interactive maps of their properties; buyers would have the option to inspect the building for structural weaknesses, damage hidden out of sight, termite infestations, and so on.
- There are potential uses as stealth technology for military apps, especially scouting ahead for enemy combatants and explosive devices. Areas could also be cleared of landmines left behind from prior conflicts.
- Likewise, police might deploy the system for surveying hostage situations, a scenario during which speed, silence and low visibility are essential for saving lives.
- The Pluribus imaging architecture will be especially well-suited for search and rescue because the Swarm can be released into small, compressed areas such as a collapsed tunnel or ruined building. We can only imagine how many people may have been located with the tireless swarm imaging tool after the earthquake last month in central Italy.

IV. CONCLUSION

Swarm Imaging provides a solution to some of the most challenging problems in data analytics today. This technology is capable of putting "eyes" into an unprecedented assortment of spaces, from the mundane area under your floorboards to the menace lurking around the corner, at the bottom of a dark stairwell, or just over the next ridge. The finely-grained architecture of Pluribus technology also works fast, providing the user a sensemaking tool responsive to rapidly changing circumstances. Whatever the nature of the business during a particular operation, Swarm Imaging executes the visual groundwork so that users can concentrate on what cannot be automated, the analysis that demands human intelligence.

Furthermore, Pluribus Technologies' emphasis on this invention's relatively low cost that makes it possible to put it in the hands of hardworking professionals who want to conduct their survey accurately at an affordable price point, to make it available for civil services charged with the quality of our community infrastructures and preservation of life, to add it to the arsenal of military and police forces so that men and women in uniform can feel more confident of success and survival on dangerous missions. From these many needs comes one visionary technology soon to be available for customers with the greatest need to see and make sense of the twenty-first century.

ACKNOWLEDGMENT

The authors would like to thank Wendy Chan, Michael Estes, Kathy Kang, Jennifer Chu, Laura Lee, Gurpreet Singh, and Laurie Taylor-Jackson for their input, support, diligence and determination in establishing our company and contributing to the Swarm Imaging model. We are also grateful to the Autodesk Forge team and the Maker Movement for providing market impetus for the components that make this possible. Thanks to Dr. Peter Weil for his invaluable suggestions and feedback during our conference preparation.

REFERENCES

[1] C. Perera, C. H. Liu, S. Jayawardena, and M. Chen, "A Survey on Internet of Things From Industrial Market Perspective," IEEE Access, vol. 2, pp.1660-1679, 2014 doi: 10.1109/ACCESS.2015.2389854

[2] D. Dougherty, "The Maker Movement," Innovations, vol. 7.3, pp. 11-14, 2012.

[3] S. Pinker, "The Cognitive Niche: Coevolution of Intelligence, Sociality, and Language," Proceedings of the National Academy of Sciences of the United States of America, vol. 107 (Supplement 2), pp. 8993-8999, 2010.

[4] D.H. Freeman, "Quantum Consciousness," Discover, p. 90, 1994.

[5] "Forge platform: the future of making things," Retrieved September 4, 2016, from https://developer.autodesk.com/

[6] J. Yu, L. McMillan, and P. Sturm, "Multiperspective Modeling, Rendering, and Imaging," Computer Graphics Forum, vol. 29.1, pp. 227–246, 2010.

Cyber Assessor: Assessment Framework to Characterize Cyber Aptitudes

A Multi-Tiered, Semi-Automated Tool for Easing Critical Organizational Challenges

Thomas J. Klemas
SimSpace Corporation
tom@simspace.com

Abstract—**Hiring, re-vectoring, and training of employees are tasks that pose an extreme challenge for Cybersecurity Officers in many organizations, and the cost of mistakes is high. As a result, some cybersecurity managers only hire personnel that they or their trusted subordinates know personally. Others are faced with insurmountable staffing deficits and must invest a nontrivial amount of subject matter experts' time and attention to aid in finding the few strong candidates from among the mass of applicants. Similar challenges complicate cross-vectoring and training of employees. In this paper, we present a semi-automated, multi-tiered platform named Cyber Assessor, which is designed to evaluate a candidate's general and specific knowledge, skills, reasoning, critical thinking, and problem solving ability. Cyber Assessor leverages advanced data analytics to achieve full mapping of performance to specialty sub-categories and thereby enable detailed understanding of an individual's areas of strength and limitations.**

***Keywords** – data analytics; cybersecurity; cybersecurity assessment; risk management; NIST; FFIEC; NERC.*

I. Introduction

There are numerous guidance documents from governmental authorities and works in the literature that describe approaches for assessment of cybersecurity for organizations, similar to [1], [2], and [3]. However, a key component of organizational cybersecurity is related to the cybersecurity operators that defend the organization and determining their level of skill and experience is not so straightforward. All organizations, commercial and government, large and small, face the challenge of hiring, re-vectoring, and training personnel for their job specialties.

This personnel challenge seems to be compounded enormously in the field of Cybersecurity, due to the field's emergence to priority and its rapid growth. Many organizations cannot hire fast enough, and when they try to accelerate their hiring, they frequently must expend even more resources to deal with the consequences of rushed hiring decisions. Two other strongly related challenges include cross-vectoring of candidates from related fields (i.e. Information Technology) into the best matching Cybersecurity specialty, as well as allocating resources for proficiency and currency training of existing cybersecurity professionals.

Suboptimal decisions in response to these critical needs can waste scarce resources and severely escalate an organizations' cybersecurity risk. Furthermore, there are two significant, additional, and frequently overlooked impacts on resources: (1) At some point, technical staff much be engaged to interview and evaluate technical candidates, either for new hire or cross-vectoring. In many organizations, a combined effort of human resources personnel and managers is utilized to screen applications and select the candidates for interview. Subsequently, most organizations then schedule technical staff that are best suited to interview the candidate in question. Unfortunately, many weak candidates slip through the human resources/management filter, and the interview process can be time-consuming and siphons the attention and time of technical experts from their primary duties. (2) Lacking any fine-grained understanding of the workforce members' expertise, training managers typically adopt a one-size-fits-all training approach. Everyone is given all training, whether or not they need it. Frequently, this sort of untargeted, carpet-bomb-approach training is also watered down so it can fit in limited time windows and the result is both less effective and partially squandered because it includes a large fraction of employees that already understand the subject matter.

The Cyber Assessor (CA) approach and technology that we present in this paper has been designed to efficiently assess an individual, to resolve the challenges discussed in the earlier paragraphs, and to provide advanced characterization of examinee skills, capabilities, general and specialty knowledge, reasoning, critical thinking, problem solving, and persistence. Cyber Assessor achieves these core capabilities, in part, through its multi-tiered design. A powerful innovation introduced with the tiered approach of the Cyber Assessor platform is the addition of multiple dimensions, each of which measures different components an examinee's ability. The capture of multi-dimensional measurements dramatically expands the Cyber Assessor system's capability to differentiate examinees, which directly enables greater insight to improve decision making.

In a previous paper, [6], the first author presented data analytic approaches that were designed to "identify important but non-evident structural groupings, resolve community clusters, develop insights based on the evolving structure and associated history, and to make sense of the raw data, the ultimate objective for Sensemaking technologies." The Cyber Assessor design team has taken a similar approach in developing advanced analytics to characterize the performance of Cyber Assessor examinees and is currently proceeding to design enhanced automation for analysis and to maximize efficiency of exam report content generation.

Cyber Assessor incorporates a relational database design that supports full mapping of every fine-grained sub-measure, whether it is a question, exercise, or complex lab problem, to every specialty category and subcategory for which it probes examinee ability or knowledge, across an arbitrary number of customer specified specialty classification systems. Current classification systems include SimSpace specialty categories, government categories, and custom customer categories. Thus, assessment reporting can be tailored to the customer's desired specialty description system and will generate a full characterization of examinee performance across every customer requested specialty categorization. This mapping and characterization capability is especially useful to understand an examinee's areas of strength and limitations, improving hiring decisions and enabling highly targeted training or retraining for maximum efficiency and improvement.

The remainder of this manuscript is arranged as described herein. Section II describes the technical details of the Cyber Assessor platform and how it achieves its objectives. Section III provides a brief description of the types of data products and a sample of result charts that are included in the evaluation report and illustrates with example examinee performance results how key insights are produced from data analytics. Section IV summarizes the key benefits of this technology and approach. Finally, the acknowledgment and reference sections complete the manuscript.

II. TECHNICAL DETAILS

The Cyber Assessor system incorporates a number of innovations that enable it to achieve a high level of examinee differentiation and deliver actionable insights to support decision making for critical actions like hiring, re-vectoring, and training. First, the CA platform consists of multiple tiers, depicted in Fig. 1, below.

Tier 1 is intended to test general knowledge, computer science, and cyber aptitude and intellectual curiosity. Tier 2 is focused on evaluating an individual's specialty knowledge in cyber subtopics, reasoning, and critical thinking. Tier 3 challenges the examinee's cyber related skills and capabilities via a series of practical lab-type problems presented in a web-based format. Finally, Tier 4 is designed to challenge and assess an individual examinee's cyber skills and capabilities on the SimSpace cyber range, which can also be used for training "near the job" or "on the job".

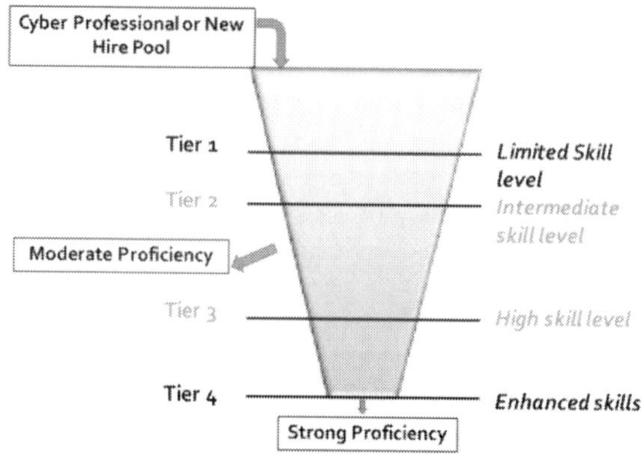

Figure 1: This figure is intended to help the reader visualize the multi-tiered structure of the Cyber Assessor platform. We highlight the Tier 2 and Tier 3 systems in green color because this paper will focus on the results and insights possible with just these 2 tiers.

Because the measures comprising each tier have key properties that are distinct from the measures of the other tiers, it is useful to think of each tier as an axis spanning a different dimension of the overall cybersecurity mastery space. The combination of the examinee performance at each tier forms a multi-dimensional score vector, as in equation 1.

$$\overline{v_{SC}} = \begin{bmatrix} v_{SC_1} \\ \vdots \\ v_{SC_5} \end{bmatrix} \quad (1)$$

It is instructive to decompose examination results to understand how the various tier 1 through 5 components contribute to describe an examinee's cybersecurity mastery. Furthermore, the CA architecture makes it possible to essentially transform coordinate systems by leveraging measure or question mappings to re-characterize examinee performance in terms of job specialty categories. This transformation starts from the individual measures or questions that comprise a particular tier scoring element. We will illustrate this transformation from tier 2 results to job specialty categories with equations 2 and 3 below. First, we show that the second element of the score arises from the tier 2 vector of measure scores which comprise scores from N_q questions in tier 2.

$$v_{SC_2} = \|\overline{v_{T2}}\| \quad (2)$$

$$\overline{v_{T2}} = \begin{bmatrix} v_{T2_1} \\ \vdots \\ v_{T2_{N_q}} \end{bmatrix} \quad (3)$$

Our goal is to transform this tier 2 measure vector into a vector of N_J job specialization category sub-scores that characterize the performance across the categories, as illustrated in equation 4.

$$\overline{v_{J2}} = \begin{bmatrix} v_{J2_1} \\ \vdots \\ v_{J2_{N_J}} \end{bmatrix} \quad (4)$$

To describe this characterization, we can leverage the transformation matrix, $\overline{\overline{M_{J2}}}$, which represents the mappings that comprise the relational database linkages between the measures and specialty categories, as illustrated in equation 5.

$$\overline{v_{J2}} = \overline{\overline{M_{J2}}}\,\overline{v_{T2}} \qquad (5)$$

Thus, with the approach shown above, it is straightforward to transform results between multiple job characterization specialty axes. The value of designing the platform for easy transformation of this kind can be visualized in figure 2 below.

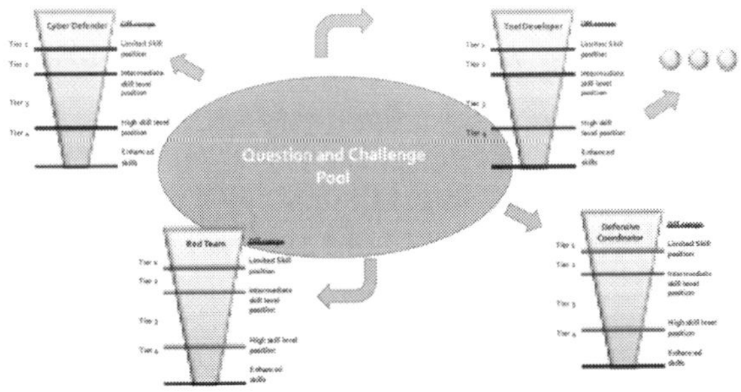

Figure 2: This figure depicts the customization enabled by flexible job specialization category mappings. A customer can identify broader job categories in which they wish to hire employees and the system will characterize performance relative to those custom job categories.

By constructing an exam with a superset combination of questions to cover every specialty category that comprises each of the broader jobs featured in Fig. 2, above, the transformations described above will be of great benefit determining a candidate's suitability for those jobs. In addition, once candidate results for multiple Tier exams are collected, it may be possible to study correlations and develop predictive tools that estimate a candidate's ability to perform on Tier 4 challenges, based simply on Tier 1 and 2 results. While this prediction approach may not be suitable for in-house candidates, in which significant resources are being invested, it can save significant resources during hiring. We also hope that these sorts of cyber assessor platform results may also enable managers to compose balanced and effective cyber teams.

The design of the measures, exercises, questions, problems also represents an area of departure from traditional knowledge retention focused approaches and an area of Cyber Assessor innovation. Although the Tier 1 and 2 exams are presented as multiple choice problems, all of Cyber Assessor's measures, exercises, questions, and problems at all Tiers were designed to probe into the examinee's fundamental skills and reasoning ability. Cyber Assessor primarily accomplishes this by posing complex challenges and evaluating the critical thinking and approach used to solve them, rather than focusing on assessing the examinee's ability to recall basic facts.

The cyber assessor analytics engine can utilize additional information about each examinee, obtained through a demographics survey, to further determine the extent of the examinees' background, level of training, and expertise and to correlate this information with exam results. The demographic survey is intended to capture relevant information pertaining to examinee backgrounds that could elucidate their performance. Towards this end, the demographic survey poses a series of questions that probe the examinee's educational background, years of interest in cybersecurity related topics years of experience in information technology, cybersecurity and various other broader areas, years of experience in a variety of narrower specialization areas, self-assessment of expertise in a variety of specialization areas, and additional accreditations or certifications that the examinee may have obtained.

The Cyber Assessor design tags each exam and each demographic survey with additional metadata that simultaneously provides their username, protects employee identity, and also link every Tier exercise and survey that the examinee completes. In this manner, it is possible to associate all of the results with the described metadata and other mappings, and these relationships are maintained in the relational database design. Furthermore, the linkages are available to the analytics engine that processes the exams, assesses performance, and characterizes the result across specialization category mappings. This capability is powerful, because frequently, it is the combination of all the available tier scoring elements with the demographic information that provides the final leap of insight as to an examinee's overall subject mastery.

The mappings illustrated in Fig. 3, below, reveals how the questions, challenges, and exercises that compose the Cyber Assessor exams and mappings encoded in the relational database are utilized by the analysis engine to characterize examinee performance across job specialty categories. The sub-result from each Cyber Assessor problem at any Tier is decomposed into that problem's contributions to each aptitude or job specialty job category, based on the relational database mappings. Thus each, examinee's results are decomposed and remapped to job specialty category sub-scores, in this example Specialty 1, Specialty 2, and each of the remaining Specialties up to Specialty N. This powerful capability enables the kind of advanced and detailed insight required to directly support leadership decision making and improve organizational cybersecurity outcomes.

III. Reporting, Example Results, and Insights

To evaluate the efficacy of our algorithms we conducted numerous Cyber Assessor engagements. The data collected from these engagements confirmed the effectiveness of the core capabilities that we designed into the Cyber Assessor platform. In this section, we utilize example data to share the insights with the reader. This example data was generated artificially to avoid sharing customer data that would compromise privacy of individuals. However, the examples were carefully designed to illustrate the identical insights that we have previously achieved during the real customer engagements.

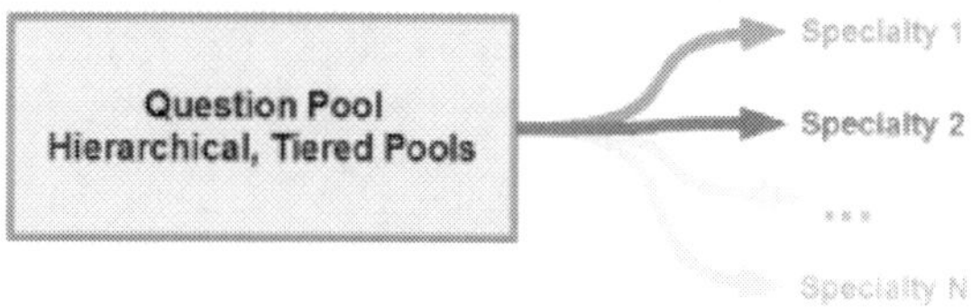

Figure 3: This figure illustrates the mapping between questions and a system for performance characterization that enables mapping to aptitude or job specialization categories. Each question is mapped to all of the categories to which it pertains.

Fig. 4, below, plots the performance distribution of examinee results from a fake organization artificially generated for this demonstration of the Cyber Assessor reporting and insight capabilities. Examinee 1 scored 100 on Tier 3 and 90 or Tier 2. Examinee 2 scored 33 on Tier 3 and 55 on Tier 2. Examinee 3 scored 59 on Tier 3 and 43 on Tier 2. Examinee 4 scored 70 on Tier 3 and 49 on Tier 2. Exam taker 5 scored 63 on Tier 3 and 33 on Tier 2. Exam taker 6 scored 100 on Tier 3 and 85 on Tier 2. Examinee 7 scored 43 on Tier 3 and 33 on Tier 2. Examinee 8 scored 22 on Tier 3 and 100 on Tier 2. Examinee 9 scored 100 on Tier 3 and 88 on Tier 2.

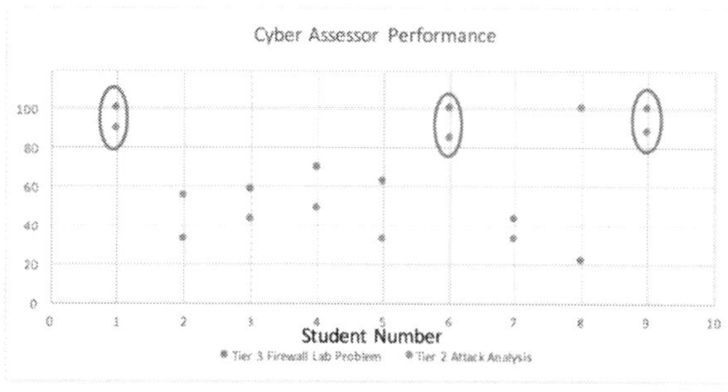

Figure 4: This charts depicts example performance data of 9 students who each took 2 exams, Tier 2 and Tier 3, is marked with green circles to indicate strong performers within the examinee distribution. These examinees, students 1, 6, and 9, performed well in both the Tier 2 knowledge and reasoning as well as the Tier 3 practical Firewall lab problem.

Since they achieved high scores in both the Tier 2 and Tier 3 Cyber Assessor platforms, this chart clearly reveals Examinees 1, 6, and 9 are high performers that demonstrated strong specialty knowledge, reasoning, skills, and problem solving, and these scores have been circled in green to highlight this insight for the reader. If these examinees were applicant candidates for hire or if these examinees were information technology specialists that were candidates for revectoring into cybersecurity, the decision maker could proceed to the next step, such as interview, with high confidence. Another potential use case: If this exercise was administered as an annual proficiency check, the leadership might consider to review these examinees as candidates for any available promotions or fast-track career programs.

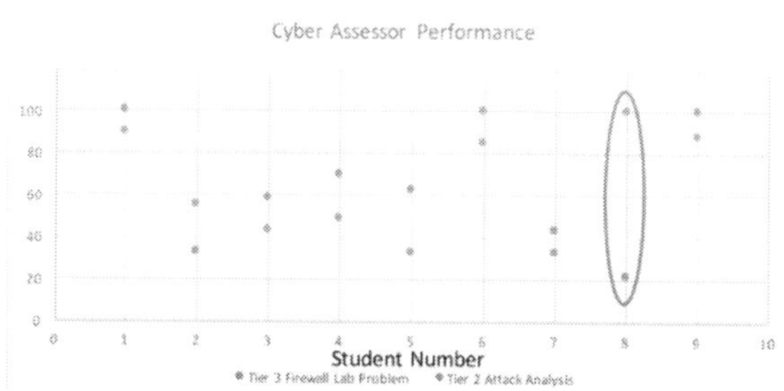

Figure 5: Sample Cyber Assessor performance data set is marked with red circle to indicate a candidate for hands-on training. Student 8 performed well on the Tier 2 knowledge and reasoning intensive exam but did not complete the practical firewall lab problem, receiving little credit.

Figure 5 represents the same results as figure 4 but is included separately to focus on an apparent anomaly that is observed in examinee 8's scores, which are circled in red to highlight this result for the reader. Examinee 8 scored a perfect 100 on the Tier 2 multiple choice knowledge and reasoning intensive exam but scored poor, only achieving 22, on the Tier 3 firewall problem solving lab exercise. This case is highly representative, not all that unusual, and is observed in customer engagements more frequently than one might initially expect. To the first glance this result seems inconsistent and it seems strange that an individual would demonstrate a high level of mastery of knowledge and reasoning and yet perform well below average in executing some of the skills that fall within his or her knowledge area.

There are several potential hypotheses that immediately come to mind when viewing the result in Fig. 3: (1) The topic of the Tier 3 exam was outside of the Examinee's expertise area. (2) The examinee was interrupted or distracted during Tier 3 exam. (3) The examinee knows a lot about his or her specialty area and has good reasoning but is very rust at actually doing things in a hands-on setting. (4) The examinee actually understood the Tier 3 problem but simply made a typo-type mistake. Several of these hypotheses, 2 and 4, can be discounted immediately by deeper dive into Cyber Assessor. Examinee exam actions can be observed in real time during the exercise, and the platform records partial results for later analysis. Either of these features are sufficient to discount that the examinee was disrupted or experienced a trivial typo-level mistake, because it is possible to observe that the examinee was repeatedly attempting to solve the lab problem throughout the exercise period.

Results like those highlighted by example examinee 8 actually have really emphasized the tremendous advantage of the multi-tiered Cyber Assessor platform to differentiate examinees that results from the multi-dimensional measurement. In the cases for which this example is representative, further understanding was obtained through a demographic survey, through anecdotal evidence, from observations, and from ensuing discussions with customer leadership when reporting results from their engagement.

It seems clear that an individual who has results like examinee 8 has the basic tools (knowledge and reasoning) to perform well in their job area but might really benefit from additional training. This very well might be a valid conclusion, but the next figure, Fig. 4, reveals some additional insight that arises when the analytics taps into the demographic survey information.

Figure 6: This chart plots example student exam performance scores versus the number of certifications that each student has achieved, captured from a demographics survey that was presented to the examinees through the Tier 2 platform. The points to the far right, corresponding to 9 certifications seems anomalous but is explained in the text of this section.

Fig. 6 plots exam performance versus number of certifications achieved by the examinee. To the far left of figure, we seem the main cluster of examinees that have accomplished between 0 and 2 certifications. The the far right, we see one outlier data pair, which corresponds to examinee 8's Tier 2 and Tier 3 scores, that indicate examinee has 9 certifications!

This is an incredible number of certifications and certainly explains examinee 8's performance on the knowledge and reasoning topics. Furthermore, it also strengthens the justification for accepting hypothesis 3. However, there are additional potential insights that a decision maker at this organization should consider. First, traditional accreditations, certifications, and exams primarily focus on examining knowledge retention and may not provide any insight into actual skill or problem solving. Skill and problem solving ability are developed through significant amounts of practice. Fortunately, CA Tier 3 is able to measure skill and problem solving. Second, given the additional information about certification, a decision would realize that employee 8 does not simply require additional training, but would benefit more from highly targeted hands-on training, individual coaching in problem solving, and perhaps additional opportunities to practice the skills associated with their specialty. We will not show an example chart that plots examinee performance versus years of experience in current job, but we ask the reader to contemplate the additional vastly different insights that would be possible if such a chart revealed employee 8 had just a few years of experience or if employee 8 had more than 15 years of experience.

Hopefully, the preceding thought experiment, following the insights from the previous charts, punctuates the asymmetric gain in value achieved by the CA platform's approach to collecting and analyzing contextual examinee background data in combination with performance data that has been designed to probe multiple dimensions of cybersecurity mastery. Finally, in figure 5, we wrap up the results section by showing how Cyber Assessor leverages the customizable specialty category mappings for each sub-measure to characterize examinee performance.

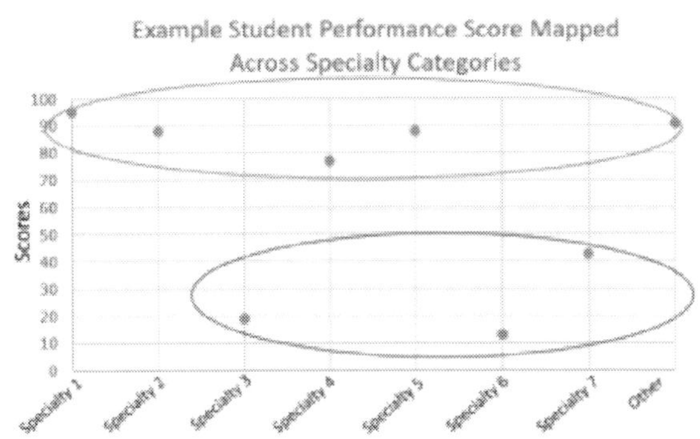

Figure 7: This chart plots an example student's performance scores versus 8 specialty categories and 1 catch-all other category to which each measure (questions, exercises, or problems) is mapped. The green circle indicates specialty categories in which the examinee performed well and might be best suited to work. The red circle indicates specialty categories in which the examinee might benefit from addition training or might not be effective to work in without additional training.

Fig. 7 maps the Tier 2 results of a particular example examinee to 7 job specialization categories, including specialties one through five and an "other" category, and the examinee scored 95, 88, 19, 77, 88, 13, 43, and 91, respectively in the measures (questions) mapped to these categories. One could imagine that the specialty descriptions might include various categories of typical cyber security operator duties such as forensics, for example. Added to the chart, a green circle was positioned to encircle scores in specialization categories where the examinee performed very well. A red circle was positioned around scores in specialization categories where the examinee struggled.

Whether in support of a hiring, revectoring or training decision, the insights revealed by the chart in Fig. 5 will be of great value to a decision maker. This examinee performed quite well in the specialty 1, specialty 2, specialty 4, specialty 5, and other specialization categories but struggled with the specialty 3, specialty 6, and specialty 7, categories. Thus, if deciding about a new hire or revector candidate, the decision maker would know what area this candidate should be directed towards and which areas to avoid. The decision maker would also know exactly how to focus the training for this examinee.

IV. Conclusion

In this research, we have developed a multi-tiered Cyber Assessment platform that was designed to evaluate cybersecurity-pertinent skills, knowledge, and other attributes of individuals. In this paper, we presented example results that illustrated how the data analytics developed to analyze the scoring organize the performance data to maximize useful insights that support critical decision making needs of any organization. The reporting, example results, and insights section demonstrated how important insights are immediately visible in the summary charts that capture the examinee performance distribution, plot the performance against various demographic survey attribute values, and characterize individual examinee performance across arbitrary specialty categorization systems. The valuable insights, which are made possible due to the differentiation achieved by the multi-dimensional measurements that are collected by the Cyber Assessor platform and generated by its analytics and reporting subsystems, will directly support key personnel decisions. Thus, we hope that Cyber Assessor will be adopted by the organizations where it can have maximal positive impact to increase efficiency, reduce cost, and improve quality of crucial hiring, re-vectoring, and training.

Acknowledgment

The authors would like to thank the SimSpace corporation for presenting us with the opportunity and means to conduct this research and solve this difficult problem and the leadership for sharing insights as to challenges facing the marketplace that we addressed in this research. Finally, the authors are very grateful to Greg Gimler, John Nelson, David Carpman and David Oyer for discussions and technical contributions related to the topics in this paper.

References

[1] FFIEC, "FFIEC Cybersecurity Assessment Tool,", https://www.ffiec.gov/cyberassessmenttool.htm, June 2015.

[2] FFIEC, "Overview for Chief Executive officers and Boards of Directors", https://www.ffiec.gov/cyberassessmenttool.htm, June 2015.

[3] National Initiative for Cybersecurity Careers and Studies (NICCS), "Professional Certifications", Department of Homeland Security, https://niccs.us-cert.gov/training/professional-certifications

[4] National Institute of Standards (NIST), "Cyber Framework", United States Department of Commerce, https://www.nist.gov/cyberframework

[5] T. Klemas and D. Rajchwald, "Evolutionary Clustering Analysis of Multiple Edge Set Networks used for Modeling Ivory Coast Mobile Phone Data and Sensemaking", Data Analytics 2014, Third International Conference on Data Analytics.

Intelligent Data Leak Detection Through Behavioural Analysis

Ricardo Costeira
Informatics Department
University of Minho
Braga, Portugal
e-mail: rcosteira79@gmail.com

Henrique Santos
Information Systems Department
University of Minho
Guimarães, Portugal
e-mail: hsantos@dsi.uminho.pt

Abstract—**In this paper we discuss a solution to detect data leaks in an intelligent and furtive way through a real time analysis of the user's behaviour while handling classified information. Data is based on experiences with real world use cases and a variety of data preparation and data analysis techniques have been tried. Results show the feasibility of the approach, but also the necessity to correlate with other security events to improve the precision.**

Keywords-Anomaly Detection; Machine Learning; Data Mining; Support Vector Machines.

I. INTRODUCTION

The evolution of technology and Information Systems has opened a phenomenal new world of possibilities for companies and organizations all over the globe, more dependent on data then ever. As an example, the advent of the Internet and development of distributed systems brought about the Cloud, which makes information accessible wherever the user is and whenever the user wants, as long as there is a connect to the service. However, this flexibility comes with some new threats related with the level of information exposure. Data leaks became one main concern a company can face. In the 2015 *Cost of Data Breach Study: Global Analysis* [1], which considers 350 companies in 11 countries, it is stated that 3.79 million dollars is the average total cost of data breaches, with a 23% increase since 2013. This study also points out that 47% of data leak incidents reported by the enquired companies are related to insider attacks.

To address data breaches, organizations have invested billions over the years mainly to secure their network perimeter with Firewalls and Intrusion Detection/Prevention systems, among other technologies. These solutions are by far insufficient, as corporate information keeps going out of the secure perimeter. As such, companies are now focusing on the concept of data-centric information protection [2]. RigthsWATCH [3], developed by Watchful Software, is an implementation of that concept. This type of system creates a protective bubble around data itself, implementing authorization rules defined by a given set of security policies. Besides, it also helps when a careless employee accidentally leaks information to the outside. However, as powerful and convenient it is, data-centric information protection is useless against a premeditated internal attack.

For this reason, behaviour analysis becomes an important concept to fight data leaks. By taking logged information about user interaction with protected data, it should be possible to create a behavioural profile, which can be used as a base of comparison during future interactions. In this paper, a framework for data leak detection through user behavior analysis is proposed. The framework collects RightsWATCH users' logs, crafting an individual behavioural profile from them. We then explored the capacity to distinguish between normal and abnormal behaviour. The research described here is part of the RightsWATCH development project.

This paper is organized into six main sections, the first of which is this introduction. The second section discusses the state of the art regarding Intrusion Detection systems, focusing mainly on Anomaly Detection. The third section provides a more detailed view of the proposed framework's architecture, and the fourth section describes the experimental environment. The fifth section discusses the obtained results, while the sixth and final section gathers the final conclusions and thoughts.

II. STATE OF THE ART

An intrusion detection system (IDS) is a tool capable of detecting possible security breaches on a system, by gathering and analysing security events. It can be designed to work with a wide range of information, such as logs from different sources (firewalls, OSs, etc.), application usage data, keyboard inputs, or network data packets. According to [4], an intrusion detection system should provide the following security functions: it has to *monitor* the computer or network, to *detect* possible threats and to *respond* to the possible intrusions.

Axelsson [5] developed a generalized IDS model, which is shown in Fig. 1: solid arrows represent data/control flow, while dotted arrows indicate a possible intrusion response. Axelsson's model is useful to describe the general, high level behaviour of an IDS, but a complete characterization and classification goes beyond this simple architecture, mainly due to the diverse technologies that can be implemented. Fig. 2 presents a more complete classification [6].

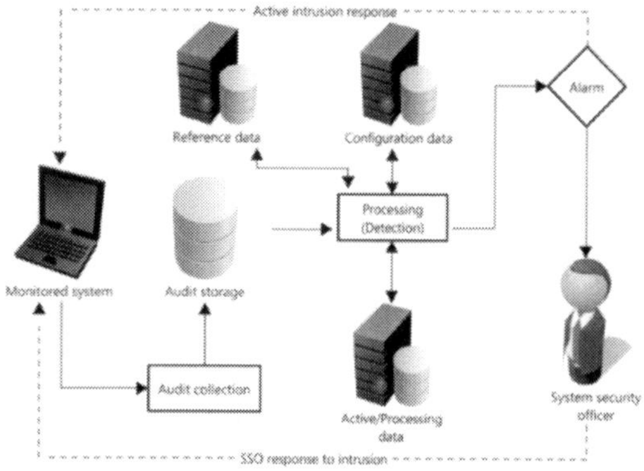

Figure 1. Generic model of an intrusion detection system.

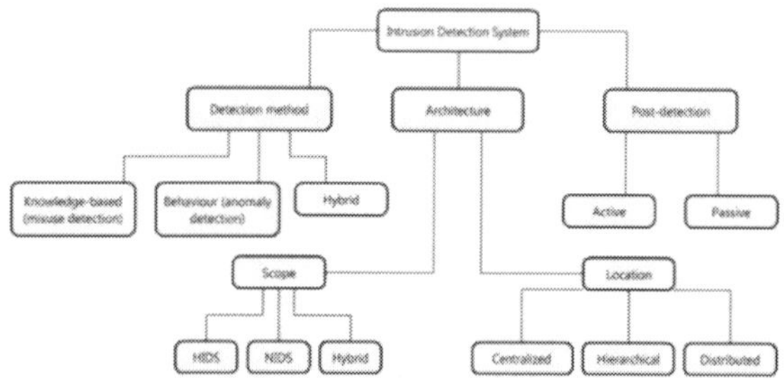

Figure 2. Characterization and classification of IDS.

This classification considers only the functional attributes of intrusion detection systems. But there is a non-functional one that should also be considered, the usage frequency [7], which is useful to distinguish an IDS from a scanner used for security assessment - the usage frequency provides a fair distinction between the two.

Each attribute has a very specific meaning, and is deeply related to the system purposes.

A. *Architecture*

The IDS architecture should be idealized considering three relevant factors: The source of the data to be analysed, the way tasks are being distributed and the processing components [6]. It is, as such, divided into two different categories: scope and location. Regarding its scope, an IDS can be host based (HIDS), network based (NIDS) or a **hybrid** system, comprising characteristics of both types.

Host based intrusion detection systems collect and analyse data from a single host. The detection software installed on the host is commonly known as agent. It can monitor a wide range of activities, such as application logs, changes in the file system, system integrity, use of resources, user access and interaction with the system, among many others.

Agents are developed to monitor servers, hosts, or even applications services. Due to the variety of implementations, de Boer and Pels consider four different main *HIDS* categories in [8]: Filesystem monitors, logfile analysers, connection analysers and kernel monitors.

The NIDS collects and analyses data from a network and usually focuses on the TCP/IP protocol. Data packets are sniffed through sensors positioned on "mission critical" spots. Sensors can be of two types [9]: appliance and software only.

In [9], the author describes some of the events detected by most of the NIDS: Application/Transport/Network layer reconnaissance and attacks, unexpected application services and policy violations.

The "location" in Fig. 2 refers to the placing of all the different modules that compose the IDS, comprising three types: centralized, where there is only one system (the manager) responsible for event analysis, detection, classification and system reaction; hierarchical, where more than one manager can exist; distributed, where there are several managers as well, but the data analysis and processing can also be done by any other component.

B. *Post-detection*

After detecting an intrusion, an IDS can perform either actively (if it reacts by its own), or passively (if it acts as a decision support system, by triggering alarms and/or notifications for the administrator).

C. *Detection Method*

Depending on the chosen methodology for analysing the audit data, IDSs can be categorized as knowledge based and/or behaviour based. Knowledge based IDSs are commonly referred to as misuse or signature detection systems, focused on attacks information, while behaviour based intrusion detection systems are usually known as anomaly detection systems (ADS), focused on information about the system behaviour [7]. The fusion of these detection methods into a hybrid system is possible.

An ADS is based on the premise that security breaches can be detected by monitoring audit data and searching for abnormal patterns of system usage, as Denning stated in [10]. The system starts by learning the general profile that describes a subject's normal behavior – learning phase. Then, during normal work, the same features are captured and a profile is deduced in a similar way – detection phase. The working profile is then compared to the stored one searching for deviations, and if they occur, and are above a given threshold, the activity is considered a possible intrusion [5]. Note that the subject in this context refers to any resource capable of access and operate the information system, typically a user, or a process on behalf of a user.

Although the concept is fairly straightforward, the actual division between anomalies and normal data is quite challenging, generating frequently a high number of false positives, which is the main drawback of this approach.

Anomaly detection is the approach chosen for the problem at hands, mainly because there are no known patterns of possible attacks – and that seems very difficult to define. Looking for possible techniques to adopt in this case, the most commonly used are statistical methods [11][12] and data mining methods [13][14], the latter usually dividing into classification or clustering [15][16], although other methods were also studied - expert systems [10][17][18], computer immunology [19], user intention identification [20][21], and a few other approaches, including combinations of different methods [11]. Following a clear tendency in the field, the scientific research potential and the authors' experience, classification was the technique selected for this work.

Classification commonly follows one of three approaches: Supervised, semi-supervised and unsupervised learning. These techniques are implemented under the assumption that a proper classifier, which can distinguish between normal and anomalous data, can be trained within the feature space available [22]. The model obtained through training can be one of two types: one-class and multi-class. In the first case, the training dataset has only one class label and the model consists of a discriminative boundary around the normal (labeled) instances, treating everything out of that boundary as anomalous. Multi-class methods are used when the training dataset has labels defining more than one normal class and, for each class, there will be a classifier. Some variants of this method associate a confidence level with the prediction made. The characteristics of the project under consideration points to one-class classification.

III. The Framework's Architecture

RightsWATCH logs every user's daily operation with protected data. The main challenge here is to discover which logs correspond to normal and abnormal activity – at first because there is no formal definition of what is normal and abnormal – and/or which features, among a large dataset, are relevant to catch dangerous activity. As already referred, the proposed anomaly detection framework follows a one-class classification model, which will be trained by a controlled dataset generated by regular user interaction (free of abnormal behaviour).

The proposed architectural design of the framework is depicted in Fig. 3 and a brief explanation of each component is given next. The *Reader* module is responsible for reading and preparing the input data. The raw data have to be previously selected by the developer and this information is embedded into the code, including formal interface rules. This way, the framework can be easily adapted to accept other data sources. The *Reader* is divided into two submodules. The first one is called *Preprocessor*, whose main function is to take raw data and prepare the desired features according to the classifier format requirements. Several logs are not in an adequate format, appearing as categorical or descriptive data. When dealing with categorical data, it is required to break it into *n* features, where *n* is the number of existent cases – a technique known as one-hot encoding.

The *Preprocessor* output feeds the second submodule, the *DatasetBuilder*, whose main function is to build the final dataset. This dataset aims to represent the user's behaviour, while preserving the user's privacy by completely transforming the data into something that cannot be tracked back to its original state - the dataset is fully composed of numeric values, whose relationship to the real data is completely eliminated.

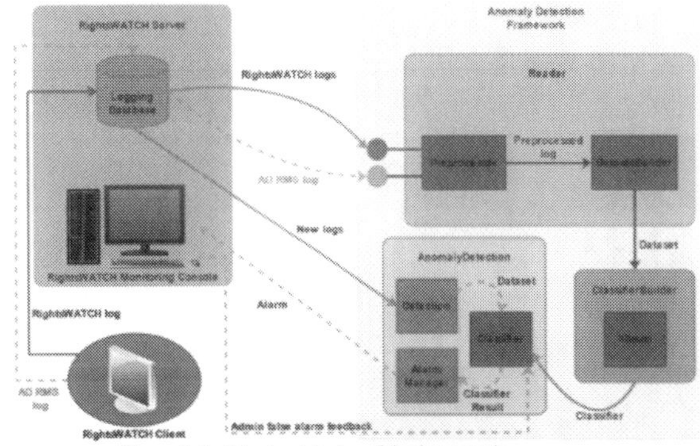

Figure 3. Architectural design of the framework.

In Fig. 3 there is a second source of logs labeled as AD RMS logs (Active Directory Rights Management Services). It corresponds to an infrastructure provided by Microsoft, which gathers all the server and client technologies to support information protection through the use of rights management in an organization. RightsWATCH uses this technology, but the associated logs are not used, for now - the dashed and greyed arrow line indicates that.

The Dataset provider by the Reader module will be the input for the *ClassifierBuilder* module. This module analyses the data and creates a model of the user's behaviour. This model, or classifier, will be used as a reference for future comparisons. To perform this task, a classification algorithm is needed. Support Vector Machines (SVM) was the chosen one for the task, by wrapping the *libsvm* library provided, by Chang and Lin [23]. This library packs the standard SVM algorithm along with the most relevant variations, such as one-class SVM and SVM for regression. Another version of the library, available in the website, also packs the Support Vector Data Description (SVDD) algorithm. The reason for choosing this library has to do with the fact that since its inception in 2001, *libsvm* was successfully integrated and used in similar problems (the full list is available on *libsvm*'s website), appearing as one of the most promising approaches to the classification problem.

To perform the detection, two different SVM algorithms were investigated, although one of them to a much greater extent than the other (the standard binary SVM classification algorithm was also used in a set of preliminary tests). As referred above, these algorithms are the one-class classification algorithm and the SVDD. This second algorithm was only considered in the final stages of the investigation, mostly for performance comparison. Both of these relate to semi-supervised learning, and are the only SVM options available for this problem.

The secondary function of the *ClassifierBuilder* module is, in the validation stage and following a conservative approach, to test different variations of the detection method, as described in the next section.

The final model will be stored and used by the *AnomalyDetection* module, which is divided into three submodules: *Detector*, *Classifier* and *AlarmManager*. The first submodule is responsible for getting logs from users in real-time, extract the features and prepare. After, the *Classifier* submodule evaluates the entry using the classifier obtained by the ClassifierBuilder module and produces a score result, which is outputted to the *AlarmManager* submodule. This submodule will react to the result, issuing an alarm to the administrator with the corresponding threat level. Shall it be the case of a false alarm, the administrator can mark the event as benign, which will also trigger an update of the classifier with the new information, to avoid similar mistakes in the future.

IV. Dataset Creation and Framework Development

RightsWATCH and the ADS framework discussed in this paper were developed at Watchful Software's office, facilitating the integration and assuring all the technical support necessary. All the testing was performed there, with data logs captured from 4 collaborators during 1 day (only 4 were chosen since only those exhibit what can be considered a typical work interaction with RightsWATCH). The available number of logs for user 1, user 2, user 3 and user 4 are, respectively, 5714, 3120, 2514 and 2365.

The logging information, initially stored in a dedicated database, is copied to a new table, called *LogTraining* (see Fig. 4), to keep original logs intact. Next we will describe in more detail the dataset creation, which, as already mentioned, raised several problems.

A. Dataset Creation

To data mining researchers, real world industrial databases can be considered one of their worst nightmares, and the reason is simple: real data is, most of the times, dirty and cluttered, and databases are not prepared at all for data mining. As this turned out to be the case, RightsWATCH logging table demanded for a preparation and cleansing process. The resulting table has thirty-eight dimensions (excluding primary key), filled with numerical, categorical and binary data. The table's structure, along with other new tables, is depicted in Fig. 4.

The most prominent problem is that thirty-five of the thirty-eight dimensions have missing values, blank spaces or null values, which affect every table record. Apart from this, there are inconsistencies between data, as well as information that should have been inserted into a different table cluttered in one single column. The logs containing email addresses that users chose as recipients in emails, are an example of the cluttered set of information – for each record, a user can have something like *email1;email2;...;emailn* for *n* "to" recipients.

The solution for these problems was quite straightforward. The missing values were substituted by actual default values, the inconsistent values were removed and the cluttered information was reorganised into different tables.

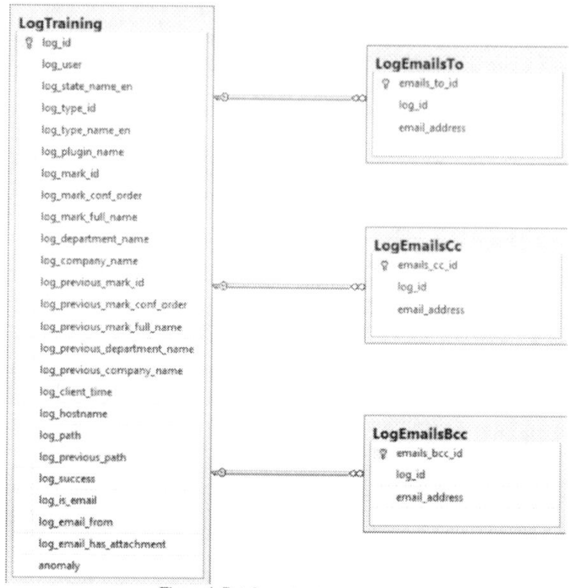

Figure 4. Database structure.

There are other features deserving particular attention, given their relevance and the amount of perturbation they may impose, namely: *log_path* and *log_previous_path*, contain a directory path of a protected file – since shared directories are avoided, this features may have an excessive weight in classification; *rule id*, that logs the id of a policy rule triggered by the user, appeared with some imprecisions due to system limitations encountered at the time. To perceive better their influence we decide to perform data analyses removing each and both from the complete dataset.

For the initial features selection and extraction stages, WEKA (Waikato Environment for Knowledge Analysis) was used, to assess the influence of each feature over the dataset. WEKA is a well-known machine learning tool wildly used for this type of data analysis and it includes *libsvm*. For each user's data we consider other users' data attacks (examples of bad behavior). Following regular recommendations, we perform a 10-cross validation operation (WEKA randomly divide the dataset in 10 subsamples, keeping one for model validation and the others for training; the process is repeated 10 times so that all subsamples are used for validation, in each time). The same process was performed with the original dataset and the ones obtained by removing the problematic features, as referred above. The results achieved are presented in tables I, II and III. Overall, the accuracy is not very high, which demands for more research.

With these results, it became obvious that a more formal way to assess feature quality was needed, which was done with PCA (Principal Components Analysis), a data analysis technique also included in WEKA.

PCA was run over the same dataset variants and it revealed that there are no outstanding features. There are, of course, features with larger coefficients (weight values) associated to them than others, but adjacent coefficients are close in value.

Table I. CLASSIFICATION ACCURACY RESULTS FOR THE FIRST VERSION OF THE DATASETS WITHOUT THE PATH FEATURES.

	Classification Accuracy Results			
Anomalous / Legitimate	User 1	User 2	User 3	User 4
User 1		67.7%	79.5%	71.1%
User 2			70.9%	67.5%
User 3				73.1%

Table II. CLASSIFICATION ACCURACY RESULTS FOR THE VERSION OF THE DATASETS WITHOUT THE RULE ID FEATURE AND STILL WITHOUT THE PATH FEATURES.

	Classification Accuracy Results			
Anomalous / Legitimate	User 1	User 2	User 3	User 4
User 1		67.7%	78.9%	70.8%
User 2			70.6%	67.6%
User 3				73.2%

Table III. CLASSIFICATION ACCURACY RESULTS FOR THE FIRST VERSION OF THE DATASETS WITH THE PATH FEATURES.

	Classification Accuracy Results			
Anomalous / Legitimate	User 1	User 2	User 3	User 4
User 1		64.7%	77.6%	70.7%
User 2			68%	63.5%
User 3				71%

Contrary to what was expected, the path features do show some classification potential. On the other hand, the email features did introduce noise in the dataset, as expected. Also, the full set of email related features correspond to approximately thirty-six percent of the whole dataset.

In all PCA executions, the correlation between features was fairly poor. Except from the obvious correlations (for instance, the *mark email* action type feature is always heavily correlated with the *Microsoft Outlook plugin* feature), most of the features have shown low correlation values between each other.

Regarding the results, the only action decided was towards the recipient email addresses. As it became clear, their presence in the dataset is a prelude of an erroneous classifier. But simply discarding the emails seems a waste of possibly useful data. As such, a more conservative solution was adopted, performing the division of the recipient emails into their respective local and domain parts. The local part is discarded, while the domain is retained as a feature. Of course, this way it is not possible to distinguish, for example, if a user is sending one hundred emails to one hundred different *Gmail* addresses, or one hundred emails to the same *Gmail* address. Still, it is better than blinding the classifier with noise or not having any recipient email address information at all.

Finally, and to conclude this section, the features produced by *PCA* or, in other words, the principal components, are often used in place of the original features.

B. *Framework Conception*

The development of the *ADS* framework started with the *Reader* module and data transformation. The categorical feature that is not one-hot encoded is the *log_client_time*. It was rendered by two new features, *day_of_the_week* and *time_of_the_day*. Both features are numeric – *day_of_the_week* goes from zero (Sunday) to six (Saturday). It is important to note that *day_of_the_week* was only added later and, by that time, *time of the day* was also modified (these changes are explained in full detail on the next section).

Two modifications regarding user names had to be implemented, by privacy reasons. The first one was ignoring the *log_user* field - it is not associated with any type of behavior; the second one occurs at runtime, and it is the removal of the user's name from every directory path, whenever it is present. For instance, for a path such as "Users\John\Sales Report.docx", the final result is just "Users\Sales Report.docx".

After the preprocessing, the *Reader* module has to build the datasets. The ratio is 70% of the total data for training, and the remaining 30% for testing (following the recommendations given in *libsvm* documentation). The datasets are created in a sequential fashion – first the training set, and then the test set. This order has to be maintained, as the features of the test set will depend on the training set. In other words, the test set will only have features that are also available in the training set, (any new feature is excluded). This condition is needed since categorical features are divided into sets of new features through one-hot encoding, and there will be cases where some of these features will exist on the test set but not on the training set.

Next, at heart of the *ClassifierBuilder* module, we use *libsvm*, as already referred. It also has methods to test and cross-validate data, and since it performs a very time consuming task, it implements some inner and heavy loops in a paralyzed way using OpenMP (Open Multi-Processing).

Apart from its main classification function, the *ClassifierBuilder* also implements new methods for performance measurement and classifier quality assessment. Essentially, the classification results regarding false/true positives/negatives are used to build a confusion matrix, and then combined together to compute the precision and recall values. These indicators evaluate different aspects of the classifier. Precision, or *positive predictive value*, is obtained with the division of true positives by the sum of all the examples that were considered positive (i.e., true positives and false positives) and represents the accuracy. It can be though as a numerical representation of the model's *exactness*. Conversely, recall or *sensitivity* is calculated by dividing true positives by the sum of true positives with false negatives, which can be seen as the model ability to classify observations from a class as cases from that actual class. It can be understood as the classifier's *completeness*. Both values vary between zero and one – zero being the worst case, and one the best case. Low precision can be a sign of a large number of false positives, and low recall can mean that the classifier is detecting too many false negatives. As such, the ideal is to have both values as closer to one as possible. Both measures are used to determine the F1 score, which can be interpreted as the weighted average of precision and recall, and its computation is achieved through the harmonic mean (F1 score = 2 · *(precision·recall)/(precision+recall)*). F1 score also varies between zero and one, with similar interpretation. These performance indicators are commonly used with anomaly detection solutions.

Finally, the *ClassifierBuilder*, was designed to test the two SVM algorithms, as stated before, and using all the four kernels available in *libsvm* - linear, RBF, polynomial and sigmoid kernels. This is achieved through a loop that performs a grid search over the algorithm parameters – *C* for *SVDD* and *v* for one-class – and kernel parameter γ (except, of course, for the linear kernel, that does not use γ). Besides, the algorithm also performs a k-fold cross validation over the dataset (as explained before), looking for the best classifier provided by each kernel. The results of the four classifiers are then evaluated, and stored along with the parameters used. Since this is done for each user, it is not viable to actually use this in a real world environment (besides, the grid search takes too much time). Still, this configuration will be maintained at the prototype level for research purposes.

V. RESULTS

For the testing methodology, it was decided to follow nearly the procedure suggested by *libsvm* authors, the difference being that all the available kernels are used.

Two very similar training datasets were used for each user, built from the same logs, which means that in total every user will have two classifiers. The difference between the two datasets is a subset of features – those features that are completely unique to each user, namely hostname and user email addresses, were removed from one dataset. Note that in a regular situation, these features would be vital in the dataset - for instance, it is possible to use the hostname to cover the anomalous cases where the user account is used on an unknown machine. In this case, as most of the test sets were composed by data from other users, labeled as anomalous behaviors, the presence of that information would introduce a strong bias on the results. For similar reasons, the username feature was completely excluded from both datasets as well.

For this testing phase, the default values for the one-class classification parameters - 0.5 to v and *1/features* to γ – were used. For the polynomial kernel we keep the default parameter value. Dataset *A* is the complete one, and dataset *B* is the one without unique features. The values for precision, recall and F1 scores were computed only for the attacks with all the available test data, and are available on tables IV and V (for visualisation purposes, every decimal value was rounded from six to two decimal places).

Let the focus be on dataset *A* results. The number of final features per user vary - 1781, 819, 377 and 761 for users 1, 2, 3 and 4, respectively. As it was expected, most of the classifiers that were trained with full featured datasets were heavily influenced by the unique features. Otherwise, it would be virtually impossible for any classifier to achieve a classification accuracy of 100%, as it happens in so many cases. However, note that this is a good thing, considering the true nature of the problem: the idea is not to have the classifier distinguishing between users, but instead having it identifying anomalous behaviour of the same user and, from that point of view, the classifier ability to decide that an example is anomalous if the hostname or the email address that the user wields are different from the usual, is very important. Regardless, it seems that most of the classifiers whilst easily recognising other users, struggle to recognise the user itself. A particularly noteworthy case of this is User 2. As a clear case of the closed world assumption point of view discussed earlier, this user has got the lowest score when tested against itself no matter the kernel used and, as a consequence, had the lowest F1 score too, given the low recall results. Also, notice that regardless of the unrealistically high classification values that this user achieved with the test dataset that comprises every user, the F1 score values resist this tendency and provide for a more grounded analysis, which ends up proving the advantage of using such a metric. As for the kernels, the *RBF* kernel achieved the overall worst results, while both linear and sigmoid kernels appear to perform better in this case.

The results are slightly different for dataset *B*. With a minimal decrease in features, the importance of the missing features becomes evident, as the overall results are much lower in quality. With this dataset, the classifiers had trouble both in distinguishing between behaviors and in recognising the target user. In addition, these results also prove that the default *SVM* parameters are, in this case, far from optimal. Finally, the kernels exhibit similar results between them, with the linear kernel slightly outstanding itself from the rest, always with the highest F1 score for all users. Note that in contrast with dataset *A*, the recall values for dataset *B* were always higher than the corresponding precision - not due to an increase in recall values, but instead because of a drastic decrease in precision.

After testing the kernels, the next challenge is to search for the best (v, γ) combination, through cross-validation. To do that, the same 70%-30% division was made for each user. The training sets were used in a 10-fold cross validation, for a grid search on twelve values for v and fifteen values for γ (again, following *libsvm*'s documentation recommendations). In the end, the best performing parameters combination for each dataset is stored, and then used to create new classification models. Then, each model is tested. The resulting performance metrics are presented on tables VI and VII.

At a first glance, and judging by the accuracy values, it seemed that these parameters would push the framework into producing overly *permissive* classifiers. This has to do with the way that one-class *SVM* works: tampering with the ν parameter has a direct impact on the number of observations that are accepted - the lower the value, the more permissive the resulting classifier will be.

Dataset *A* still demonstrates the importance of the user unique features. Also outstanding is the clear difference in the ability to correctly classify both anomalous and legitimate instances between the linear kernel and the remaining three. The quality of this kernel was already noticed before, but not to this extent. For every user, this kernel attained the best F1 score. In fact, the F1 scores for this kernel are, for every user, better than those reported in the results before the grid search. Although, it was the only kernel to achieve such feat, as the remaining F1 scores are mostly low. Finally, the recall values for this dataset were substantially higher than before, due to the classifier accepting more samples as normal ones (i.e., being more permissive).

The results for dataset *B* turned out to be even worse than before. Without the unique features, and with such forgiving ν parameters, the classifiers declare a large part of the attacking users' instances as legitimate. In this dataset, apparently, no kernel stands out from the others, and even with the high recall values, the F1 scores are simply unacceptable.

At a first glance, this investigation could end here. The linear kernel achieved better results with dataset *A*, after the grid search. However, this does not prove that the linear classifier will do a good job detecting anomalies. In fact, without the unique features (dataset *B*), the classifier does not perform so well. What if the user himself leaked valuable information, from his usual machine, with his usual email? Thanks to the unique features, the classifier would likely detect the resulting log as legitimate. As such, it is not time to finish, but to stop for a while. Time to pause and think about the causes of the results obtained with dataset *B*. Was it the classification algorithm, or the data itself? It might have been both.

The ν parameter controls how many observations get misclassified, and how many turn into support vectors. For instance, if the ν parameter is set to 0.1, it is guaranteed that at most 10% of the training instances will be misclassified, and at least 10% of them will become support vectors. Before the grid search, ν was the default *libsvm* value of 0.5. This is a conservative value, which created classifiers incapable of correctly recognising a legitimate user by setting a high upper bound for the outlier ratio. Then, the grid search chose the parameters that allowed for the highest F1 scores. With such low ν values, the upper bound of outliers decreased, therefore letting more examples fall on the correct side of the hyperplane. On the other side, assuming too small outlier ratios, can easily allow anomalous instances to fall on the legitimate side of the hyperplane, which indeed happened. Of course, the γ parameter also influences everything as well. This parameter defines how *far* the influence of a single training example reaches: low values mean *far* and high values mean *close*. Before the grid search, the value was dictated by the number of features, which means that it varied, depending on the dataset, between ≈ 0.0006 and ≈ 0.001. After the grid search, most of the γ parameters achieved values that were higher, which in turn diminished the influence of the training instances. All of this leads to one thought: The grid search method might prove effective with two class problems, but the same might not apply to one-class classification, given the actual nature of the optimisation problem, when performing it with cross-validation.

Taking this into consideration, a new grid search was performed: The classifiers were tested against data from both the user and the other users and, instead of returning the parameters with the highest F1 score, the algorithm was modified to output all the data it produces for each parameter combination, so that each of the 552 classifiers (12 for the linear kernel and 180 for each of the other kernels) could be individually examined. The perusal of the data confirmed the worst: with dataset *B* there were no cases where any of the classifiers managed to successfully separate anomalous from legitimate records. The classifiers mostly bounced between the two extremes - either classifying most of the cases as legitimate or as anomalous. When this is not the case, the classification accuracy values just revolve around the 50% mark, with very low standard deviation values.

With these results, it was inevitable to think about the quality of the data. One of the first impressions that arose when contacting with the available data for the first time, during the data cleansing and data selection phases, was that it would be possible it be too **fine grained** for the *SVM* algorithm. The features are poorly correlated between them, and with the naked eye, at least, it is next to impossible to distinguish between examples, if we ignore users' unique features. Although this granularity-level issue is not confirmed, the obtained results do allow to consider it as a reason for the classifiers poor quality. As such, it seems appropriate to rethink the way the dataset is built, and how the information is used. Hence, the next section describes the final dataset transformation.

Table IIV. PERFORMANCE METRICS FOR DATASET A.

	User 1 Metrics			User 2 Metrics			User 3 Metrics			User 4 Metrics		
Kernels	Precision	Recall	F1 Score	Precision	Recall	F1 Score	Precision	Recall	F1 Score	Precision	Recall	F1 Score
Linear	1	0.65	0.79	1	0.11	0.19	1	0.53	0.69	1	0.58	0.73
RBF	0.16	0.68	0.26	0.10	0.25	0.14	1	0.52	0.68	0.24	0.74	0.37
Polynomial	0.26	0.84	0.39	1	0.09	0.17	1	0.55	0.71	1	0.25	0.40
Sigmoid	1	0.65	0.78	1	0.11	0.20	1	0.46	0.63	1	0.58	0.74

Table V. PERFORMANCE METRICS FOR DATASET B

	User 1 Metrics			User 2 Metrics			User 3 Metrics			User 4 Metrics		
Kernels	Precision	Recall	F1 Score	Precision	Recall	F1 Score	Precision	Recall	F1 Score	Precision	Recall	F1 Score
Linear	0.14	0.65	0.24	0.08	0.57	0.14	0.22	0.53	0.31	0.06	0.55	0.11
RBF	0.14	0.78	0.24	0.07	0.71	0.14	0.18	0.41	0.25	0.06	0.71	0.10
Polynomial	0.15	0.76	0.25	0.07	0.49	0.12	0.22	0.51	0.30	0.05	0.21	0.08
Sigmoid	0.14	0.65	0.24	0.08	0.53	0.13	0.22	0.47	0.30	0.06	0.60	0.11

Table VI. PERFORMANCE METRICS FOR DATASET A AFTER GRID SEARCH

	User 1 Metrics			User 2 Metrics			User 3 Metrics			User 4 Metrics		
Kernels	Precision	Recall	F1 Score	Precision	Recall	F1 Score	Precision	Recall	F1 Score	Precision	Recall	F1 Score
Linear	0.99	0.97	0.97	1	0.2	0.33	0.99	0.99	0.99	0.99	0.99	0.99
RBF	0.17	0.98	0.29	0.04	0.54	0.08	0.17	0.97	0.28	0.06	0.99	0.11
Polynomial	1	0.95	0.98	1	0.19	0.32	0.2	0.72	0.31	1	0.97	0.98
Sigmoid	0.17	0.99	0.3	0.07	0.48	0.12	0.24	0.99	0.39	0.06	1	0.11

Table VII. PERFORMANCE METRICS FOR DATASET B AFTER GRID SEARCH.

	User 1 Metrics			User 2 Metrics			User 3 Metrics			User 4 Metrics		
Kernels	Precision	Recall	F1 Score	Precision	Recall	F1 Score	Precision	Recall	F1 Score	Precision	Recall	F1 Score
Linear	0.16	0.98	0.27	0.07	0.97	0.14	0.11	0.99	0.2	0.05	0.99	0.1
RBF	0.16	0.98	0.28	0.07	0.99	0.13	0.09	0.99	0.17	0.05	0.99	0.1
Polynomial	0.16	0.93	0.27	0.08	0.94	0.14	0.16	0.72	0.27	0.06	0.95	0.1
Sigmoid	–	0	–	0.07	1	0.13	0.09	1	0.17	0.05	1	0.1

A. *Dataset Refactoring*

The current dataset is composed of *point anomaly* records. Following the reasoning explained before, the framework will now aggregate data points into larger sets, thus producing new features that, in essence, **summarise** the attribute values from every example that comprises the given aggregated set, this way creating a different, *collective anomaly* dataset.

The log aggregation process was performed considering each set of logs that was generated in an hour. In other words, the set of logs generated in an hour became one collective log. The starting time was defined by the very first log. This time frame was chosen for two reasons. Firstly, it is feasible that a user generates more than one log in an hour. Secondly, it is still a small enough time frame to allow for mitigating measures in case of a data leak.

With the aggregation, the number of available observations diminished significantly. Users 1, 2, 3 and 4 now have, respectively, 1576, 1722, 469 and 1466 total observations. The number of features has also changed, as it was expected with the changes regarding the path features, not to mention the fact that the features themselves are different. Using the same distinction between datasets, dataset *A* now consists of 642, 355, 485 and 398 records for the four users (in that order), while dataset *B* contains 635, 349, 482 and 394 records. Note that with this dataset, the training set of user 3 will have a number of features higher than the number of observations, which can reshape the final results.

The testing process was the same one used before. The 70%-30% division between training and test sets still remains, but note that this division was established only in the individual logs. A lot of work would be needed in order to apply this process to the new data, as it is created dynamically. Fortunately, with the division between the individual logs, the final ratio of the new data between training and test sets is roughly 80%-20% for users 1 and 3, and 75%-25% for users 2 and 4, which are still acceptable boundaries. Also, this will be an opportunity to test the impact of different division ratios between the data.

Despite the expectative, results are not very different from those obtained before – for that reason we think it is not necessary to present them in new tables. Next we will discuss the small details that deserve some attention.

Dataset *A* exhibits the same high precision and low recall values, while dataset *B* displays the same drop in precision, while maintaining the recall values. Even the different kernels performed in an identical fashion. On the other hand, the variation between the F1 scores of both dataset types is not wide enough to allow for any kind of conclusion just yet. Since the default parameters were used, these results are not unexpected.

The grid search for this dataset was slightly different from before. This time, every parameter combination was manually examined. Also, instead of performing the search through cross-validation, the algorithm tested each of the 552 classifiers with the test sets that contain information about all users. This was done so that the obtained parameters were more adequate to the validation process. Indeed, in a normal situation, the parameters would be generated via cross-validation, as the data belonging to the user would be the only data used. However, it was already seen that the classifiers are able to accept logs as being legitimate, and thus the purpose now is to search for parameters that can aid the classifiers into defining the best plane possible between both legitimate and anomalous instances. Concerning dataset *A*, the only thing to point is the superior performance of the polynomial kernel over all the others. This kernel managed to obtain good results even when the others wavered.

Recall that the only reason for working on a completely different dataset had to do with dataset *B* disappointing results. As it turns out, the new dataset *B* error metric results are similar to the old ones - although, from a more optimistic point of view, when looking at both the classification and confusion matrices results, these classifiers performed clearly better, with no exception. In fact, these are good news, since there are still so many possible ways to perform the log aggregation that were not investigated. In other words, one (or more than one) of these other options might prove itself to be more successful.

A curious pattern emerged with both datasets. With only two exceptions - users 1 and 3 always scored the top classification results. This is most certainly related to the data division between training and test sets. Recall that these two users are the ones with the 805-20% division – more data to train the classifier and less data to test it. As it is known, the more data there is, the more accurate should the classifier be. However, this same pattern is noted, although to a lesser extent, on dataset *B* classification result, which might suggest that there is more to it than the data division.

Finally, a last attempt was made with the SVDD method, using the initial datasets, *A* and *B*. However, the obtained results were worst most of the times. Besides, it suggests that this algorithm has a stronger resistance to the unique features, as results from both datasets were quite similar. This is actually a good omen if we think in terms of generalisation capabilities.

Now the only question remaining is whether the optimal parameters are able to improve the classifier's accuracy or not. Similarly to what happened before, both datasets produced similar results, with dataset *A*'s classifiers sometimes underachieving when compared to those of dataset *B*, but most of the times surpassing them and, in some instances, by a large margin. With dataset *A*, the *RBF* kernel was always ahead of the other three, while this distinction was not so clear with dataset *B*, where it was even surpassed by the polynomial kernel on the tests with user 4.

A noticeable aspect of the tests with this classification method is that, for each user, the *C* regularisation parameter is mostly constant throughout the different kernels, which leads to the belief that this regularisation parameter is stronger and more influential than the v on the one-class classification method, which might be directly involved in this method's resistance to the unique variables. In other words, it is possible that the classifiers produced by *SVDD* are more stable than the ones generated through the one-class classification *v-SVM*, but this result require more research.

VI. Conclusions and Future Work

As the obtained results suggest, and even if they are less conclusive then expected, it is possible to define a user behaviour pattern based on the features generated by *RightsWATCH*, which can be used to identify possible data leaks linked to abnormal behaviour. Regardless, there is still so much more to do. With the knowledge about what has already been done and how, it becomes easy to define a high level roadmap for the framework. The first step is to test additional different options for log aggregation – tests for aggregating logs considering different time frames, considering a fixed number of logs and considering the use of a sliding window. If the classifier's performance does not improve, it might be advisable to start testing with different classification methods, other than *SVM*. There is actually an alternative machine learning technique that worth to compare with *SVM* (the only reason why it was not tested already is because it would give birth to a whole new project). This technique is called online learning. Online or incremental (online learning and incremental learning are considered to be the same thing as often as they are not) machine learning is similar to the standard "offline" machine learning, with the difference that the model is updated after the initial training, as new data points arrive. This would allow the framework to continuously improve the classifier, even if the user changed is behavioural pattern. In a very interesting article, Laskov suggests a way to extend the already known one-class and *SVDD* classification methods to this learning method [24], but of course, there are many more implementation suggestions, considering both linear and non-linear kernels.

Acknowledgments

This work has been supported by FCT – Fundação para a Ciência e Tecnologia within the Project Scope UID/CEC/00319/2013.

References

[1] "2015 cost of data breach study: Global analysis," Ponemon Institute LLC, 2308 US 31 North, Traverse City, Michigan 49686 USA, Tech. Rep., May 2015.

[2] J. Bayuk, "Data-centric security," Computer Fraud & Security, vol. 2009, no. 3, 2009, pp. 7 – 11.

[3] Watchful software's RightsWATCH. https://www.watchfulsoftware.com/en. Retrieved: August, 2016.

[4] D. V. C. Venkaiah, D. M. S. Rao, and G. J. Victor, "Intrusion detection systems - analysis and containment of false positives alerts," International Journal of Computer Applications, vol. 5, no. 8, August 2010, pp. 27–33, published by Foundation of Computer Science.

[5] S. Axelsson, "Research in intrusion-detection systems: A survey," 1998.

[6] A. Pathan, The State of the Art in Intrusion Prevention and Detection. Taylor and Francis, January 2014.

[7] H. Debar, M. Dacier, and A. Wespi, "Towards a taxonomy of intrusiondetection systems," Computer Networks, vol. 31, no. 8, 1999, pp. 805–822.
[8] P. de Boer and M. Pels, "Host-based intrusion detection systems," Amsterdam University, 2005.
[9] K. Scarfone and P. Mell, "Guide to intrusion detection and prevention systems (idps)," NIST Special Publication, vol. 800, no. 2007, 2007, p. 94.
[10] D. E. Denning, "An intrusion-detection model," Software Engineering, IEEE Transactions on, no. 2, 1987, pp. 222–232.
[11] H. S. Javitz and A. Valdes, "The sri ides statistical anomaly detector," in Research in Security and Privacy, 1991. Proceedings., 1991 IEEE Computer Society Symposium on. IEEE, 1991, pp. 316–326.
[12] C. Manikopoulos and S. Papavassiliou, "Network intrusion and fault detection: a statistical anomaly approach," Communications Magazine, IEEE, vol. 40, no. 10, 2002, pp. 76–82.
[13] W. Lee and S. J. Stolfo, Data mining approaches for intrusion detection. Defense Technical Information Center, 2000.
[14] L. Portnoy, E. Eskin, and S. Stolfo, "Intrusion detection with unlabeled data using clustering," in Proceedings of ACM CSS Workshop on Data Mining Applied to Security (DMSA-2001, 2001, pp. 5–8.
[15] T. Lane and C. E. Brodley, "An application of machine learning to anomaly detection," in Proceedings of the 20th National Information Systems Security Conference, vol. 377. Baltimore, USA, 1997.
[16] T. Shon and J. Moon, "A hybrid machine learning approach to network anomaly detection," Information Sciences, vol. 177, no. 18, 2007, pp. 3799–3821.
[17] H. S. Vaccaro and G. E. Liepins, "Detection of anomalous computer session activity," in Security and Privacy, 1989. Proceedings., 1989 IEEE Symposium on. IEEE, 1989, pp. 280–289.
[18] C. Dowell and P. Ramstedt, "The computerwatch data reduction tool," in Proceedings of the 13th National Computer Security Conference. University of California, 1990, pp. 99–108.
[19] S. Forrest, S. A. Hofmeyr, and A. Somayaji, "Computer immunology," Communications of the ACM, vol. 40, no. 10, 1997, pp. 88–96.
[20] P. Spirakis, S. Katsikas, D. Gritzalis, F. Allegre, J. Darzentas, C. Gigante, D. Karagiannis, P. Kess, H. Putkonen, and T. Spyrou, "Securenet: A network-oriented intelligent intrusion prevention and detection system," Network Security Journal, vol. 1, no. 1, 1994.
[21] T. Spyrou and J. Darzentas, "Intention modelling: approximating computer user intentions for detection and prediction of intrusions." in SEC, 1996, pp. 319–336.
[22] V. Chandola, A. Banerjee, and V. Kumar, "Anomaly detection: A survey," ACM Computing Surveys (CSUR), vol. 41, no. 3, 2009, p. 15.
[23] C.-C. Chang and C.-J. Lin, "Libsvm: a library for support vector machines," ACM Transactions on Intelligent Systems and Technology (TIST), vol. 2, no. 3, 2011, p. 27.
[24] P. Laskov, C. Gehl, S. Kruger, and K.-R. M ¨ uller, "Incremental support vector learning: Analysis, implementation and applications," The Journal of Machine Learning Research, vol. 7, 2006, pp. 1909–1936.

Quantifiable Measurement Scheme for Mobile Code Vulnerability Based on Machine-Learned API Features

Hyunki Kim*, Joonsang Yoo*, Jeong Hyun Yi†
*Department of Software Convergence
Soongsil University, Seoul, 06978, Korea
Email: {hitechnet92,phoibos92}@gmail.com
†School of Software
Soongsil University, Seoul, 06978, Korea
Email: jhyi@ssu.ac.kr

Abstract—**Owing to open market policies and self-signed certificates, any malicious application developer can easily insert malicious code into Android mobile applications and then distribute them in the Google Play market. Furthermore, even applications that are known to be benign or safe are collecting private information without asking users. Thus, there is a need for a quantifiable measurement scheme that can evaluate the degree of risk posed by an application beyond applications simply being classified as normal or malicious. In this paper, by using ensemble learning, we develop a quantifiable measurement scheme to assess the sensitivity of the Android framework API, and we experimentally evaluate the feasibility of this scheme.**

Keywords–Android; Vulnerability; Application Assessment

I. INTRODUCTION

With the increasing number of mobile devices, such as smartphones, tablets, and wearable devices, based on the Android operating system, the use of the Google Play market has also dramatically increased. However, owing to open market policies such as self-signed certificates, the number of users suffering from malicious applications has also greatly increased. For example, a malicious application developer can download an application registered in the market and then re-upload the application with added malignant behavior codes, resulting in many problems such as private information leakage and financial threats [1][2]. These applications can be installed on a users devices and can secretly steal the users location information or encrypt personal information and request money in return for decryption. To implement these behaviors, framework Application Programming Interfaces(API) or user-defined methods are used. User-defined methods also use framework APIs provided by the operating system. Therefore, to understand the behaviors of the application, the APIs used by the application must be analyzed.

In this paper, we generate an API sensitivity ranking by using machine learning with API metadata. API metadata includes the package name, class name, and API name, each of which comprises words that reflect the behavior of the API [3]. Thus, the learning model creates classification rules based on these words, thereby predicting new input data [4]. On the other hand, because the ensemble learning model is more accurate than a single model, we use various learning models in an ensemble to produce a high-accuracy result [5].

This is the first attempt to actually generate API sensitivity ranking. API sensitivity ranking can be used for criteria measuring the risk of an application, thus alert user to potentially risky application. Also, It can make developers refrain from abusing the sensitive API, and therefore spend more attention to secure programming. Previous work has been done to distinguish applications into normal and malicious [6]. However, users might use malicious application because it is distinguished as a normal application. Therefore, applications must be evaluated in a degree of risk to prevent harm.

The remainder of this paper is organized as follows. Section 2 describes the method used to generate the API sensitivity ranking. Section 3 presents the experimental result of generated ranking. Section 4 concludes the paper.

II. PROPOSED SCHEME

The API sensitivity ranking generator, as shown in the following Figure 1, consists of an API Metadata Extractor, Data Preprocessor, and Predictive Model via Ensemble Machine Learning.

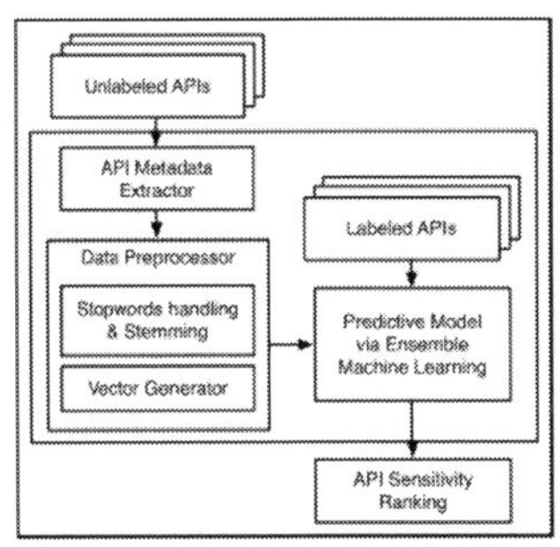

Figure 1. Framework of API sensitivity ranking generator

To generate the API sensitivity ranking, first, we build training data for the nonsensitive and sensitive APIs. To do so, we analyze more than 6,000 malicious applications collected from Contagio [7] and VirusShare [8].

A. API Metadata Extractor

The API Metadata Extractor crawls the metadata of the API in the Android developer site. The API metadata consist of the API name, package name, class name, and API description, which reflects the behavior of the API and the resources that the API accesses. For example, the GetDeviceID method belongs to the TelephonyManager class under the android.telephony package. Through this, it can be seen that GetDeviceID accesses the telephony service. In addition, the

API description Returns the unique device ID of a subscription, for example, the IMEI for GSM and the MEID for CDMA phones explicitly states that it is used to retrieve the device ID, such as IMEI and GSM. When this metadata extraction process is finished, the vocabulary tokenization process is performed for the package name, class name, API name, and API description.

B. Data Preprocessor

1) Stop Words and Stemming: The extracted API Metadata includes stop words such as this, that, and who that, by themselves, do not provide any useful information. Because these words could degrade the performance of the learning model, in this paper, they are removed by defining the following words as stop words [9].

TABLE I. Defined stop words list

```
'i', 'me', 'my', 'myself', 'we', 'our', 'ours',
'ourselves', 'you','your', 'yours', 'yourself',
'yourselves', 'he', 'him', 'his', 'himself',
'she','her', 'hers', 'herself', 'it', 'its',
'itself', 'they', 'them', 'their', 'theirs',
'themselves','what', 'which', 'who', 'whom',
'this', 'that', 'these', 'those', 'am', ...
```

Stemming is a process by which a word is reduced to its word root. It is usually performed by removing any suffixes and prefixes from the word. For example, in the API metadata, some words have the same meaning but in different forms, such as retrieve, retrieved, retrieving, and retrieval. Because these words could also degrade the performance of the learning model, the stemming process proceeds in accordance of the rules [10].

2) Vector Generator: After pre-processing the metadata, they are transformed into a vector that is capable of machine learning. To generate a vector from the metadata, first, a dictionary of all words is created. Then, the metadata is matched with the dictionary.

C. Predictive Model via Ensemble Machine Learning

Ensemble learning is a composite learning model that is constructed by combining various learning models. When new data is given, the individual learning model that makes up the ensemble class votes the class label of the data, and then, the ensemble model collects the votes of the individual learning model and finally predicts the outcome. Under the condition that the classifier outputs are independent, it was proved that the voting combination will always result in a performance improvement compared to a single classifier. The API sensitivity ranking is generated by using the result of the majority voting. As a simple example, assume that there exist five learning models. When new data is entered, if four learning models classify it as sensitive and one learning model classifies it as non-sensitive, then it is given a ranking of 0.8.

III. EXPERIMENT

We generate the API sensitivity ranking using ten learning models, in which the highest performance ten learning models were selected using the cross-validation method. The following table shows the API sensitivity ranking created by the ensemble model. The most sensitive APIs are assigned a rank of 1.0 as shown in Table II. For higher ranks, mainly SMS, File, Network, and Contact related APIs are found, whereas for lower ranks, data type, painting, and weather related APIs are found. Our experimental results demonstrate that the top rank results were actually confirmed to be mainly used for malicious applications such as ransomware and Trojans.

TABLE II. Sensitivity API Ranking

Ranking	API List
1.0	URLConnection.getPermission(), TelephonyManager.getDeviceID(), SmsManager.sendDataMessage(), SmsManager.sendTextMessage(), TelephonyManager.getLine1Number(), ...
0.9	LocationProvider.requiresNetwork(), AppWidgetHost.deleteHost(), BasicHttpResponse.getStatusLine(), UserManager.getUserForSerialNumber(), SendSmsResult.getSendStatus(), ...
...	...
0.0	PictureDrawable.getPicture(), DateFormatSymbols.getEras(), TextView.getCompoundDrawablePadding(), Deflater.getAdler(), NumberFormat.getIntegerInstance(), Resources.getColor(), Resources.Theme.getDrawable(), ...

IV. CONCLUSION

In this paper, we propose a scheme for quantitatively evaluating the risk of an application by generating the sensitivity ranking of the API. Because the API is mainly used to implement the functionality of applications, it is expected that risk assessment using the sensitivity ranking of the API can be more objective compared to conventional risk assessment methods.

ACKNOWLEDGMENT

This research was supported by the Global Research Laboratory (GRL) program through the National Research Foundation of Korea (NRF) funded by the Ministry of Science, ICT, and Future Planning (NRF-2014K1A1A2043029).

REFERENCES

[1] J. H. Jung, J. Y. Kim, H. C. Lee, and J. H. Yi, "Repackaging attack on android banking applications and its countermeasures," Wireless Personal Communications, vol. 73, no. 4, 2013, pp. 1421–1437.

[2] A. P. Felt, M. Finifter, E. Chin, S. Hanna, and D. Wagner, "A survey of mobile malware in the wild," The 1st ACM Workshop on Security and Privacy in Smartphones and Mobile Devices, 2011, pp. 3–14.

[3] Android API Reference, https://developer.android.com/reference/packages.html, Apr. 2015.

[4] P. Domingos, "A few useful things to know about machine learning," Communications of the ACM, vol. 55, no. 10, 2012, pp. 78–87.

[5] T. G. Dietterich, "Ensemble methods in machine learning," International Workshop on Multiple Classifier Systems, 2000, pp. 1–15.

[6] M. Lindorfer, M. Neugschwandtner, and C. Platzer, "Marvin: Efficient and comprehensive mobile app classification through static and dynamic analysis," The 39th IEEE Annual International Computer Software and Applications Conference, 2015, pp. 422–433.

[7] Contagio, http://contagiodump.blogspot.kr/, Apr. 2015.

[8] VirusShare, https://virusshare.com/, Apr. 2015.

[9] H. Saif, M. Fernandez, Y. He, and H. Alani, "On stopwords, filtering and data sparsity for sentiment analysis of twitter," The 9th International Conference on Language Resources and Evaluation, 2014, pp. 810–817.

[10] D. A. Hull, "Stemming algorithms: A case study for detailed evaluation," Journal of the American Society for Information Science, vol. 47, no. 1, 1996, pp. 70–84.

Single Sign-On Webservice with Adaptable Multi Factor Authentication

Sandra Kübler, Christian Rinjes, Anton Wiens and Michael Massoth
Department of Computer Science
Hochschule Darmstadt – University of Applied Sciences
Darmstadt, Germany
e-mail: {sandra.kuebler | christian.rinjes | anton.wiens | michael.massoth}@h-da.de

Abstract—**Cybercrime activities have led to a global cost of 445 billion USD in 2014. Potential and attractive targets of cybercriminals are identity and access management systems. These are especially used by enterprises to better organize their employees' credentials and privileges. Part of such a system can be a single sign-on service to reduce the number of different accounts/credentials of a user. To enhance security, multi factor authentication is slowly becoming more present in identity and access management systems and single sign-on services. In this paper, we will present a new approach to multi factor authentication in a web-based single sign-on service called SecureAID. This service is thought to be extensible and easy to implement for service providers, who are able to define their own (minimum) security levels. A security level defines which factors are required for a login to the service of a service provider. For a user, it is possible to define their own order in which factors are used, thus further improving usability. Additionally, a user is able to use an arbitrary number and type of factors, as long as the minimum security level defined by a service provider is met. This paper concludes with an evaluation of our approach.**

Keywords-web-based single sign-on; multi factor authentication; digital identity; security levels.

I. Introduction

Through the help of identity and access management (IAM) systems, enterprises are trying to meet the demands of user account, privilege and password management, as well as single sign-on (SSO) services. With the growing digitalization, the need for secure cyber systems is bigger than ever, as cybercrime activities are growing as well. According to the internet security company *McAfee*, the global cost of cybercrime in 2014 has been estimated to be 445 billion USD [1]. Identity theft is one of the threats companies and their employees, as well as a person in private have to face. To enhance security of IAM systems, the use of multi factor or at least two factor authentication is growing. On the one hand, multi factor authentication combined with a SSO service in an IAM system must meet basic and additionally defined security aspects. On the other hand, these IAM systems must provide ease of use for a company and its employees, for users in general (private) and have to be practicable.

In this paper, we will present a new approach to combine an arbitrary number of authentication methods with distinct strengths to one identity. A service provider is given the possibility to support a large number of factors without having to implement them in their own platform. Only the minimum requirements concerning the required security level in total have to be defined by a service provider. A *factor* is an *identity* the user already possesses, e.g., a social login (Facebook, Twitter, etc.) of a third-party supplier or his own palm which can be scanned. A service provider using the system cannot derive the user's *distinct identities* from the single identity given by the system.

The paper is structured as follows. Subsequent to the introduction, a definition of terms is given. Section III shows related work, as in products and papers concerning multi factor authentication in an identity and access management system and single sign-on service. Following this, Section IV introduces attack vectors in general on web-based services. Our approach, SecureAID, is presented in Section V. How big of a threat the described attack vectors of Section IV are to our service is shown in Section VI. Section VII ends this paper with a conclusion and future work.

II. Definitions

In this section, we will introduce definitions of terms helpful for understanding this paper.

Security (own definition): The term security can be defined in many different ways, depending on the actual context. As our goal is to provide a web-based single sign-on system with multi factor authentication, our definition is as follows: The system is viewed as *secure*, if no other individual (or robot, artificial intelligence, etc.) can impersonate the actual user, who wants to log into the service. It has to be pointed out that such a system consists of several possibly safety-critical components. This further bears the question whether one or more compromised components can lead to an insecure system as a whole.

Identity and Access Management (IAM) System: An IAM system is defined to be able to combine user account, privilege and password management, as well as single sign-on (see definition below) across all platforms and for all application types. It is a so-called *multiproduct approach*. [2]

Web-based single sign-on (WebSSO) service: A web-based SSO service is "used to move the authentication and authorization of users out of individual web applications, to a shared platform" [3]. Typically, when a user wants to sign in to a website or web application using a WebSSO service, the service first checks if the user is already authenticated. If this is not the case, the user is able to sign in using the required methods (e.g., username + password or a smartcard) at an authentication server [3].

Multi factor authentication: Using two or more independent factors for an authentication is seen as multi factor authentication. Generally, the more factors are used, the more secure it is. A hacker has more "obstacles" to overcome, meaning the hacker has to be able to gain access to all of the factors used to impersonate a person.

III. RELATED WORK

There exist several products offering multi factor authentication in identity and access management systems and single sign-on services. PalmSecure truedentity from Fujitsu [4] is a product offering a mutual authentication of services and users, while the users' identities are kept in their possession. The authenticity of both parties is verified by a server. Several different factors, such as smartcards or biometric factors, can be used, but their palm vein scanner, PalmSecure, has to be used as one of the factors. IBM offers identity and access management systems and has several products in their product family. One of those is the IBM Security Access Management. IBM provides an integrated platform for web, mobile and cloud, offering "multiple strong authentication schemes", including one-time passwords (OTP) and SMS verification codes [5]. CA Technologies offers "CA Strong Authentication", which provides "multi-factor authentication for web applications, portals and mobile apps" [6]. Several factors are supported and security levels are introduced. These are dependent on the application the user wants to gain access to and it is not possible to choose custom factors within a category. As for the factors, they do not include external identity providers and all user data is saved on their own repositories (users and 2F credentials, as well as audit data).

Aloul et al. propose a method, which uses mobile phones for two factor authentication [7]. A mobile phone is used for generating an OTP being composed by using factors unique to the user and the mobile phone. This OTP is only valid for a user-defined period of time. They use a SMS-based mechanism for back-up and synchronization purposes.

Bhargav-Spantzel et al. use a two-factor biometric authentication in the first phase for a two-phase authentication mechanism for federated identity management systems [8]. Other authentication factors are combined with the biometric factor in the second phase. Their focus lies on the generation of a biometric key using vector-space modeling.

In [9], a modular framework for multi factor authentication and key exchange is proposed and a tag-based method is used.

In all solutions or approaches presented in related work, external identity providers were not included. In some cases, multi factor authentication is used as a synonym of two-factor authentication. Proprietary solutions often demand the use of at least one factor which has to be used, for instance PalmSecure in combination with truedentity. Our approach is designed to include external providers to be more extensible and to grant more flexibility. Furthermore, the possibility to use more than two independent factors is granted.

IV. ATTACK VECTORS

Multiple possibilities to perform attacks on web-based systems do exist. In this work, we will focus on rudimentary attack vectors possible on such systems and will not delve into details.

We distinguish between attacks on our service/platform, the used interfaces (third-party provider) and the user. The purpose of such attacks is to gain access to user accounts and, therefore, compromise them. Depending on the system, a hacker can gain access to additional services. Concerning our approach, the hacker could have the intent to gain the digital identity of a certain user.

Several methods can be used to perform attacks. The act of *social engineering* consists of using a social disguise, a cultural ploy or a trick, mostly psychological towards a computer user in order to gain illegal access to, e.g., a computer or a network [10]. *Brute force* is the most basic method to perform an attack. An attacker uses "brute force" to gain access to a system, mostly by sequentially trying all possible variations of a password concerning the order of numbers, letters, etc. The method of performing *Man-in-the-Middle attacks* (user- and third-party supplier side) is defined as a situation, in which "an adversarial computer between two computers [is] pretending to one to be the other" [11]. Concerning attacks against a database (gaining access), be it one at a third-party supplier side or of the service provider, there exist several possibilities to do so. Having gained access to a database can potentially, e.g., enable an attacker to impersonate a customer/user, to alter existing data (changing administration controls), to add new content (giving the attacker full access to the system) or to simply delete or extract existing data.

V. SECUREAID

Our approach, *SecureAID* (Secure N-Factor-Authentication and IDentity Management), is to combine several factors into one single identity of a user while securing the user's (data) privacy and identity. It is an independent web-based single sign-on service enabling multi factor authentication and is thought to be extensible and easy to implement for service providers. A web interface enables the user interaction, providing the possibility to register, login and configure an account. Service providers can integrate SecureAID as a service and define, which factors a user is required to have and use for the login to the provider's service. Users are able to register themselves to SecureAID using existing external factors, such as a login to a social network, etc., so that they can easily login via SecureAID, given the service provider they want to login to has integrated our service.

In this section, we will first provide an overview of SecureAID's architecture, followed by registration and authentication processes. Afterwards, possible factors for a multi factor authentication are organized in types of factors. These types are then further categorized into security levels, before a definition of the term "digital identity" is given. This section ends with an example of a login process, as well as advantages and disadvantages concerning the usability of SecureAID.

A. *Architecture overview*

An overview of the architecture of SecureAID is shown in Fig. 1.

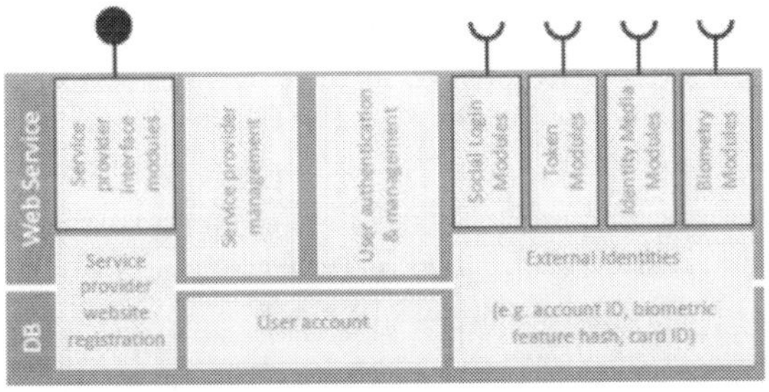

Figure 1. Overview of the architecture of SecureAID.

SecureAID is a modular web-based single sign-on service. It provides modules for factors to retrieve or verify user identities from social login services, identity media, biometric devices and security tokens (external identities). Other modules exist to allow service provider websites to request authentication and retrieve a unique user identity. A database stores the identities and no credentials, as well as an ordered list of all identities used for authentication with service provider websites. A web interface allows users to create a new account and add, remove and rearrange the order of factors for the platform and service providers. It also allows for registration and configuration of new and existing service providers under the current user's account.

B. *Registration and authentication processes*

In order to use SecureAID and before an authentication can take place, users have to register themselves to the service. In the following, we distinguish between user and service provider, the latter being a specialization of the former, as every user can potentially be a service provider.

1) User registration process

Users trying to sign in with an identity not present in the database are given the option to create a new account using the third-party identity provided. This new account can then immediately be used for authentication and be further extended with additional factors and ordered login lists for service providers.

2) User authentication process

For service provider authentication, a website redirects a user to the SecureAID platform to provide their credentials, which are then matched against the registered information. To modify their SecureAID account, a user simply opens the platform's website. The user then selects the first module he chose for the given service to start the authentication process and, in order, verifies and confirms all factors. After the requirements for the login list have been met, the user is then signed in to SecureAID or, if the required security level is met, authorizes the service provider website to retrieve their specific user ID. Furthermore, a user is able to define multiple paths for authentication. Each path is an order in which factors are used. With multiple possible paths for authentication, a user is provided with alternatives for the authentication process, for instance, if the user forgets one of the factors or is not able to use one. The alternative login processes have to meet the service provider's requirements concerning the security level.

3) Service provider registration/authentication process

Any user authenticated to SecureAID is able to register a new service provider website by specifying a display name, minimum security level and further authentication method specific credentials. In the case of OAuth2 (delegation protocol), a valid redirect URI must be specified and the user/service provider will be provided with a client ID and secret.

A sequence diagram of an authentication process of a user is shown in Fig. 2. In this example, a social login is used for authentication. Preliminary to the shown authentication process, the service provider a user wants to login to has registered its service to SecureAID. Upon starting the authentication process, the user is able to see SecureAIDs web interface and do further actions to authenticate.

Upon choosing, in this example, "login with social login X", a user gets redirected to the interface of the social login X (SLX), together with a client ID, redirect URI and the requested scopes belonging to the ID. The SLX first checks whether client ID and redirect URI are known. Upon a match, the user has to login to the social login. Given the credentials of the user are correct and the user wants to login for the first time with SLX using SecureAID, the user is asked if SecureAID is allowed to have access to the scopes of the ID. The confirmation is saved into a database to allow the access to the scopes for longer range, given the user allowed it. If the confirmation has been already given, the next step is for SLX to generate an authentication code which is, using the redirect URI, redirected to SecureAID. At last, SecureAID is given an ID token from SLX in order to request user data.

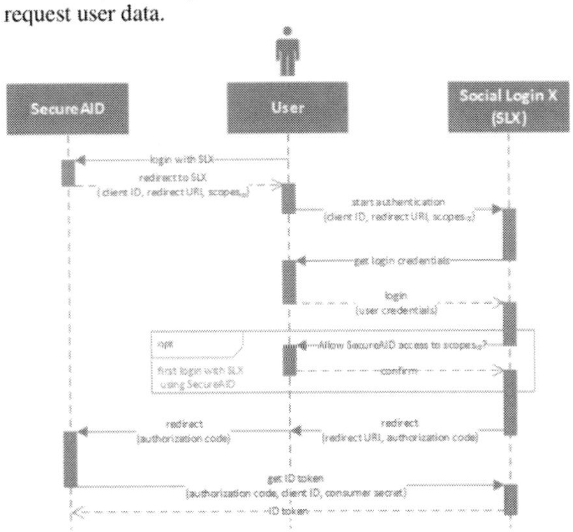

Figure 2. The authentication process of a user using a social login X.

C. *Factors for multi factor authentication*

There can be several factors for a multi factor authentication. In the following, the authors provide a list of factors grouped into different types.

1) Social logins

Already existing user accounts from external providers are defined as social logins. For example, Facebook, Google or Twitter accounts count as such. Usually, the login process is based on knowledge of the user (username + password). Therefore, it is a factor the user knows.

2) Token

A token is something users have in their possession and a factor from an external device. One example for tokens are time-based one-time passcode generators (software), such as Google Authenticator [12] or even a SMS with a passcode send to a mobile device. These passcodes can be used for a two-factor authentication by combining a conventional login of a user with a username and password with the generated passcode as a second factor. The FIDO (Fast IDentity Online) Alliance's hosted Universal Second Factor (U2F) protocol can be used for a strong two-factor authentication, too, for instance with a FIDO U2F device [13] via USB with a button or NFC (hardware token).

3) Identity media

A user has an identity medium. This possession is often combined with knowledge of a PIN or password. Such a medium can be a smartcard or electronic identity (eID) card. Further, it is possible to have other features saved on an identity medium, such as a fingerprint or a vein scan.

4) Biometry

A biometric factor is something a user is. The most prominent biometric factors are fingerprints, iris scans or even vein scans of, e.g., a palm (see Fig. 3).

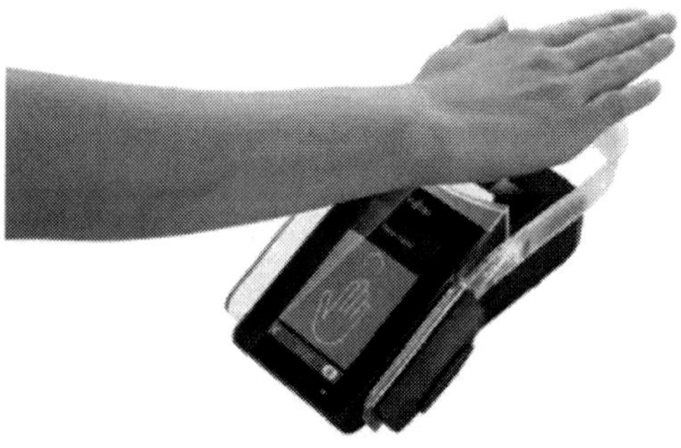

Figure 3. Example of a (palm) vein scanner: Fujitsu's PalmSecure ID Match [14].

D. *Security level*

As a means to further improve security of the service, *security levels* are introduced. A service provider has the possibility to define a minimum security level, which all of its users shall meet using a set of pre-defined *types of factors*. The combination of the chosen types of factors results in the minimum security level.

For instance, a security level is set to only allow authentications that include the two types of factors "identity medium" and "unforgeable biometric" (e.g., palm scan). A user can now only authenticate to this service provider when using at least these two types of factors.

Fig. 4 shows a pyramid of possible types of factors (see Section V.C). The higher its position in the pyramid, the more secure the type is. This ranking does not exclude the possibility to combine different types of factors, resulting in a higher security level. For instance, it is still possible for a service provider to demand a social login, as well as vein scan (unforgeable biometric factor) of a user for the login process.

Social logins are seen by the authors as the least secure of the shown types of factors. The credentials of a user are typically stored in databases by external providers of a social login. A database itself is a likely target by a hacker. Besides the database, there exist varying levels of personal security concerning the chosen passwords, which lead to them being regularly compromised. Additionally, social networking accounts are a common target for social engineering attacks. The next factor, *tokens*, are relatively easy to obtain, e.g., hardware tokens can be easily stolen, lost or even broken. They require access to another device or even physical access.

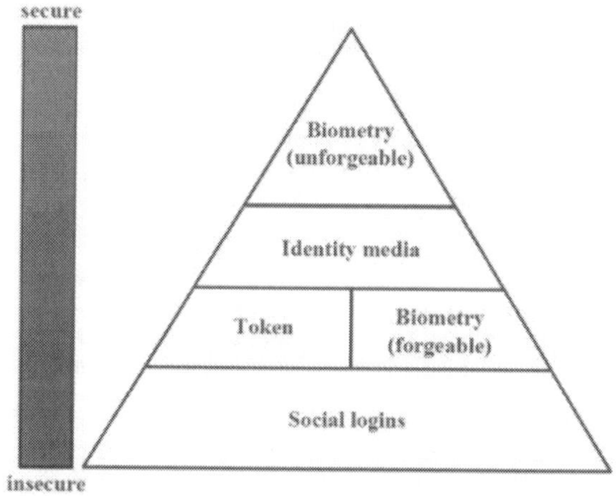

Figure 4. Pyramid of possible types of factors, in which each layer corresponds to a higher grade of security.

Biometric factors have been divided into *forgeable* and *unforgeable*. *Forgeable biometry*, for instance, a fingerprint can be copied by another person using a tape or a high resolution picture. Using an iris scan as a factor is viewed as forgeable as well, as a high resolution picture can suffice to tamper with an access gain system, too. On the other hand, a fingerprint or a picture of an iris is still needed beforehand in order to copy and use the factor, which is per se more difficult than obtaining credentials of a social login. *Identity media* are, in total, ranked higher than forgeable biometry and tokens. It is possible to save biometric factors, for instance, a fingerprint or a vein scan, which makes the identity medium itself less possible to be forged. In most cases, a PIN is required as well when utilizing an identity medium. *Unforgeable biometry* is at the top of the pyramid and, therefore, seen as the safest out of the mentioned factor types. For instance, using a vein scan as a biometric factor to gain access to a system is currently seen as unforgeable. A vein scan, be it of a palm or an iris, requires a flow of blood, meaning, a person wanting to gain access to a system has to be alive and therefore making it more difficult to forge.

E. Digital identity

Each user has their own *digital identity*. After using the service to authenticate themselves with an arbitrary number of factors, a service provider is given a hash value – the digital identity. Besides the number and types of factors, a user is able to choose the order in which the factors are used. Due to the digital identity being a hash value, a service provider is not able to derive any factors and the order in which these factors were used by a user during the authentication process. Additionally, no two service providers receive the same digital identity for the same user.

F. Example of a login process

Fig. 5 shows the login process with SecureAID using a social login and another factor from the second layer upwards of the pyramid (see Fig. 4) for the authentication.

A user from a service provider website wants to login using the service SecureAID (1). Using a social login and getting the approval of the service (2), the user can now use a second factor to authenticate. The second factor is used to verify that the user trying to login is truly the user. After the verification using the second factor is approved (3), SecureAID communicates the approval to the website of the service provider (4).

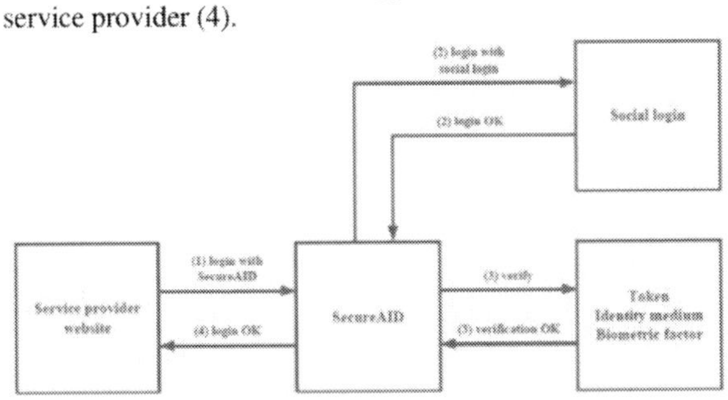

Figure 5. Example of a login process with SecureAID.

G. Usability

In the following, possible advantages and disadvantages of SecureAID concerning usability are presented.

1) Advantages

Both a service provider and a user can profit from the customizable security level. For instance, if the required authentication security level of another service enabling the use of multi factor authentication is regarded as not high enough, a user can choose the use of SecureAID. Another point is the configuration through the web interface of the system. As already mentioned in Section V.A, it is possible to add, remove and rearrange the order of factors. This is done via drag and drop, which is more intuitively and comfortable for a user. The registration of new and existing service providers can also be done via web interface. A service provider only needs to indicate a redirect URI and is able to choose the types of factors for the minimum security level via checkboxes.

2) Disadvantages

More factors and diversity for authentication may lead to a decrease in usability. For instance, a service provider chose more than two types of factors – e.g., palm vein scan (biometric), eID (identity medium) and Facebook login (social login). Logging in with all three factors can lead to a user to be on edge, as the most common form of authentication is to type in a username and password or, especially concerning employees, by using an identity medium, e.g., a smartcard, which is less time consuming.

VI. ATTACK VECTORS AGAINST SECUREAID

In Section IV, an overview of attack vectors against web-based systems has been given. In this section, we will elaborate theoretically how big a threat these attack vectors are to our approach and whether it is possible to impersonate a user or not.

A. Social engineering

This attack vector – or rather method to perform an attack – strongly depends on the user. It is possible for a hacker to trick users into revealing all of their factors. A next step would be to get all login credentials. Now, it strongly depends on the used factors and the security level defined by the service. For instance, if only a social login and an OTP were required as factors, the possibility of a hacker being able to impersonate a user after using social engineering would be very high. If an unforgeable biometric factor like a palm vein scan were to be required, a hacker would not be able to impersonate the user, as this factor is bound to a "sign of life" of the user.

B. Brute force

Using the method of brute force to perform an attack on SecureAID requires the knowledge of SecureAID as a service. If a hacker knows about a user's profile in our service, the hacker could possibly acquire as much pieces of information as when he has access to the database. From here on, hackers can extend their "research" on other services, such as social logins, and eventually acquire the login credentials and, therefore, possibly impersonate the user.

C. Man-in-the-Middle attack

A Man-in-the-Middle attack can be distinguished between user-side and third-party supplier side. On the user's side, an attacker would be able to acquire the login credentials of a user of different services (e.g., social logins like Facebook or Twitter). Using *SecureAID* would not change the fact that acquiring such credentials is still possible for an attacker. The attacker would still have to gain the knowledge that a service like *SecureAID* exists and that there are additional pieces of information and data to be collected.

On the side of a third-party supplier, the digital identity of a user would be exposed for an attacker. The digital identity per se is not usable for a hacker, as it is only a hash value. However, the attacker could be able to monitor the user and possibly back trace the user's actions. This would lead to the attacker knowing about the service SecureAID and that the user is using this service. But the attacker would not know about the service provider the user wants to login to using SecureAID. Nevertheless, without any additional data, the attacker would not be able to fully impersonate the user, as the attacker does not have the *whole identity* and would still have to bypass the other factors used by the user.

D. Attack against database (gaining access)

At this point, we are not going into detail about defense strategies in various aspects of a database holder, but we are assuming the fact that a hacker actually *has gained access* to a database. Potential targets of an attack could be a database of a third-party supplier or SecureAID's database.

Having access to a database of a third-party supplier is giving a hacker as much information as a Man-in-the-Middle attack. The attacker gets the third-party supplier's digital identity of a user and gains knowledge about SecureAID, but still has to do further "research".

Access to the database of SecureAID is providing a hacker with more pieces of information. All user's digital identities (user IDs) and corresponding third-party suppliers are stored in a database. With this data, a hacker is able to recreate a user's profile, but still has to get login credentials of a user and **is not able to impersonate** a user. Hacking the database of SecureAID does not come with a loss of a user's login credentials.

The success of a hacker is strongly dependent on the type of the factors used and, therefore, the defined security level of a service provider. For instance, if only social logins are used, a hacker could easily impersonate a user.

VII. Conclusion and Future Work

In this paper, we presented a new approach for multi factor authentication using an arbitrary number of independent factors as a web-based SSO service SecureAID with a customizable level of security.

The ***unique characteristics and features*** of our approach are the following: Service providers can define their own minimum security level by choosing which types of factors have to be at least used. A user is able to freely choose the order and amount in which the factors are used. The choice of factors is only limited to the ones supported by SecureAID and the security level defined by a service provider using SecureAID. Another strength is, given a hacker has gained access to the digital identity (hash value) of a user, having the digital identity alone is not sufficient to impersonate a user. For instance, if one social login of a user is compromised, the hacker knows that the hacked user is using our system. This knowledge alone is not sufficient enough to impersonate the user, as the hacker still has to bypass all other factors/systems. Potential shortcomings can possibly lie in the usability and user-friendliness, as those can decrease with the number of used factors.

Concerning ***future work***, the list of possible attack vectors can be extended. Additionally, several and extensive tests concerning our approach's defense against these attack vectors have to be conducted.

References

[1] McAfee, Net Losses: Estimating the Global Cost of Cybercrime, Economic impact of cybercrime II. Center for Strategic and International Studies. June 2014. Available from: http://www.mcafee.com/us/resources/reports/rp-economic-impact-cybercrime2.pdf, 2016.05.29.

[2] R. Witty, A. Allan, J. Enck, and R. Wagner, "Identity and Access Management Defined" Research Note, 04 November 2003, Note Number SPA-21-3430. Available from: http://www.bus.umich.edu/KresgePublic/Journals/Gartner/research/118200/118281/118281.pdf, 2016.05.11.

[3] Hitachi ID Systems, Inc., Web Single Sign-on. [Online] Available from: http://hitachi-id.com/resource/concepts/web-sso.html, 2016.05.30.

[4] Fujitsu, PalmSecure truedentity. White paper. [Online] Available from: http://sp.ts.fujitsu.com/dmsp/Publications/public/wp-palmsecure-truedentity-de.pdf, 2016.05.30.

[5] IBM, IBM Security Access Manager, data sheet. [Online] Available from: http://www.ibm.com/common/ssi/cgi-bin/ssialias?subtype=SP&infotype=PM&htmlfid=SED03160USEN&attachment=SED03160USEN.PDF, 2016.05.31.

[6] CA Technologies, CA Strong Authentication, data sheet [Online] Available from: http://www.ca.com/content/dam/ca/us/files/data-sheet/ca-strong-authentication.pdf, 2016.05.31.

[7] F. Aloul, S. Zahidi, and W. El-Hajj, "Multi Factor Authentication Using Mobile Phones" In International Journal of Mathematics and Computer Science, vol. 4, no. 2, pp. 65-80, 2009.

[8] A. Bhargav-Spantzel, A. C. Squicciarini, S. Modi, M. Young, E. Bertino, and S. J. Elliot, "Privacy Preserving Multi-Factor Authentication with Biometrics" In Journal of Computer Security, vol. 15, no. 5, pp. 529-560, 2007.

[9] N. Fleischhacker, M. Manulis, and A. Azodi, "A Modular Framework for Multi-Factor Authentication and Key Exchange" In Security Standardisation Research: First International Conference, Proceedings, Springer International Publishing, pp. 190-214, 2014.

[10] S. Abraham and I. Chengular-Smith, "An overview of social engineering malware: Trends, tactics, and implications" In Technology in Society 32, pp. 183-196, 2010.

[11] Yvo Desmedt, Man-in-the-Middle Attack. Reference work entry in Encyclopedia of Cryptography and Security. 2011, Springer US, pp. 759-759. ISBN 978-1-4419-5906-5, doi:10./1007/978 -1-4419-5906-5_324.

[12] Google Authenticator OpenSource, project side. [Online] Available from: https://github.com/google/google-authenticator, 2016.05.19.

[13] FIDO Alliance official homepage, Specifications Overview. [Online] Available from: https://fidoalliance.org/specifications/overview/, 2016.05.19.

[14] Fujitsu PalmSecure ID Match, product description. [Online] Available from: http://www.fujitsu.com/de/products/computing/peripheral/accessories/security/palmsecure-id-match/, 2016.06.08.

Forensic Analysis of the Recovery of Wickr's Ephemeral Data on Android Platforms

Thomas Edward Allen Barton and M A Hannan Bin Azhar
Computing, Digital Forensics and Cybersecurity
Canterbury Christ Church University
Canterbury, United Kingdom
Email: tb1150@canterbury.ac.uk; hannan.azhar@canterbury.ac.uk

Abstract—**This paper documents anti-forensics techniques of a secure messaging application named "Wickr" on the Android platforms. Advertised as an application that focusses on security, Wickr provides many anti-forensics features, such as ephemeral messaging and end-to-end encryption. This paper analyses Wickr in detail using experimental research methods. The results revealed how Wickr's file deletion consisted of distinct stages beginning with a simple logical deletion and progressing to overwriting deleted files as the application operated.**

Keywords- wickr; android; ephemeral messaging; forensic analysis; data sanitization; mobile forensics

I. INTRODUCTION

The advent of smartphones has allowed for a huge range of third party applications to be developed [1]. Third party applications used to commit crimes present a challenge to digital forensic investigators as vital digital evidence is obscured by their unknown nature and structure. This challenge creates the need for research into how these applications operate. The opportunity for malicious actions presented by third party applications, especially those that emphasize security, is obvious. In the last two years, two large terror attacks were carried out in Europe [2] [3]. These acts are highly coordinated in a fashion that could not occur without technology. Reports on usage of the social media by the Islamic State group (ISIS), for example, have demonstrated how a small group of individuals can fully utilise technology to their advantage, for the purposes of recruitment [4], coordination [5] and communication [6].

One category of the communication applications is an Ephemeral Messaging Application (EMA) that uses transient data [7]. Transient data are only permitted to exist for a limited amount of time. An example of an EMA that rose to huge popularity among the eighteen to thirty-four year old age range (which happens to be statistically the largest demographic for smartphone ownership in the United States [8]) was SnapChat [9], an application that allowed users to send photos and images that would be deleted after opening. In SnapChat's case, the use of ephemeral messaging provided a novel social networking platform that quickly attracted many users. After SnapChat's popularity, other applications began to adopt the feature, including Wickr [10], which aims to provide a service that goes beyond simple social networking. Wickr's use of transient data is part of its professional dedication to security; other features concurrent with this theme include end-to-end encryption [10]. Third party applications with a focus on security thus pose a challenge to digital forensics investigators in retrieving artefacts especially when an application like Wickr incorporates anti-forensics features, such as ephemeral messaging and encryption, in its core functionality. To investigate the organization of the data and to understand how the deletion process works in secure messaging applications like Wickr, a series of experiments were conducted on the Android based platforms. A number of forensic tools were used to inspect different areas of the platforms including data storage, Random Access Memory (RAM) and the Wickr application itself. The experiments reported in this paper are listed in chronological order, each one building on from the last.

The remainder of this paper is organized as follows: Section 2 explains the objectives of this research in relation to previous work completed, and Section 3 goes on to detail the experimental setup and tools used in this project. Sections 4 to 8 detail the experiments, one per section. These experiments follow a pattern of acquisitions and analyses on various areas of interest on the target platform, including the data storage, RAM and the Wickr application itself. Finally, conclusions and future work are discussed in Section 9.

II. OBJECTIVES

Research into the forensic analyses of social media applications often focusses on the most popular applications at the time [11, 12]. Ephemeral data techniques first emerged after the previously mentioned SnapChat gained popularity. The methods used in [7] were successful in recovering artefacts, using physical image analysis of the test platforms. The work reported in [7] demonstrated the ability of forensic investigators to overcome the deletion and obfuscation of artefacts by an ephemeral messaging application. Since SnapChat, other applications have adopted ephemeral messaging as part of their features. Wickr, a secure messaging application, employs anti-forensics tactics, including ephemeral messaging [10]. In the face of such tactics, the use of standard forensic methodologies, such as string searches, may yield challenges in recovering artefacts. Previous investigations reported in [13] have focused on using such plaintext searches to look for artefacts, but Wickr's extensive use of encryption hampered the results.

The aim of the research presented in this paper was to analyse the data storage, removal and sanitization techniques used by Wickr, in order to provide digital forensics investigators some insight on how Wickr operates and also to provide some useful techniques for analysing a secure mobile application like Wickr. The methodology adopted in this investigation took into account that previous attempts to retrieve artefacts, for example searching a backup of the Android data directory for matching strings were not successful as string searches for known artefacts in Wickr revealed no matches [13]. Our investigation overlooked the encryption problem in Wickr and focused instead on how Wickr stores and treats its transient data. To achieve the aim of this research, a number of experiments and analyses were performed on Wickr and its relevant data. These actions can be categorized into two distinct classes. Firstly, forensically sound analysis, which refers to techniques used by forensic investigators in a real-world case with the aim of presenting evidence in court [14], in conjunction with the Association of Chief Police Officers (ACPO) guidelines [15]. Secondly "experimental" analysis, which takes advantage of the freedom of academic research. Results presented in this paper identified the files that Wickr used to store its transient data. Experiments were also conducted to observe how these files could change as the app removed them.

III. EXPERIMENTAL SETUP

In order to establish an experimental setup, Wickr had to be installed on two different Android Platforms. The Samsung Galaxy S4 Mini [16] was the primary platform used. The AllWinner A13 Android tablet [17] was used as a backup platform to ensure the repeatability of all experiments performed. The choice of platform in this case, a phone from Samsung's flagship galaxy range, reflects the current state of the worldwide smartphone market, which is dominated by Android [18], the market for which is in turn dominated by Samsung [18]. Another reason Android was chosen was its huge online developer community, which stems from its open source status. Table 1 lists the detail of platforms, including the versions used in the experiments for Android, kernel and Wickr.

TABLE I. ANDROID PLATFORMS

Name	Specifications			
	Model Number	***Android Version***	***Kernel Version***	***Wickr Version***
Samsung Galaxy S4 Mini [16]	GT-I9195I	4.4.4 (KitKat)	3.10.28-5334500	2.6.4.1
AllWinner A13 [17]	Q8	4.4.2 (KitKat)	3.4.39	2.6.4.1

In order to access all areas of the platform's data storage systems, they needed to be rooted. In the Android developer community, rooting refers to the process of gaining administrator privileges on the device through exploitation of weaknesses in the operating system [13]. This was done via an application called Kingo Root [19], which offers a simple rooting solution. In a real-world scenario, the option of rooting may not be available as it involves changing data on a captured device, which goes against the ACPO guidelines for handling digital evidences [15], and should only be used as a last resort. Investigators may need to use another method to gain access, such as "chip-off" forensics [20]. This involves removing the memory chip of a device and reading the stored data using a bespoke hardware interface. This bypasses any restrictions as it can be performed directly and independently of the platform's operating system.

A. *Forensic Worksation and Software tools*

Two forensic workstations were used, listed in Table 2, the first with Windows, which makes accessing specific tools easier. The second had a distribution of Linux named Kali which came with forensic tools pre-installed on the system.

TABLE II. FORENSIC WORKSTATIONS

Name	Specifications	
	Operating System	***Installed Software***
RM Desktop Core i3	Windows 7	Android Debug Bridge [21] Dex2Jar [22] Java Decompiler [23] File Manager (ZIP Extractor) Autopsy 3.0.8 [24]
Toshiba Sattelite L450D	Kali	Android Debug Bridge [21] Cat (Linux) Strings (Linux) BASH (Linux) Sleuth Kit [24] Mount (Linux)

Most of the software tools used to perform analyses were specific to the experiments. Android Debug Bridge (ADB) is a tool that allows for access to the mobile platform via USB cable [21]. This is a useful tool as it allows command line execution on the platform from the forensic workstation. The Wickr application itself was examined once the "classes. dex" artefact was extracted and converted to a Java Archive (see Section 4). Java Archives have a custom format and are not easily readable in text editors, so a specific tool for Windows, Java Decompiler [23], was used to examine this artefact. Java Decompiler presents the archive in a tabulated format that makes analyses easier.

To examine the data storage, Sleuthkit was used. Sleuthkit is an open-source digital forensics toolkit that revolves around the recovery of deleted files [24]. It is a set of command line tools for Linux. Autopsy was developed by creating a Graphical User Interface (GUI) for Sleuthkit, combining all of the included tools into one seamless package. Autopsy performs very much the same functionality as Sleuthkit, but in GUI form, offering advantages such as file previews. The analysis of acquired data with standard forensics tools previously reported such as Hex Workshop [13], Encase and DCode [11] was not suitable in our experiments, as initial tests confirmed the lack of any artefacts available for recovery. Instead, the experiments searched for alternate artefacts, such as the location and status of files. To do this, simple terminal commands, such as "ls", "strings" and "cat", which are all included in the forensic workstations' distribution of Linux, were used to examine acquired files and directory structures.

IV. EXPERIMENT 1: WICKR.APK DECONSTRUCTION

The objective of the first experiment was to explore the installation package for Wickr in order to understand how it functioned. Android uses installation packages to install new software on the platform. The installation packages used are file archives with the extension ".apk". These contain all the compiled code that is needed to run the application, including both core and third party libraries. Included in these libraries are the functions that Wickr uses to store data. This experiment accessed the data storing functions contained in these libraries so they can be comprehensively understood. A useful artefact contained in the archive is the "classes.dex" file, which contains all the definitions for classes used by Wickr. The "classes.dex" file is composed of compiled code that cannot be analysed using a plaintext analysis method. However, the tool "dex2jar" from the dex2jar project [22] was used to convert this file into a Java archive. The Java Archive was opened using a specialized tool, "Java Decompiler" [23]. There were four steps to this procedure: acquiring the ".apk" using an ADB pull command as seen in Fig. 1, extracting the "classes.dex" file from the archive, converting this file to a Java archive using the tool "dex2jar", and lastly examining the archive using the windows tool "Java Decompiler".

```
Windows PowerShell
Copyright (C) 2015 Microsoft Corporation. All rights reserved.

PS C:\Users\Thomas> adb pull /data/app/com.mywickr.wickr2-1.apk <Local destination>
```

Figure 1: ADB Pull command for Wickr's APK

Android stores applications under "/data/app" [25] and the filename for Wickr is "com.mywickr.wickr2-1.apk". The resulting parameters for the "adb pull" command are displayed in Fig. 1. After opening the "com.mywickr.wickr2-1.apk" file using a ".zip" archive extractor (for example 7-zip or Windows Explorer) the "classes.dex" file was extracted. Using the tool "dex2jar" [22] the "classes.dex" file was converted into a Java archive.

```
WickrDBAdapter.class

package com.mywickr.wickr;

import android.app.Application;
import android.content.Context;
import android.content.SharedPreferences;
import android.content.SharedPreferences.Editor;
import com.mywickr.helpers.SharedPreferencesHelper;
import java.io.File;
import net.sqlcipher.Cursor;
import net.sqlcipher.database.SQLiteDatabase;
import net.sqlcipher.database.SQLiteDatabaseHook;
import net.sqlcipher.database.SQLiteOpenHelper;
import timber.log.Timber;
```

Figure 2. WickrDBAdapter.class header

Data was stored in a database file, which was managed by an SQL Helper class. Shown in Fig.2, the SQL helper class found in the system was "net.sqlcipher.database.SQLite OpenHelper". SQLCipher is an extension to the SQLite database engine that incorporates encryption into its functionality [26]. An extract from the "WickrDBAdapter. class" directory, as shown in Fig. 3, includes variable names such as DATABASE_NAME and their respective values.

```
private static final String DATABASE_NAME = "wickr_db";
private static final int DATABASE_VERSION = 12;
static final String Partner_User_KEY_Wickr_User = "wickrUser";
static final String Partner_User_KEY_avatarUrl = "avatarUrl";
static final String Partner_User_KEY_id = "_id";
static final String Partner_User_KEY_isHidden = "isHidden";
static final String Partner_User_KEY_status = "status";
static final String Partner_User_KEY_userName = "userName";
static final String TABLE_Partner_User = "Partner_User";
public static final String TABLE_Wickr_Account = "Wickr_Account";
```

Figure 3. Extract from WickrDBAdapter.class

V. EXPERIMENT 2: ACQUIRING AND ANALYSING WICKR DATA DIRECTORY

A key part of how an application functions is how and where it stores data in permanent secondary storage. Analysing the data stored by Wickr revealed exactly how the data was stored. To analyse this data, it first had to be acquired. On Android platforms, all data for Wickr is stored in the "com.mywickr.wickr2" directory within the "/data/data" directory [25]. This area of storage is inaccessible unless the investigator has administrative privileges, i.e. the platform is rooted (see Section 3). To acquire this directory and its contents, an external SD card was mounted in the phone. Fig. 4 shows how the UNIX "cp" (copy) command was used recursively to acquire the directory.

```
1|root@serranovelte:/data/data/com.mywickr.wickr2 # cp -av /data/data/com.mywi>
/data/data/com.mywickr.wickr2 -> /mnt/sdcard/Documents/wickr.directory/com.mywic
cp: symlink: /data/app-lib/com.mywickr.wickr2-1: Operation not permitted
/data/data/com.mywickr.wickr2/cache -> /mnt/sdcard/Documents/wickr.directory/com.
/data/data/com.mywickr.wickr2/cache/bugsnag-errors -> /mnt/sdcard/Documents/wick
/data/data/com.mywickr.wickr2/cache/bugsnag-errors -> /mnt/sdcard/Documents/wick
/data/data/com.mywickr.wickr2/cache/com.android.opengl.shaders_cache -> /mnt/sdc
s_cache
```

Figure 4. Dumping Wickr Data Directory to SD card

Upon inspection of the contents of these files using the UNIX "*cat*" command, it becomes clear that files such as "wickr_db" and the ".wic" files lack normal file headers. The resulting conclusion was that Wickr uses encryption, confirming the hypothesis of experiment 1. There were two areas of interest in the directory, including "databases" and "files", both were the subdirectories of the "com.mywickr. wickr2" directory, as seen in Fig. 5.

app_sfs	06/06/2016 15:15	File folder
app_webview	06/06/2016 15:15	File folder
cache	06/06/2016 15:15	File folder
databases	06/06/2016 15:15	File folder
files	06/06/2016 15:15	File folder
no_backup	06/06/2016 15:15	File folder
shared_prefs	06/06/2016 15:15	File folder

Figure 5. Wickr Data Directory Structure

The "databases" directory, shown in Fig. 5, contained a file called "wickr_db", which was an encrypted database. Upon examination of the "WickrDBAdapter.class" file shown in Fig. 3, it became clear that this database was used to store account information, such as usernames of the user and their contacts, IDs, public and private keys. The "files" directory is where Wickr stores its received messages, including both text and attachments. This will be explored in the next experiment.

VI. Experiment 3: Wickr's Data Removal and Sanitization Methods

The nature of transient data requires an ongoing process consisting of at two logical stages. Firstly, the data must be created and stored. Wickr's data is generated by receiving messages. The second stage is the removal of data. This experiment will explore how Wickr achieves the second logical stage, data removal, by examining the data both when they are present and after they have been removed. One of Wickr's features is a "secure shredder" that offers removal of deleted data. Copies of the data directory were be taken when messages were present (opened) in Wickr, after messages had expired, and after the "secure shredder" function had been executed. This experiment used the acquisition method described in experiment 2. Table 3 shows the disparities in the structure and contents of the data directories that revealed how the data was being treated during the handling of transient data.

TABLE III. Data directory analysis results

Stage of File Removal (Arbitrary)	*Secure Shredder Status*	*Copy Taken*	*Files Directory and Further Observations*
1	Before	Before images were received	Only two ".wic" files, "pcc.wic" and "pcd.wic" were present in the files directory.
2	Before	After images were received	Two ".wic" files, each with 64 character string file names, were present in the files directory. Their sizes were 47488 and 54136 bytes respectively.
3	Before	After images were removed	Two ".wic" files were not present.
4	After	After images were removed	Two ".wic" files were not present.

These disparities can be monitored using general-purpose UNIX tools such as "ls" for directory listing and "cat" for the examination of the contents of files. The concurrence of the amount of received messages and the amount of "*.wic" files in the files subdirectory reveals that Wickr stores its received attachments as ".wic" files. From the observations in Table 3, a record of Wickr's file decay were established, as seen in Table 4. After the received messages had been deleted, the corresponding ".wic" files were no longer present. The type of acquisition performed in this experiment by using the command "cp" relied on the file headers to locate blocks of data on the storage media. The files did not show up after expiry, which indicates that Wickr had removed the files, at least from the logical filesystem. To check if the files were completely removed without any trace of the data anywhere in the device, a low-level data acquisition had to be performed; the outcome of this will be discussed in the next experiment.

TABLE IV. Wickr's file decay

Stage of file removal	*1*	*2*	*3*	*4*
Status of received file	N/A	File present, encrypted, stored in ".wic" file	File present, encrypted, filesystem header removed	File overwritten with random or null data
Process required to recover file	N/A	Logical level acquisition, for example copy.	Low level acquisition, such as device data dump or chip-off analysis	File unrecoverable .

VII. Experiment 4: Low Level Data Analysis

The results from the experiment 3 showed that there were multiple stages to Wickr's removal of files. A crucial stage in the recovery of expired files is when their filesystem headers have been removed, so they cannot be accessed via the application, but their contents still reside in unallocated space, as they have not been overwritten. To examine unallocated space on the "userdata" partition, a low-level logical acquisition was performed. Low-level acquisition captures deleted data that resides in unallocated space, something that could not be achieved using the filesystem alone.

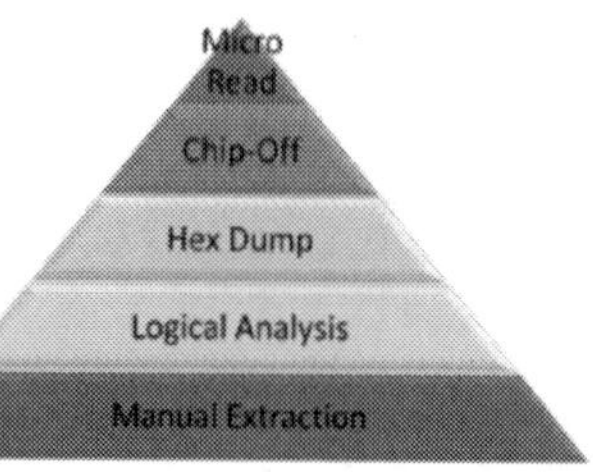

Figure 6. Cellular Phone Tool Levelling Pyramid [27]

Fig. 6 shows the cellular phone tool-levelling pyramid [27], which is a model used to describe the increasingly complex, expensive and forensically sound levels of mobile forensic acquisitions and analyses. The previous experiments performed have relied on the filesystem which is also a type of logical analysis situated the second level of the pyramid.

In Fig. 7, the listing for "/dev/block/bootdevice/by-name/", shows the mount points of various android partitions. For this experiment, the target partition was the data directory, which contains all user created data [25]. In this case, the "userdata" partition was mounted on the block device "/dev/block/mmcblk0p27".

```
root@serranovelte:/dev/block/bootdevice/by-name # ls -l
lrwxrwxrwx root     root              2014-01-01 00:57 aboot -> /dev/block/mmcblk0p5
lrwxrwxrwx root     root              2014-01-01 00:57 apnhlos -> /dev/block/mmcblk0p1
lrwxrwxrwx root     root              2014-01-01 00:57 backup -> /dev/block/mmcblk0p19
lrwxrwxrwx root     root              2014-01-01 00:57 boot -> /dev/block/mmcblk0p16
lrwxrwxrwx root     root              2014-01-01 00:57 cache -> /dev/block/mmcblk0p25
lrwxrwxrwx root     root              2014-01-01 00:57 ddr -> /dev/block/mmcblk0p4
lrwxrwxrwx root     root              2014-01-01 00:57 efs -> /dev/block/mmcblk0p13
lrwxrwxrwx root     root              2014-01-01 00:57 fota -> /dev/block/mmcblk0p18
lrwxrwxrwx root     root              2014-01-01 00:57 fsc -> /dev/block/mmcblk0p20
lrwxrwxrwx root     root              2014-01-01 00:57 fsg -> /dev/block/mmcblk0p9
lrwxrwxrwx root     root              2014-01-01 00:57 hidden -> /dev/block/mmcblk0p26
lrwxrwxrwx root     root              2014-01-01 00:57 modem -> /dev/block/mmcblk0p2
lrwxrwxrwx root     root              2014-01-01 00:57 modemst1 -> /dev/block/mmcblk0p14
lrwxrwxrwx root     root              2014-01-01 00:57 modemst2 -> /dev/block/mmcblk0p15
lrwxrwxrwx root     root              2014-01-01 00:57 pad -> /dev/block/mmcblk0p11
lrwxrwxrwx root     root              2014-01-01 00:57 param -> /dev/block/mmcblk0p12
lrwxrwxrwx root     root              2014-01-01 00:57 persdata -> /dev/block/mmcblk0p23
lrwxrwxrwx root     root              2014-01-01 00:57 persist -> /dev/block/mmcblk0p22
lrwxrwxrwx root     root              2014-01-01 00:57 qhee -> /dev/block/mmcblk0p8
lrwxrwxrwx root     root              2014-01-01 00:57 qsee -> /dev/block/mmcblk0p7
lrwxrwxrwx root     root              2014-01-01 00:57 recovery -> /dev/block/mmcblk0p17
lrwxrwxrwx root     root              2014-01-01 00:57 rpm -> /dev/block/mmcblk0p6
lrwxrwxrwx root     root              2014-01-01 00:57 sbl1 -> /dev/block/mmcblk0p3
lrwxrwxrwx root     root              2014-01-01 00:57 sec -> /dev/block/mmcblk0p10
lrwxrwxrwx root     root              2014-01-01 00:57 ssd -> /dev/block/mmcblk0p21
lrwxrwxrwx root     root              2014-01-01 00:57 system -> /dev/block/mmcblk0p24
lrwxrwxrwx root     root              2014-01-01 00:57 userdata -> /dev/block/mmcblk0p27
root@serranovelte:/dev/block/bootdevice/by-name #
```

Figure 7. List of partitions mounted on the Android platform

To acquire this partition, the UNIX tool "dd" (data dump) was used to create a bit-for-bit copy on an external SD card, using the command "dd if=/dev/block/mmcblk0p27 of=/mnt/extSdCard/userdata.dd". While performing this type of acquisition it is important to have a correctly formatted SD card, because some filesystems impose upper size limits with the file creation. The appropriate filesystem to use in this case was exFAT, which has no limits on file size. The resulting raw data file came to around 5 GB, which was then transferred to a forensic workstation for analysis using an "adb pull" command. The "userdata.dd" image's filesystem was analysed using the Autopsy forensic suite, which uses Sleuthkit. Upon mounting the "userdata" image in Autopsy and navigating to the "/data/com.mywickr. wickr2" directory, several references to deleted ".wic" files were found in unallocated space, as seen Fig. 8. Using the deleted files' meta addresses (i-nodes), the forensic examiner could see where these files were previously stored, and use this information to recover their contents.

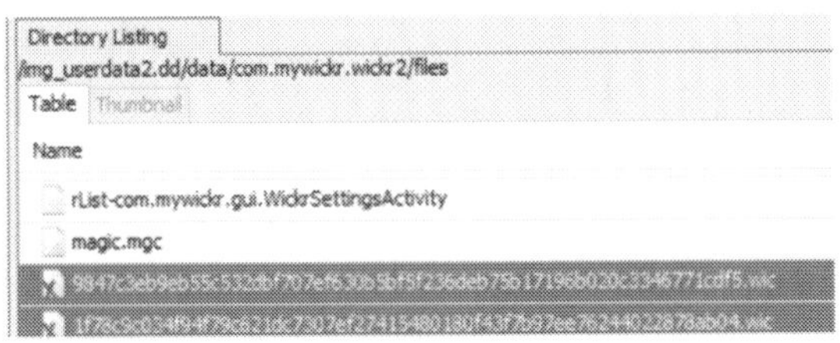

Figure 8. Wickr's "files" directory in Autopsy

VIII. Experiment 5: Wickr RAM Dump

As no plaintext artifacts were recovered from the internal storage so far, our next approach was to analyse device's RAM to look for evidences which could be in the un-encrypted form [28]. The analysis of RAM involved the acquisition of data while the application was running and this falls into the category of "live forensics" [29], which refers to any actions taken when the device is in full operation. This has a huge amount of risk involved as an investigator could accidentally remove key bits of data or change data so that it is no longer viable in court. The important aspect with this is to follow ACPO guidelines for handling digital evidence [15]. The second and third principles of the ACPO guidelines state that any competent investigator must be able to explain their actions and keep an audit trail of any actions taken, for the sake of accountability. In the case of this experiment, the Android tool Memory Dump [30] was used while the test platform was turned on. Eventually the Wickr application was running while the acquisition occurred. During this process to preserve authenticity and integrity we followed ACPO guidelines using supporting documentation with minimal change of the original evidence where possible.

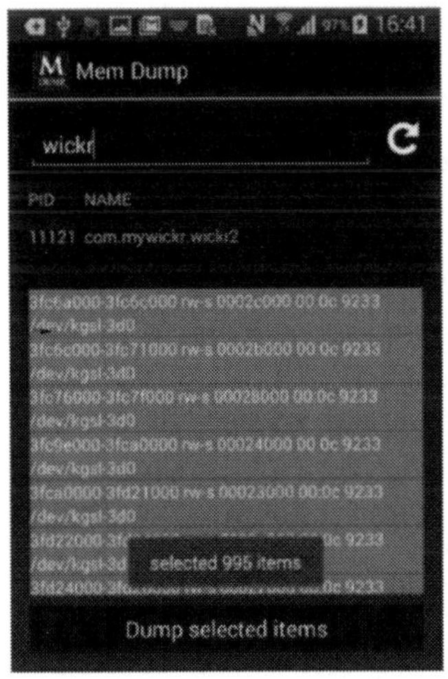

Figure 9. Memory Dump process

Memory Dump, as shown in Fig. 9, is an Android tool that allows the investigator to dump the information used by any specific running process. The resulting "MEMDUMP" directory was transferred to the Linux forensic workstation and analysed with a string search. To do this, the Linux tool "strings" was run on all files in the directory. A simple Linux bash script, as seen in Fig. 10, was created to search the output from a list of keywords. This list includes the username and password used to sign up to Wickr, as well as other accounts that had been used to communicate using the test scenario, names of files transmitted, and excerpts of transmitted messages.

```
#!/bin/bash

for ITEM in $(cat item_list.txt)
do

cat /media/xubuntu/7AEF-B34E/MEMDUMP/memdump_strings.txt | \
grep $ITEM > ~/searchresults/memdump_strings_$ITEM.txt

done
```

Figure 10. Bash Script to search strings

The files in the resulting output directory showed matches with the list of keywords used by the search script. These files were viewed in a text viewer. Although most of the search terms returned no matches, there was a match for the account name used to sign up to Wickr in the "dumped__7428b000-7428e000_rw-p" dump file. This is a pertinent artefact as if acquired could be used, in co-operation with Wickr and telecomms services, to locate the user that signed up to Wickr using a captured device.

IX. CONCLUSIONS

The results of the experiments documented in this paper give insight into the function of Wickr, a highly secure application, as well as the exploration of mobile digital forensics techniques that revolve around third party applications. The results found that Wickr stores data using extensive encryption with the CryptSQL extension for SQLite, and storing received messages in encrypted ".wic" files. Wickr removes its data by removing file headers. The experiments in this paper provided understanding of the manner in which Wickr stores its data by analyzing artefacts recovered from the Wickr application itself, as well as understanding the ephemeral messaging function by analyzing directory structures on the test Android platform's internal storage and the RAM. Interesting lines of research for the future include the recovery of encrypted artifacts, as well as the application of methods used in this paper to analyse similar applications on other platforms, such as iOS and Windows Phone.

REFERENCES

[1] Statista, "Number of apps available in leading app stores as of June 2016," http://www.statista.com/statistics/276623/number-of-apps-available-in-leading-app-stores/, [retrieved: August, 2016].

[2] S. Almasy, P. Meilhan, J. Bittermann, "Paris Massacre: At least 128 killed in gunfire and blasts, French officials say," http://edition.cnn.com/2015/11/13/world/paris-shooting/, November 2015 [retrieved: August, 2016].

[3] M. Madi, S. Ryder, J. Macfarlane, A. Beach, and V. Park "As it happened: Charlie Hebdo attack" January 2016 [retrieved: August, 2016].

[4] A. Roussinous, "The social media Accounts of British Jihadis in Syria just got a lot more distressing," http://www.vice.com/en_uk/read/british-jihadis-beheading-prisoners-syria-isis-terrorism, April 2014 [retrieved: August, 2016].

[5] R. Torok, "How social media was key to Islamic State's attacks on Paris," http://theconversation.com/how-social-media-was-key-to-islamic-states-attacks-on-paris-50743, November 2015 [retrieved: August, 2016].

[6] L. Vidino, S. Hughes, "ISIS in America: From retweets to Raqqa," http://www.stratcomcoe.org/download/file/fid/2828, December 2015 [retrieved: August, 2016].

[7] C. Wu, C. Vance, R. Boggs, and T. Fenger, "Forensic Analysis of Data Transience Applications on IOS and Android," http://www.marshall.edu/forensics/files/Wu-Poster.pdf, September 2013 [retrieved: August, 2016].

[8] M. Anderson, "The demographics of device ownership," http://www.pewinternet.org/2015/10/29/the-demographics-of-device-ownership/, October 2015 [retrieved: August, 2016].

[9] M. Wilbourn Partners, "Snapchat is now the third most popular social network among millennials," http://mwpartners.com/snapchat-is-now-the-third-most-popular-social-network-among-millennials/, 2014 [retrieved: August, 2016].

[10] Wickr Official Website, https://www.wickr.com [retrieved: August, 2016].

[11] D. Walnycky, I. Baggili, A. Marrington, J. Moore, and F. Breitinger, "Network and device forensic analysis of Android social-messaging applications," Digital Investigation, vol. 14, pp. 77-84, August 2015.

[12] K. M. Ovens and G. Morrison, "Forensic analysis of Kik Messenger on iOS devices," Digital Investigation, vol. 17, pp. 40-52, 2016.

[13] T. Mehrota and B. M. Mehtre, "Forensic Analysis of Wickr on Android Devices," IEEE International Conference on Computational Intelligence and Computing Research, December 2013.

[14] D. B. Garrie, "Digital Forensic Evidence in the Courtroom: Understanding Content and Quality," Northwestern Journal of Technology and Intellectual Property, vol. 12, pp. 121-128, 2014.

[15] Association of Chief Police Officers, "ACPO Good Practise Guide for Digital Evidence," https://www.cps.gov.uk/legal/assets/uploads/files/ACPO_guidelines_computer_evidence[1].pdf [retrieved: August, 2016].

[16] Samsung Galaxy Mini, http://www.samsung.com/uk/consumer/mobile-devices/smartphones/galaxy-s/GT-I9195ZKABTU, [retrieved: August, 2016].

[17] Allwinner A13 User Manual, http://linux-sunxi.org/A13, [retrieved: August, 2016].

[18] V. Woods and R. V. D. Meulen, "Gartner Says Worldwide Smartphone Sales Grew 3.9 Percent in First Quarter of 2016," http://www.gartner.com/newsroom/id/3323017, Feburary 2016 [retrieved: August, 2016].

[19] Kingo Root Tool, https://www.kingoapp.com, [retrieved: August, 2016].

[20] S. Bommisetty, R. Tamma, and H. Mahalik, "Practical Mobile Forensics," Packt Publishing, 2014.

[21] ADB tool, https://developer.android.com/studio/command-line/adb.html, [retrieved: August, 2016].

[22] Dex2Jar tool, https://github.com/pxb1988/dex2jar, [retrieved: August, 2016].

[23] Java Decompiler tool, http://jd.benow.ca, [retrieved: August, 2016].

[24] SleuthKit tool, http://www.sleuthkit.org, [retrieved: August, 2016].

[25] Wei-Meng Lee, "Beginning Android 4 Application Development," John Wiley & Sons, 2012.

[26] SQLCipher tool, https://www.zetetic.net/sqlcipher/, [retrieved: August, 2016].

[27] S. Brothers, "How Cell Phone "Forensic" Tools Actually Work - Proposed Leveling System," Mobile Forensics World Conference, Chicago, Illinois, 2009.

[28] E. Casey, G. Fellows, M. Geiger, and G. Stellatos, "The growing impact of full disk encryption on digital forensics," Digital Investigation, vol. 8, no. 2, pp. 129-134, 2011.

[29] A. Shortall and M. A. H. B. Azhar, "Forensic acquisitions of WhatsApp data on popular mobile platforms," Sixth International Conference on Emerging Security Technologies (EST). IEEE Press, Technische Universitaet Braunschweig, Germany, pp.13-17, 2015.

[30] Memory Dump tool, https://play.google.com/store/apps/details?id=com.cert.memdump&hl=en, [retrieved: August, 2016].

Designing An IEC 61850 Based Power Distribution Substation Simulation/Emulation Testbed for Cyber-Physical Security Studies

Eniye Tebekaemi * and Duminda Wijesekera†
Volgenau School of Engineering
George Mason University
Fairfax, USA
Email: *etebekae@gmu.edu, †dwijesek@gmu.edu

Abstract—**The present traditional power grid system is slowly migrating to an interactive, intelligent power grid system (smart grid or future grid) driven by information and communication technology. The smart grid functions are expected to improve the reliability, efficiency, operations and control of the electric power grid. The smart grid functions are realizable through power communication networks that interface with traditional computer networks often connected to the Internet. This situation makes cyber-physical security a serious concern in the design, development, and implementation of smart grid functions in power grid systems. Understanding the physical behavior, cyber security challenges, physical security challenges, impact of cyber/physical security breaches, and security requirements of time-critical cyber-physical systems like the smart grid is critical in designing a robust security solution that ensures its safe and reliable operation. This work focuses on the design and implementation of a simulation testbed that would support extensive analysis of communication protocols, cyber-physical security functions, intelligent electronic device (IED) vulnerabilities, network configuration, and physical security requirements of an IEC 61850 based power distribution substation.**

Keywords–Cyber Security; Communication Protocols; Simulation Testbed; Cyber-Physical Systems; Smart Grid; Power Substation Automation.

I. Introduction

Simulation of cyber-physical systems is fast becoming a popular method for analyzing the behavior of hybrid systems and testing out new functionalities before deployment in the real world. In power systems, simulation testbeds have been used extensively for fault analysis, testing of protection and control functions, and in the testing and analysis of new technologies. The future grid (or smart grid) represents one such new technology that incorporates data communication network into existing power networks to provide a more efficient and resilient power grid system. Simulating the smart grid functions for cyber-physical security studies requires three major parts: 1) Simulation of the physical power system, 2) Simulation of the communication network, and 3) The interaction between the physical power system and the communication network. There exist several power systems simulation software used for the design, evaluation, and analysis of powers systems that supports real-time simulation, discrete event simulation, and hardware in the loop (HIL) simulation. Most research work focuses on the use of network simulators to simulate network communication between components, and either implement the smart grid functions in the simulated network nodes or as functions in the power system simulator. This approach helps researchers to determine suitable network topology and configuration that supports the real-time communication requirements for the smart grid. For cyber security studies, the approach helps in studying the effects of packet delay, packet loss, packet injection and data manipulation on the simulated power systems.

The major objective of this work is to expand the scope of cyber-physical security studies using simulation testbeds to perform real-time analysis of smart grid communication network and security protocols, analyze the impact of physical disturbance (deliberate and accidental), provide a realistic environment for implementing and testing new and existing smart grid functions through virtual IEDs, perform vulnerability analysis of physical IEDs used in smart grid systems, test new Internet of Things (IoT) services, and analyze security protocols and security controls for the smart grid. To achieve this, the physical system, IEDs and communication network must be independent and support relevant standards and protocols to ensure interoperability when implementing smart grid functions. Implementing IEDs as nodes in network simulators or as procedures in power system simulators in the smart grid simulation testbed makes it tough to perform studies that meet our objectives.

In this work, we make use of virtual IEDs, which are computing units implemented as either virtual machines (VMs) or standalone computers with full network support capabilities. The virtual IEDs can be connected through a physical, simulated or software-defined network (SDN). The virtual IEDs depending on the smart grid function they implement, can read values from the simulated power system, communicate with other IEDs through the communication network, and write control instructions to the simulated power system. Fig. 1 shows the high-level graphical representation of the simulation testbed.

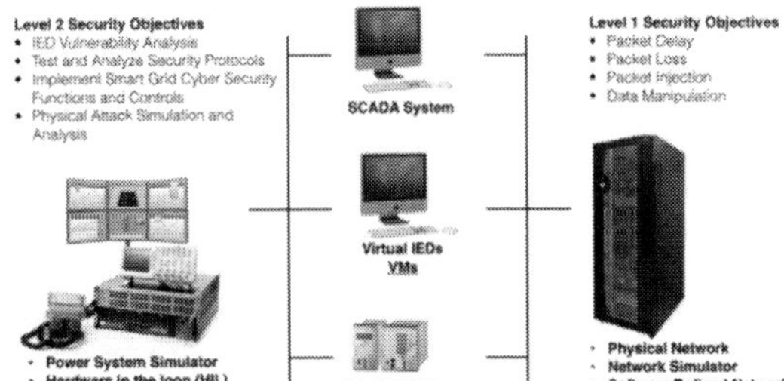

Figure 1: High-level representation of the proposed testbed.

The simulation testbed presented in this work enables cyber-physical security research objectives at level 2. Some of the other advantages of this model include:

1) *Modular Design* - The modular structure used in our testbed enables components to be easily replaced with newer and more efficient components, making it easy to test new technologies, upgrade and replace existing components, and perform scale up operations seamlessly.
2) *Scalability* – The testbed can easily be scaled out to support more smart grid functions, HIL co-simulations, distributed simulations, and remote IoT operations.
3) *Cost* – Using virtual IEDs makes it cheap and convenient to implement practical smart grid functions. The testbed can be set up on a small scale in a purely virtual environment, using a single host computer with multiple VMs costing a few hundred dollars; or large scale using real-time HIL simulators such as RTDS Simulator and OPAL-RT Simulator with real IEDs and actual communications and networking equipment.
4) *Ease of Setup and Use* – Both network and power simulators come with APIs written in a specific programming language that must be learned to use the simulator. Using these network simulators means that one can hardly take advantage of already existing smart grid libraries when using network simulators. Our testbed allows users to implement smart grid functions using libraries, programming languages, and applications they are comfortable with in the virtual IEDs.
5) *Interoperability* - The testbed is based on IEC 61850 standards and related protocols, which makes it relatively easy to perform system in the loop (SIL) and HIL simulations with systems and devices that support IEC 61850.

The remainder of this work is organized as follows: Section II discusses the cyber and physical vulnerabilities of the smart grid, and related work is discussed in Section III. Section IV reviews related smart grid standards, software, and tools that are frequently used in designing simulation testbeds. In Section V, we present our simulation testbed model. Section VI focuses on the implementation of the model and presentation of some of our results. We conclude in Section VII by discussing the accomplishments and limitations of this work, and potential future work.

II. Cyber and Physical Vulnerabilities of Smart Grid

Over the years, we have seen series of cyber-attacks of massive scale against government organizations and private companies alike. Cyber-Physical systems like the smart grid, are vulnerable to both cyber and physical acts that could critically impact their safe and reliable operation. Also, the high availability, tight coupling of components, and time sensitive communication requirements of power systems make them even more vulnerable.

A. Physical Vulnerabilities

Attacks on Physical Components - Power systems have components distributed over a large geographical area, and some of their components are installed in areas where it is difficult to guarantee physical security. An attacker can physically attack sensors, actuators and other components that may result in faulty measurements causing errors in the system state estimation and control operations [1], [2].

Faults and Failure of Components - Devices may fail during operation. These failures could be caused by some accumulated faults or the device reaching its end of life. In most cases, power system components degenerate progressively giving facility managers enough time to respond and in some cases, failure is abrupt with little or no indication.

Accidents and Acts of Nature - Severe weather conditions could cause instability in power systems and power disruption. Power systems frequently suffer from trees falling on power lines, storms, lightning and thunder strikes destroying power installations and causing power outages.

B. Cyber Vulnerabilities

Software and Firmware Bugs - IEDs rely on software to provide the much-needed functionality. Software often comes preinstalled which determines the (primary) behavior of the IED without any need for human interaction (firmware and drivers), while others can be installed by the user to extend the functionality of the smart device. Since software is written by humans, we cannot rule out errors in the implementation, and attackers look for such errors to exploit the system [3]. An example of this was the Heartbleed vulnerability of 2014 caused by bugs in the OpenSSL implementation of the secure sockets layer (SSL) protocol [4].

IED and Network Misconfiguration - Misconfiguration of network components and IEDs are huge security risks to the smart grid. Some of these misconfigurations include: 1) Using default settings and default passwords even when the device is operational, 2) poorly maintained security and software patches, 3) using short and guessable passwords, 4) poorly configured firewall [5], or some other configuration issues. All these can put the network at risk.

Data Manipulation and Falsification - Data manipulation and falsification attacks border on data integrity. By altering certain bits of the signal, an attacker alters the meaning of the control signal. An attacker with knowledge of how the system works can generate packets or replay previously recorded packets to change the correct behavior of the system. Data manipulation attacks are countered by proper application of cryptographic controls in the authentication and integrity checks of communicating nodes and data.

Malware and Advanced Persistent Threat (APT) - Malware are pieces of software with malicious intent. Malware could open covert communication channels to the remote attacker so that the attacker can take control of the host, send vital information about the system to a remote attacker, or just perform preprogrammed malicious actions [6]. APTs are unique forms of malware and attacks that use various stealthy techniques to gain remote access while staying undetected on the host system for a long time.

Communication Channel - power systems are distributed and span multiple locations requiring communication links between the various parts of the system. This communication network can be wired or wireless, although the wireless connection is most often used. One weakness of wireless communication is that of visibility. Anyone in proximity to the wireless network and operating on the same frequency and channel can see the network traffic. Power systems rely on the timeliness of communication packets to operate (e.g., interlocking and switching functions in power distribution systems) and a mere delay or loss of packets may yield undesired results. Typical attacks include signal jamming, wormhole attacks, and signal diversion attacks.

C. *Coordinated Cyber-Physical Attacks*

Another possibility is a coordinated cyber-physical attack, exploiting both the physical and cyber vulnerabilities of the power system in a contemporary way to maximize the impact. This kind of attack could be a collusion between an insider with access to the physical power system components, and a cyber attacker at a remote location with knowledge of the power communication network working together to cause cascading failures and service disruption.

III. Related Work

There are a few substation simulation testbeds designed primarily for cyber-physical security related research. These testbeds are either too expensive to reproduce or lack the capability for level 2 cyber security work. This is a significant setback for researchers who need a realistic simulation testbed for cyber-physical security studies in power systems but do not have a large budget. Other issues are the lack of implementation of existing information security standards, which means these information security protocols cannot be evaluated for vulnerabilities and possible impact on the substation. For example, the IEC 62531-9 uses the group domain of interpretation (GDOI) protocol for key management, but what happens if the key management server is down or compromised? Hahn et al. [7] developed the PowerCyber testbed at Iowa State University that supports level 1 and 2 cyber security objectives. In their work, they use the RTDS Simulator platform and the PowerFactory power simulation software to simulate the physical power system. The RTDS Simulator provides real-time HIL simulation and interfaces directly with the IEDs, while the PowerFactory is used mainly for non-realtime analysis and connects to the RTDS Simulator through the open platform communications (OPC) protocols. The IEDs are either actual physical IEDs or virtual machines (VMs), and they communicate with remote terminal units (RTUs) that aggregate their data and send it to the controller. For the communication network part, they use the Internet-Scale Event and Attack Generation Environment (ISEAGE), a multimillion-dollar research at Iowa State University dedicated to designing a security testbed to emulate the Internet for the purpose of researching, designing, and testing cyber defense mechanisms.

Yang et al. [8] presented a testbed that simulates the power system using the RTDS Simulator, actual IEDs and communication devices. Using only real IEDs makes it difficult to implement and analyze new substation security protocols and functions, and gives little room for scalability. Liu et al. [9] designed a reconfigurable testbed for analyzing the impact of specific cyber-attacks on the power systems. They implemented their substation testbed using RTDS Simulator to simulate the power system, and used network simulator 3 (NS3) and the defense technology experimental research laboratory (DeterLab) to simulate the communication network. Their testbed was not implemented according to the IEC 61850 standards, and their controllers were modeled as nodes in the network simulator. Koutsandria et al. [10] simulated the power system with Matlab/Simulink and used simulated and actual programmable logic controllers (PLC) for control. They also used an actual local area network (LAN) setup for the network communication part. Their objective was to validate the continuous, reliable operation of network intrusion detection systems (NIDS) in exposed network environments.

Jarmakiewicz et al. [11] used labVIEW software to simulate the power system and used real IEDs connected to a real LAN. Hong et al. proposed in [12] a cyber-physical security testbed to simulate attacks and validate security controls. Their proposed testbed although not yet implemented, would be based on RTDS and support HIL simulations. Deng et al. in [13] designed their testbed to test the operation, control and protection functions of the substation using RT-LAB, actual and virtual IEDs. Their testbed is not intended for cyber security analysis and lacks an appropriate communication network model. Chen et al. [14] used RTDS and OPNET to simulate the power system and communication network respectively, but implemented the bay-Level IEDs as functions in RTDS and the station-level IEDs as nodes in OPNET, and not as standalone devices. The works [15]–[19] all have similar software based testbeds. The major differences are in their choice of software combination used in the co-simulation of power and communication network systems. The IEDs used in their simulation is either modeled as nodes in the network simulator or as functions in the power system simulation.

IV. Review of Standards, Libraries and Tools

Understanding the standards for substation automation necessary to set up a simulation testbed for research in power systems could be daunting, as it requires one to have adequate knowledge of both the power systems and communications network domain. The international organization for standardization (ISO) and the international electrotechnical commission (IEC) are the two primary organizations that define standards for power systems. In this section, we will discuss the IEC 61850 Standards (communication networks and systems for substations), the ISO/IEC 9506 (MMS – Manufacturing Message Specification), the IEC 62351 (Information Security for Power System Control Operations), the RFC 6407 (GDOI - Group Domain of Interpretation) and the relevant parts of the open systems interconnection (OSI) communication model.

IEC 61850 (Communication Networks and Systems in Substations) is the most popular internationally accepted standard for substation automation. It describes the structure, functions, and interface for substation devices, as well as the communication protocol for process-level, bay-level, and station-level communication necessary for substation automation.

ISO/IEC 9506 (MMS – Manufacturing Message Specification) is an application layer messaging standard based on the OSI communication model. MMS is designed for controlling and monitoring devices remotely through remote terminal units (RTU) and programmable logic controllers (PLC). It defines functions common across distributed automation systems and acts as a concrete object to implement the abstract IEC 61850 standards.

IEC 62351 (Information Security for Power Systems Control Operations) is the current security standard and defines the end to end cyber security requirements for securing power management networks. It specifies the security requirements for secure data communication and processing in power systems in regards to data confidentiality, data integrity, authentication, and non-repudiation.

RFC 6407 (GDOI - The Group Domain of Interpretation) is the internet engineering task force (IETF) protocol used to provide group key management for secure group communications. The IEC 62351 standard specifies the use of the GDOI for managing security associations and distributing security transforms in power systems.

Open Systems Interconnection (OSI) Model is the communication model that standardizes the communication functions necessary for computer network communication. The OSI model consists of 7 abstraction layers and defines communication functions and requirements for each layer. It serves as an abstract structure through which network communication protocols are defined.

A. *Intelligent Electric Devices (IEDs)*

Understanding how the IEC 61850 standard defines the naming structure, data structures, services, and command sets for read, write, and control is necessary to design virtual IEDs. Substation automation consists of functions that facilitate monitoring, protection, and control in the substation. Each substation automation function performs dedicated tasks and is referred to as a logical node in the IEC 61850 standard. A logical node (LN) is defined as the smallest part of the IED that exchanges data and performs some functions [20]. An IED is composed of one or more LNs and must implement all the necessary data structures, services, and interfaces to support each LN it contains. LNs are the building blocks for IEDs and have standardized names, data structures, abstract service interfaces, and behavior models.

1) Naming Structure: LNs exchange data by reading and writing values to memory locations referenced to by their data attribute (DA). The IEC 61850 standard uses a hierarchical naming convention that uniquely identifies each DA in the substation. The first letter of the LN name identifies the group to which the LN belongs, and suffixes can be used to identify each instance of the LN in the IED. An IED name is unique within the substation, and LN name is unique within the IED. Using Fig. 2, we can determine the status value (stVal) of the switch position (Pos) of the circuit breaker Relay1 by referencing *"Relay1/XCBR2.ST.Pos.stVal"*, where "2" represents an instance of the circuit breaker LN (XCBR) in "Relay1", "X" identifies its LN group as switchgear, and "ST" represents the functional constraint (FC) for status value.

2) Data Structure: The compatible data class (CDC) template specifies the data type of each data attribute (DA) allowed for the given data object (DO). For example, if the CDC specifies that the controllable double point (DPC) template be used for the Relay1/XCBR1.Pos data object, then the data attribute for Relay1/XCBR1.ST.Pos.stVal will have a type "coded enum" with four possible states intermediate-state, off, on, bad-state [21]. The timestamp attribute "t" referenced by Relay1/XCBR2.ST.Pos.t will have a data type of either int32 or unsigned int24 based on the chosen time quality [22]. Both IEC 61850-7-2 and IEC 61850-7-3 should be consulted for the detailed definition of all data types and recommended values used in the CDC template.

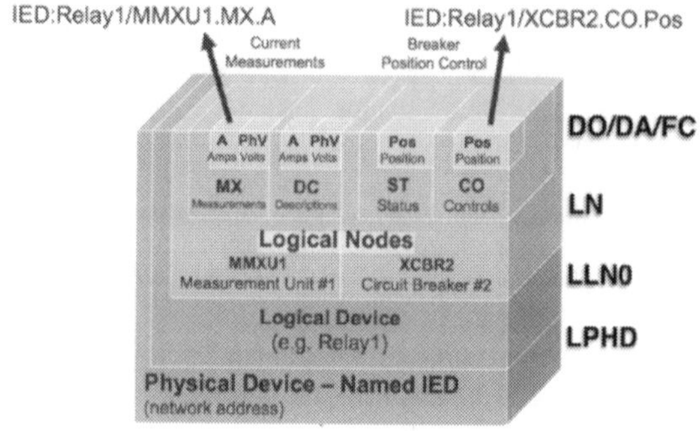

Figure 2: Structural Composition of an IEC 61850 based IED

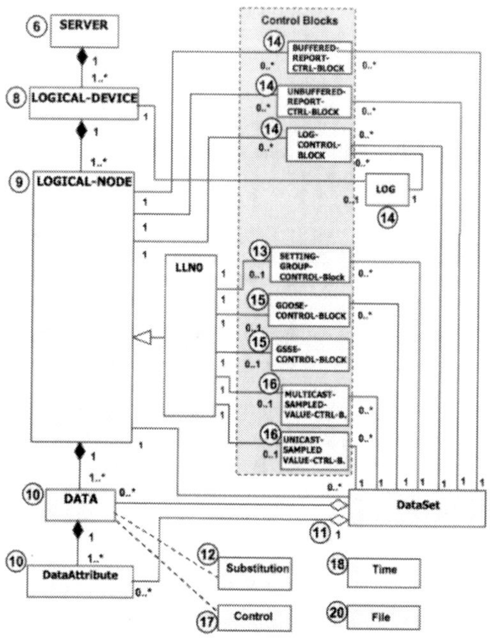

Figure 3: Conceptual service model of the ACSI [22]

3) Services and Interfaces: IEC 61850-7-2 defines an abstract communication service interface (ACSI) for IEC 61850 based IEDs. All IEDs must implement some of the services and interfaces defined by the ACSI if they require real-time cooperation in the substation. ACSI defines abstract interfaces for client/server remote communication that supports real-time data access, remote control, event reporting and more. It also defines the subscriber/publisher communication abstract interface for fast and reliable system-wide event distribution and transmission of sampled values. Interfaces represent communication points, IEDs communicate with one another using these interfaces. Services are activities that run on interfaces, the kind of interface an IED supports determines the type of service the IED can provide.

Fig. 3 summarizes all the abstract interfaces available defined in [22]. IEDs can implement all or a subset of interfaces. The type of interface an IED implements determines the kind of services it can provide and the type of communication protocol it can use. For example, an IED needs to implement the Generic Object Oriented Substation Event (GOOSE) control block interface to use the GOOSE communication protocol to send GOOSE messages.

B. Protocol for Data Communication

Communication protocols are necessary for IEDs to send and receive messages in a power communication network. IEC 61850 based IEDs rely on the 7-layer OSI reference model which specifies the functional requirements for each layer. The IEC 61850 standard groups the seven abstract OSI layers into two profiles; 1) the ISO application profile (A-Profile) composed of the three upper layers, and 2) the ISO transport profile (T-Profile) composed of the four lower layers. It is important to draw the distinction between an application program and an application protocol. An application program provides a set of functions and an interface through which users can interact with the application, while an application protocol provides a communication structure through which applications interact with other applications irrespective of their internal system representation. Application protocol provides interoperability and universality, which means that application programs can be written in different programming languages, run on different operating systems and still be able to communicate as long as the implement the same application protocol.

The IEC 61850 standard defines all requirements needed to design IED application programs, but not application protocols. Instead, it relies on existing application protocols, and defines mappings from ACSI services to the communication protocol (A-Profile and T-Profile). [23] and [24] describe in detail the mappings from ACSI to MMS, ACSI to Generic Substation Events (GSE/GOOSE), ACSI to Generic Substation State Event (GSSE), and ACSI to sampled value (SV) for both application and transport profiles (A-Profile and T-Profile).

C. Data and Communication Security

Information security is a grave concern for power management systems. Many standards have been proposed over the years, and the IEC 62531 standard [25] is the only globally accepted standard for securing power management systems. The IEC 62531 standard suite defines information security requirements for the various communication profiles used in substation automation necessary to provide confidentiality, integrity, availability, and non-repudiation. The IEC 62531 standard identifies potential threats and vulnerabilities for power automation systems, and other aspects of information security relevant to power automation systems.

1) TCP Profile: IEC 62531-3 specifies the use of transport layer security (TLS) 1.0 or higher to protect TCP/IP profiles and provides protection against eavesdropping through encryption, spoofing through Security Certificates (Node Authentication), replay through TLS encryption, and man-in-the-middle security risk through message authentication [25]. It mandates the support for Rivest, Shamir, and Alderman (RSA) and digital signature standard (DSS) signature algorithms with RSA key length of 2048 bits and also mandates the support for regular and ephemeral Diffie-Hellman key exchange with a key length of 2048 bits. For authentication, it mandates the use of the X.509 certificates with support for multiple certificate authority (CA). As observed by Schlegel et a. [26], IEC 62531-3 can protect against rogue certificates but not against already compromised IEDs which would have valid certificates.

2) MMS Profile: IEC 62531-4 defines the security requirements for all profiles that include MMS. It provides authentication through the use TLS based X.509 certificates but does not cover message integrity and confidentiality. If encryption is to be employed then IEC 62531-3 should be used. The IEC 62531-4 by itself only protects against unauthorized access to information.

3) GOOSE and SV: IEC 62531-6 defines the security requirements for IEC 61850 communication profiles. GOOSE and SV profiles use multicast and non-routable messages that run on the substation LAN, and must be transmitted within 4ms. IEC 62531-6 does not recommend the use of encryption or certificate based authentication as it may increase the transmission time and add more processing overhead. For GOOSE profile, encryption can be used only if the processing and transmission time is less than 4ms. For message authentication and integrity protection of GOOSE and SV messages, the IEC 61850 supports the use of HMAC digital signatures.

4) Access Control and Certificate Management: IEC 62531-8 specifies the use of role-based access control (RBAC) for power systems. RBAC defines roles and set of rights associated with each role. Users/Entities are assigned to roles, and they inherit all the rights associated with that role. The IEC 62531-8 standard defines a list of roles and associated rights for power systems. For certificate/key management, the IEC working group is currently working on the IEC 62351-9 standards, which will specify the use of the Group Domain of Interpretation (GDOI) protocol (RFC 6407).

D. Libraries, Software and Tools

In this section, we will discuss IEC 61850 libraries, network and power simulation software, and other tools frequently used to simulate substation automation functions.

1) IEC 61850 Libraries and Tools: Software libraries are a collection of prepackaged functions and resources used to help reduce the time and effort needed to implement applications that share common properties. Since IEDs implement IEC 61850 services, libraries have been developed by individuals and organizations for some or all of the IEC 61850 services. The libiec61850 [27] and the OpenIEC61850 [28] are two of the most popular open source IEC 61850 libraries in use. The libiec61850 is a c library written by Michael Zillgith under the GPLv3 license and provides a server and client library for the IEC 61850/MMS, IEC 61850/GOOSE, and IEC 61850-9-2/Sampled Values communication protocols. It supports the static implementation and dynamic creation of IED models using substation configuration language (SCL) files or through API calls. It also provides full ISO protocol stack on top of TCP/IP, and publisher and subscriber models used for GOOSE and SV applications. The OpenIEC61850 is an open source implementation of IEC 61850 standard suite written in Java under the Apache 2.0 license. OpenIEC61850 provides IEC 61850/MMS client and server libraries but does not provide native support for the subscriber/publisher model based GOOSE and SV communication protocol. Organizations like Systemcorp, Xelas Energy, SISCO, and SmartGridware all have their implementation of the IEC 61850 standard suite available for purchase.

Development IEC 61850 based IED models could be a complicated process. Creating virtual IEDs requires the application developer to have a thorough understanding of data objects (DO), data attributes (DA), compatible data classes (CDC), interfaces, and services that apply to all the LNs to be implemented in the IED. IED modeling applications such as IEDModeler and OpenSCLTools amongst others, help reduce the complexity and programming errors associated with designing IEDs by visualizing the IED modeling process and generating the corresponding IED Capability Description (ICD) files. Like most of the other IEC 61850 libraries, the libiec61850 library suite has individual tools that parse ICD files into c classes corresponding to the IED model.

2) Power Simulation Software: IEDs implement substation automation functions (protection, monitoring, and control) used inside substations as part of the power management ecosystem. There are several applications used to simulate power systems, some of them are MATLAB/Simulink, GridLab-D, and PSS/E amongst others. MATLAB/Simulink produced by Mathworks is one of the most popular simulation software used for power system simulation experiments today. MATLAB/Simulink uses a very intuitive, graphical component-based code generation process to create models of systems. For power systems simulation, MATLAB/Simulink has a specialized toolbox called Simscape Power Systems (SimPowerSystem). SimPowerSystem provides component libraries and tools for modeling and simulating physical power systems. GridLAb-D is an open source multi-agent based power system distribution simulation and analysis tool developed by the U.S. Department of Energy (DOE). Gridlab-d is very useful in power simulations that involve distributed energy resources (DER), distribution automation, and retail markets interaction and evolution. PSS/E is a power system planning and analysis tool used primarily for power transmission systems [29].

Other popular platforms for power systems simulation are the specialized real-time digital simulators like those produced by RTDS [30] and OPAL-RT [31] Technologies. These are custom hardware and software solutions specialized for continuous real-time digital simulations. They can be used to design, test, analyze and optimize control systems and support personal computer and field programmable gate array (PC/FPGA) based real-time HIL simulations.

3) Communication Network Simulation Software: IEC 61850 based IEDs exchange messages over data communication networks. OPNET, NS2, NS3, OMNET++, and NetSim are some of the most popular network simulation and analysis application used in simulating the communication network part of the power systems automation network. Siraj et al. [32] give a comprehensive analysis of these network simulators, their features, advantages, and disadvantages.

V. TESTBED MODEL

Our testbed model consists of the power model, IED model, communication model, and attack model. The power model for this work is a single bay power distribution substation as shown in Fig. 4.

A. IED Model

IEDs have physical properties such as names, network interfaces, and ON/OFF states. IEDs also have logical behavior which aggregates the behavior of the all the LN's functions that make up the IED. IEC-61850 mandates all IEDs to implement the two system LNs; 1) the physical device LN (LPHD), which abstracts the physical properties of the IEDs, and 2) the Logical node zero (LLN0), which aggregates all the mandatory DAs of the LNs in the IED to provide a single consistent point of access/update. These two system LNs are mandatory for all IEDs whether they are process-level, bay-level or station-level devices as shown in Fig. 2.

1) Process Level:
Switchgear Devices - Make use of circuit breaker LNs (XCBR) and circuit switch LNs (XSWI) that directly control power systems actuators to open or close the breakers and isolators. XCBR and XSWI are process-level devices and subscribe to switch controller (CSWI) for open or close instructions. Each instance of XCBR or XSWI represents one circuit breaker or isolator and controls the operations of that breaker or isolator. Switchgear devices communicate with bay-level IEDs through GOOSE messages and support the GOOSE communication protocol with keyed-hash message authentication code (HMAC) for authentication and integrity protection. All devices in the substation connected to the same process bus share a single group key. The group key is managed by the key management server and must be changed periodically.

Measurement Devices - Make use of current transformer LNs (TCTR) and the voltage transformer LNs (TVTR) to obtain current and voltage measurements from the power system. Each instance of TCTR or TVTR represents one phase measurement from the current or voltage instrumentation transformer in the power system. The TCTRs and TVTRs are aggregated into merging units (MU) that operates a publisher/subscriber service. Merging units support SV multicast communication protocol and transmit voltage and current measurements to subscribers. Merging units also support HMAC for authentication and integrity protection, and TLS protected MMS connection for key management services.

2) Bay Level:
Control IEDs - Control operations like bay-level interlocking functions, fault isolation functions, load management switching functions, voltage/VAR control, frequency control, and power quality control functions are all designed as control IEDs and form part of the "Bay Controller." At the minimum, all control IEDs implement the switch controller LN (CSWI), and sometimes implement the bay-level interlocking LN (CILO) if interlocking functions are to be provided at the bay level. The CSWI controls the operations of switchgear devices (XCBR and XSWI), and the CILO provides the bay-level interlocking rules.

Protection IEDs - Make use of protection function LNs like the time overcurrent protection (PTOC), time overvoltage protection (PTOC), instantaneous overcurrent protection (PIOC), and distance protection (PDIS). Protection IEDs subscribe to the MU and monitoring IEDs to obtain necessary data values needed to make protection decisions. Protection IEDs also implement CSWI for controlling switchgear operations in response to protection decisions. *Monitoring IEDs* - Make Use of sensor-based monitoring LN like the monitor and diagnostics for arc LN (SARC) that monitors gas volumes of gas insulated switchgear devices. Monitor IEDs obtain information from sensors that monitor power system equipment to obtain their state information.

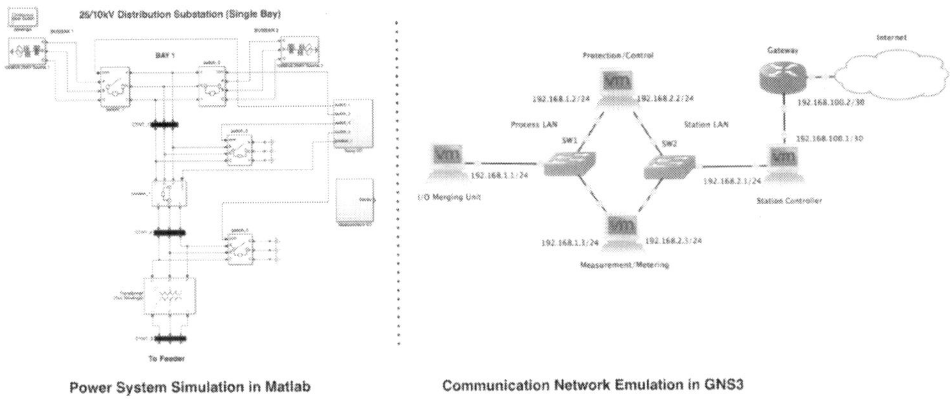

Figure 4: Single Bay IEC 61850 Power Distribution Substation Simulation Testbed

Bay-level IEDs could also implement measuring and metering LNs (MMXU and MMTR), and other LNs to provide additional functionalities that may be required at the bay level. Bay-level Control IEDs support GOOSE and SV protocols for communication with the process and bay-level devices, and MMS protocol for communication with the station-level devices.

3) Station Level: Station-level devices provide monitoring, control, and remote terminal functions for the substation. Functions at this level include human machine interface LN (IHMI), group control/key server (GCKS), remote terminal unit (RTU), and supervisory control and data acquisition (SCADA) services. Station-level devices support TLS protected MMS communication with devices at the station and bay level.

B. Communication Model

The communication model consists of the process network and the station network. Each bay has a dedicated process network, which is a switched or hub-based 10/100Base-T LAN, that supports GOOSE and SV multicast/broadcast protocols and isolate from that of other bays in the substation. The substation has one station network connecting all the bay-level devices and the station-level devices. The substation network is a switched 10/100Base-T LAN redundantly configured.

C. Attack Model

Attacks on the smart power grid could be physical-based, cyber-based, or both physical and cyber based.

1) Physical Attack Model: - There are two types of physical attacks; 1) the incremental attack where the attack occurs slowly and is spaced over time, and 2) the abrupt attack where the impact is sudden. Let C_i be the current state of the device, X be the set of all normal operating states, and Y be the set of faulty states and $Y = \bar{X}$, then we can model an abrupt attack as

$$C_1 = \{C_0 + A\} \in Y \qquad (1)$$

Where A is the attack value, and C_0 is the state of the device just before the start of the attack. If A is spread over n duration such that $a = A/n$ be the attack value for each iteration, then we can model the incremental attack as

$$C_i = \{C_{i-1} + a\} \in X \mid 0 \leq i \leq n-1\} \quad and \quad \{C_0 + a.n\} \in Y \qquad (2)$$

2) Network Attack Model: An attacker may be able to access the substation network from the process LAN, station LAN, or from a remote network. The type of traffic at each access level is different, and requires different attack strategies for each access level. *Process-Level Attacks* - We assume that the attacker can gain physical access to the process LAN, and the network traffic is predominantly broadcast and multicast GOOSE and SV packets. *Station-Level Attacks* - We assume that the attacker can gain physical access to the substation LAN, and the network traffic is a mixture of multicast GOOSE and unicast MMS packets. *Remote Attacks* - These are attacks that seek to compromise the substation RTUs, IDS, and firewall to gain access to the station network.

VI. Implementation and Results

Our testbed is implemented as shown in Fig. 4, and consists of a single bay with the associated substation devices. The simulation testbed runs on an Intel corei7 MacBook Pro computer, with a processor speed of 2.5ghz, 16GB of RAM, and 512GB SSD.

A. Implementation Details

1) Physical Power System: The power substation system is simulated in Matlab/Simulink. The substation consists of a single bay (Bay1) connected to two three-phase power transmission lines from two different power generation sources using two busbars (Busbar1 and Busbar2). The busbars are controlled by isolator switches (switch_1 and switch_2), and the bay is protected by a circuit breaker (breaker_1). The Bay also has two earthing switches (switch_3 and switch_4) and three three-phase voltage/current measurement units. The simulated power system uses two functions; Measurement I/O, and Relay to send and receive messages from the communication network system through UDP ports. The measurement I/O function receives voltage and current measurements from all the measurement units, converts them into a data communication compatible format and sends them to the communication network. The relay function receives switchgear control messages from the communication network and converts them into control signals for the simulated switchgears.

2) Process-Level IEDs: At the process-level, we implemented a single VM (I/O Merging Unit) that performs the measurements merging and switchgear control functions. The measurements merging function is composed of nine TVTR and nine TCTR corresponding to each phase in the three three-phase voltage/current measurements received from the measurement I/O. The switchgear control function consists of four XSWI and one XCBR necessary to control the switches and the circuit breaker in the simulated power system.

3) Bay-Level IEDs: We implemented two VMs at the bay level. The first VM (Protection/Control) consists of five CSWIs, two MMXUs, and two CILOs. The CSWIs are configured to publish their status information to all the XSWI and XCBR subscribers in the I/O merging unit using the GOOSE control blocks. The MMXUs subscribe to the TVTRs and TCTRs in the I/O merging unit VM using SV message blocks. The two CILOs contain state and interlocking information about the two isolator switches. The second VM (Measurement/Metering) consists of three MMXUs and subscribes to the TVTRs and TCTRs in the I/O merging unit using SV message blocks.

4) Station-Level Devices: At the station-level, we have the offline CA server VM (not shown in Fig. 4) and the station controller VM. The station controller runs the CSWI client applications for all the switchgear devices and connects to the bay-level IEDs through MMS. The CA server is run offline and its only function is to issue certificates.

5) Communication Network: The communication network simulation comprises of 4 VMs that are identically configured (Ubuntu 14.04.4LTS 1GB RAM, 1 Core Processor, 20GB HDD), the process LAN, and the station LAN. The IEC 61850 standard is implemented using the libiec61850 API modified to support MMS over TLS. The process and station LAN infrastructure are simulated using the GNS3 network emulator. The GNS3 is a network emulation software that emulates network devices (switches and routers) to use VMs without modification as shown in Fig. 4.

6) Attacker: The attacker is implemented as a Kali VM (not shown in Fig. 4). Kali is an advanced penetration testing Linux distribution tool used for penetration testing, hacking, and network security assessments. The Kali VM comes preinstalled with applications frequently used in network security testing and exploitation. The Kali VM is configured to have access to the process and station LAN.

B. Preliminary Results

We tested the testbed against some well-known network attacks at the process and network LAN.

1) Process LAN Attacks: Process-level traffic is predominantly multicast/broadcast and publisher/subscriber ethernet messages. An attacker having access to the process LAN can read and write GOOSE and SV messages. Using wireshark and tcpreplay from the attacker VM, we were able to capture and replay GOOSE messages from the protection/control VM to the I/O merging unit VM. By observing the stNum (status number) and sqNum (sequence number) of the goose messages for switchgear control, we were able to create custom GOOSE messages using scapy (a packet manipulation tool) to control the switchgear devices.

2) Station LAN Attacks: At the station level our single bay implementation only supports MMS unicast client-server messages. To gain access to the network traffic, we did a man-in-the-middle attack by spoofing the ARP messages of the station controller and protection/control VMs. Then we configured our attacker VM to intercept and forward the MMS messages between the station controller and protection/control VMs using the ettercap tool.

The attacks were first performed when the IEC-62531 standard was not implemented, and then when the IEC-62531 standard was implemented. The attacks were not successful when the IEC 62531 standard was implemented. However, the attacker can still see the process LAN messages in plain text, and can learn useful information concerning the behavior of the system.

VII. Conclusion

Cyber-physical systems have both physical and cyber components, and any security solution for cyber-physical systems must take this into consideration. Building an IEC 61850 based substation simulation testbed for cyber-physical security studies requires independence between the physical system, the IEDs, and the communication network to realistically represent the IEC 61850 power substation. This work presents a cost effective testbed model that can be easily implemented and scaled according to budget constraints. Our modular and independent design enables various IEC 61850 functions and configurations that supports security to be implemented and tested using virtual IEDs. Our model enables testing and tuning of network configuration to enhance security and performance, and study the effects of physical attacks and disturbances on the security posture of the substation network.

In our future work, we would expand our substation testbed to use real IEDs, and implement multiple bays like actual substation with full SCADA functions using IEC 61850 standards. We would also simulate physical attacks to study its effects on the security posture of the substation network, analyze existing and proposed smart grid security protocols and controls, and develop cyber-physical security solutions that would take into consideration the physical and cyber behavior of intelligent power systems.

References

[1] R. Smith, "Assault on California power station raises alarm on potential for terrorism," Wall Street Journal, vol. 5, 2014.

[2] E. I. Bilis, W. Kröger, and C. Nan, "Performance of electric power systems under physical malicious attacks," IEEE Systems Journal, vol. 7, no. 4, 2013, pp. 854–865.

[3] Y. Li, J. M. McCune, and A. Perrig, "Sbap: Software-based attestation for peripherals," in International Conference on Trust and Trustworthy Computing. Springer, 2010, pp. 16–29.

[4] Z. Durumeric, J. Kasten, D. Adrian, J. A. Halderman, M. Bailey, F. Li, N. Weaver, J. Amann, J. Beekman, M. Payer, and V. Paxson, "The matter of heartbleed," in Proceedings of the 2014 Conference on Internet Measurement Conference, ser. IMC '14. ACM, 2014, pp. 475–488.

[5] C.-C. Liu, A. Stefanov, J. Hong, and P. Panciatici, "Intruders in the grid," IEEE Power and Energy magazine, vol. 10, no. 1, 2012, pp. 58–66.

[6] R. Langner, "Stuxnet: Dissecting a cyberwarfare weapon," IEEE Security & Privacy, vol. 9, no. 3, 2011, pp. 49–51.

[7] A. Hahn, A. Ashok, S. Sridhar, and M. Govindarasu, "Cyber-physical security testbeds: Architecture, application, and evaluation for smart grid," IEEE Transactions on Smart Grid, vol. 4, no. 2, June 2013, pp. 847–855.

[8] Y. Yang et al., "Cybersecurity test-bed for IEC 61850 based smart substations," in 2015 IEEE Power & Energy Society General Meeting. IEEE, July 2015, pp. 1–5.

[9] R. Liu, C. Vellaithurai, S. S. Biswas, T. T. Gamage, and A. K. Srivastava, "Analyzing the cyber-physical impact of cyber events on the power grid," IEEE Transactions on Smart Grid, vol. 6, no. 5, Sep. 2015, pp. 2444–2453.

[10] G. Koutsandria et al., "A real-time testbed environment for cyber-physical security on the power grid," in Proceedings of the First ACM Workshop on Cyber-Physical Systems-Security and Privacy. ACM. ACM Press, 2015, pp. 67–78.

[11] J. Jarmakiewicz, K. Maślanka, and K. Parobczak, "Development of cyber security testbed for critical infrastructure," in 2015 International Conference on Military Communications and Information Systems (ICMCIS). IEEE, May 2015, pp. 1–10.

[12] J. Hong et al., "Cyber-physical security test bed: A platform for enabling collaborative cyber defense methods," 2015. [Online]. Available: http://taocui.info/docs/TestBed.pdf

[13] W. Deng, W. Pei, Z. Shen, and Z. Zhao, "IEC 61850 based testbed for micro-grid operation, control and protection," in 2015 5th International Conference on Electric Utility Deregulation and Restructuring and Power Technologies (DRPT). IEEE, Nov. 2015, pp. 2154–2159.

[14] B. Chen, K. L. Butler-Purry, A. Goulart, and D. Kundur, "Implementing a real-time cyber-physical system test bed in RTDS and OPNET," in North American Power Symposium (NAPS), 2014. IEEE, Sep. 2014, pp. 1–6.

[15] M. A. H. Sadi, M. H. Ali, D. Dasgupta, and R. K. Abercrombie, "OPNET/simulink based testbed for disturbance detection in the smart grid," in Proceedings of the 10th Annual Cyber and Information Security Research Conference. ACM. ACM Press, 2015, pp. 1–4.

[16] D. Bian, M. Kuzlu, M. Pipattanasomporn, S. Rahman, and Y. Wu, "Real-time co-simulation platform using OPAL-RT and OPNET for analyzing smart grid performance," in 2015 IEEE Power Energy Society General Meeting. IEEE, July 2015, pp. 1–5.

[17] J. Nivethan, M. Papa, and P. Hawrylak, "Modeling and simulation of electric power substation employing an IEC 61850 network," in Proceedings of the 9th Annual Cyber and Information Security Research Conference, ser. CISR '14. ACM. ACM Press, 2014, pp. 89–92.

[18] A. Razaq, B. Pranggono, H. Tianfield, and H. Yue, "Simulating smart grid: Co-simulation of power and communication network," in Power Engineering Conference (UPEC), 2015 50th International Universities. IEEE, Sep. 2015, pp. 1–6.

[19] K. Mets, J. A. Ojea, and C. Develder, "Combining power and communication network simulation for cost-effective smart grid analysis," IEEE Communications Surveys & Tutorials, vol. 16, no. 3, 2014, pp. 1771–1796.

[20] IEC 61850-5:2003, "Communication networks and systems in substations - part 5: Communication requirements for functions and device models," first Edition. [Online]. Available: https://webstore.iec.ch/publication/20075

[21] IEC 61850-7-3:2003, "Communication networks and systems in substations - part 7-3: Basic communication structure for substation and feeder equipment - common data classes," first Edition. [Online]. Available: https://webstore.iec.ch/publication/20075

[22] IEC 61850-7-2:2003, "Communication networks and systems in substations - part 7-2: Basic information and communication structure - abstract communication service interface (ACSI)," first Edition. [Online]. Available: https://webstore.iec.ch/publication/20075

[23] IEC 61850-8-1:2004, "Communication networks and systems in substations - part 8-1: Specific communication service mapping (SCSM) - mappings to MMS (ISO 9506-1 and ISO 9506-2) and to ISO/IEC 8802-3," first Edition. [Online]. Available: https://webstore.iec.ch/publication/20075

[24] IEC 61850-9-2:2004, "Communication networks and systems in substations - part 9-2: Specific communication service mapping (SCSM) - sampled values over ISO/IEC 8802-3," first Edition. [Online]. Available: https://webstore.iec.ch/publication/20075

[25] IEC TS 62351-1:2007, "Power systems management and associated information exchange - data and communications security - part 1: Communication network and system security - introduction to security issues." [Online]. Available: https://webstore.iec.ch/publication/6903

[26] R. Schlegel, S. Obermeier, and J. Schneider, "Assessing the security of iec 62351," in Proceedings of the 3rd International Symposium for ICS & SCADA Cyber Security Research, ser. ICS-CSR '15. Swinton, UK, UK: British Computer Society, 2015, pp. 11–19.

[27] Michael Zillgith. libIEC61850 | open source library for IEC 61850. [Online]. Available: http://www.libiec61850.com/libiec61850/ (2016)

[28] Stefan Feuerhahn, Marco Mittelsdorf, Dirk Zimmermann, Albrecht Schall, Philipp Fels. OpenIEC61850 | open source library for IEC 61850. [Online]. Available: https://www.openmuc.org/index.php?id=35

[29] SIEMENS. PSS®E - Power Transmission System Planning Software. [Online]. Available: http://w3.siemens.com/smartgrid/global/en/products-systems-solutions/software-solutions/planning-data-management-software/planning-simulation/Pages/PSS-E.aspx (2016)

[30] RTDS Technologies. RTDS - Real Time Digital Simulation. [Online]. Available: https://www.rtds.com (2016)

[31] OPAL-RT Technologies. OPAL-RT - PC/FPGA Based Real-Time Digital Simulators. [Online]. Available: http://www.opal-rt.com (2016)

[32] S. Siraj, A. Gupta, and R. Badgujar, "Network simulation tools survey," International Journal of Advanced Research in Computer and Communication Engineering, vol. 1, no. 4, 2012, pp. 199–206.

Exchanging Database Writes with Modern Crypto

Andreas Happe, Thomas Loruenser
Department Safety & Security
AIT Austrian Institute of Technology GmbH
Vienna, Austria
email: {andreas.happe|thomas.loruenser}@ait.ac.at

***Abstract*—Modern cryptography provides for new ways of solving old problems. This paper details how Keyed-Hash Message Authentication Codes (HMACs) or Authenticated Encryption with Associated Data (AEAD) can be employed as an alternative to a traditional server-side temporal session store. This cryptography-based approach reduces the server-side need for state. When applied to database-based user-management systems it removes all database alteration statements needed for confirmed user sign-up and greatly removes database alteration statements for typical "forgot password" use-cases. As there is no temporary data stored within the server database system, there is no possibility of creating orphaned or abandoned data records. However, this new approach is not generic and can only be applied if implemented use-cases fulfill requirements. This requirements and implications are also detailed within this paper.**

***Index Terms*—Internet, Network security, Web services**

I. Introduction and Problem Statement

A common web-application user-interaction pattern is *Request-Verification-Execution*. An example can be seen in Fig. 1: the user requests an server-side operation and transmits needed data to the server. The server validates the information and stores the user-submitted data temporally on the server. To verify the user request a challenge is transmitted through a separate communication channel. After the user fulfills the challenge the operation is executed and finalized on the server. An example of this pattern is a user registration (we are basing all examples upon Ruby on Rails' *Devise* framework): after a potential new user entered her data on a website, she is presented with an confirmation email and the user account is only activated after the user has confirmed her identity through a confirmation link within this email. Similar examples are typical "user registration", "password reset" or "delete account" functions.

Problems arise if the user fails to perform the verification step or automated tools request the initial operation thousands or millions of times without ever performing the corresponding confirmation step. During the initial request temporary data is stored within the server: this data is "dead" and must be eventually removed from the database. Furthermore, additional server-side data is needed for the implementation of the verification process. For example, commonly used implementations (depicted in Fig. 2) generate and store a random token within a server-side database. This token is included within the confirmation email and later matched against the database record.

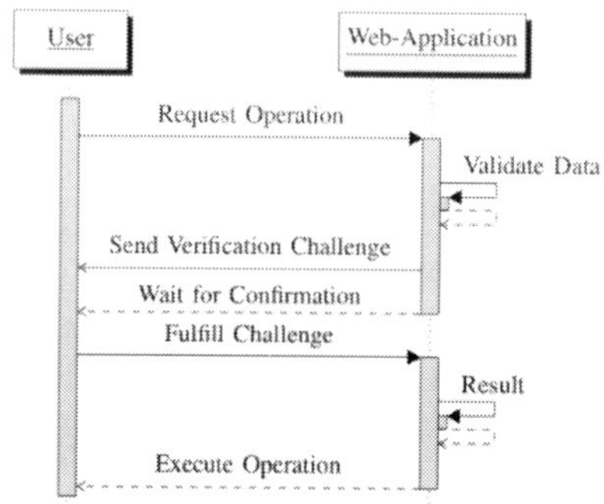

Fig. 1. Generic "Request-Verification-Execution" Work-Flow

Server-side temporary data is commonly stored within databases and therefore leads to I/O overhead. In this paper, we propose an cryptographic alternative utilizing HMACs [1] or AEAD that inherently prevents stale database entries and removes the need for both data alteration operations and additional database fields.

The tow approaches are detailed in Section II and Section III. This work is compared with existing solutions in section IV. Section V showcases advantages and disadvantages of this approach while section VI concludes this paper.

II. Database-centric Approach

The database-centric approach stores all temporary data within the server-side database as can be seen through the multiple database calls in Fig. 2.

The web-application must track confirmed and unconfirmed operations. For example, during user registration the application must separate confirmed from unconfirmed users as the latter must not be able to login. To differentiate between those either an explicit or implicit state is used. The former can be implemented through an additional *state* field. The latter can be implemented through additional metadata, e.g., a *confirmed_at* field. Those fields must be added to each user record but are unused most of the time.

Typically, an additional database field *created_at* is used to store the timestamp of the original request. This allows detection of orphaned operation that never have been confirmed. Subsequently, the user might be sent an reminder-email, but

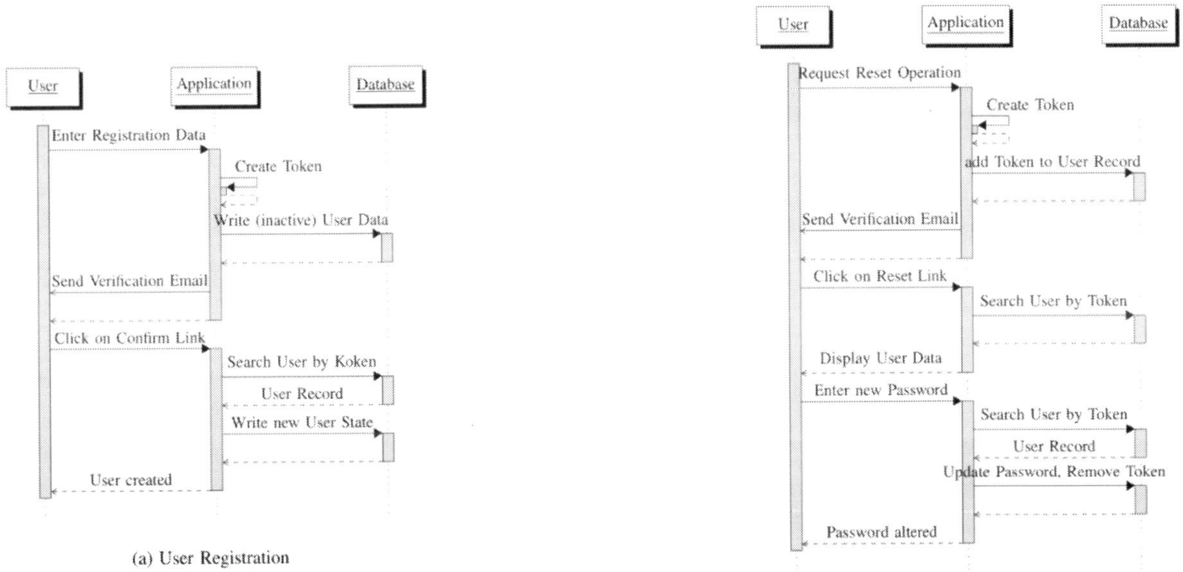

(a) User Registration

(b) Resend Password Functionality

Fig. 2. Sequence Diagrams for database-centric work flows.

eventually the stale user record has to be removed if the user does not interact.

The "user registration" use-case shows three distinct database interactions. 1) During user registration all mandatory user data is captured and stored within the database. Additional fields (e.g., *confirmation_token* and *confirmed_at*) are needed to perform the registration and are thus added to the database. If the new user never confirms his registration, the whole data set is "dead" data. 2) when the user clicks on the confirmation link contained in the mail, the user record has to be retrieved from the database and 3) after confirmation the user record's state is set and meta-information is cleaned up.

The "password reset" use-case does not depend upon record creation but alters the existing user record multiple times. To perform the action two new fields are added to the user record: *reset_password_sent_at* and *reset_password_token*. Typically, four phases of database access can be seen: 1) a new reset token is generated and stored within the user record, 2) when the user clicks on the verification link, the database is queried for it's validity and then a password entry formula is shown 3) when the user submits a new password the token is again verified and 4) the password is finally updated within the database and meta-information is cleaned up. Even if the data is retrieved directly from a in-memory data store, the session verification commonly entails database access.

III. Alternative: Usage of HMAC/AEAD

Our proposed alternative approach does not depend upon server-side storage of temporary state but uses cryptography to authenticate data presented by the user during the verification step. Cryptography is used to ensure that neither users nor third-parties are able to tamper data passed on by the server.

HMACs[1] offer a solution to this problem. A MAC combines the plain-text data with a secret-key and produces a tag that verifies the plain-text data's integrity and authenticity. In our case, the server creates the tag and transmits the plain-text data and the tag within the verification challenge. When the user fulfills the challenge, the tag verifies that the data has not been tampered with. The secret-key never leaves the server. The transmitted data has to be careful chosen to prevent replay attacks as will be detailed later on.

HMACs provide authentication and integrity but not data confidentiality as all input data is transmitted in plain sight. AEAD in contrast provides confidentiality, integrity and authenticity. An AEAD algorithm uses the plain-text and a secret key as input, and produces a cipher text and authentication tag as output. The overall protocol is similar to the HMAC-based protocol but replaces the plain-text data with the cipher text to additionally provide data confidentiality. Also similar to the HMAC-based algorithm, the encoded data must be sufficient to prevent replay attacks.

Fig. 3 details two possible AEAD-based workflows. Instead of storing temporary state within the server-side database, the state is encrypted and attached to the verification challenge, e.g., encoded in the verification link contained in the sent verification email. The usage of HMACs/AEAD prevents users or third-parties from maliciously altering the transmitted data. During verification, the server verifies and decrypts the received encrypted data and uses it as intermediate state that finally is committed to the database. Note that only a single

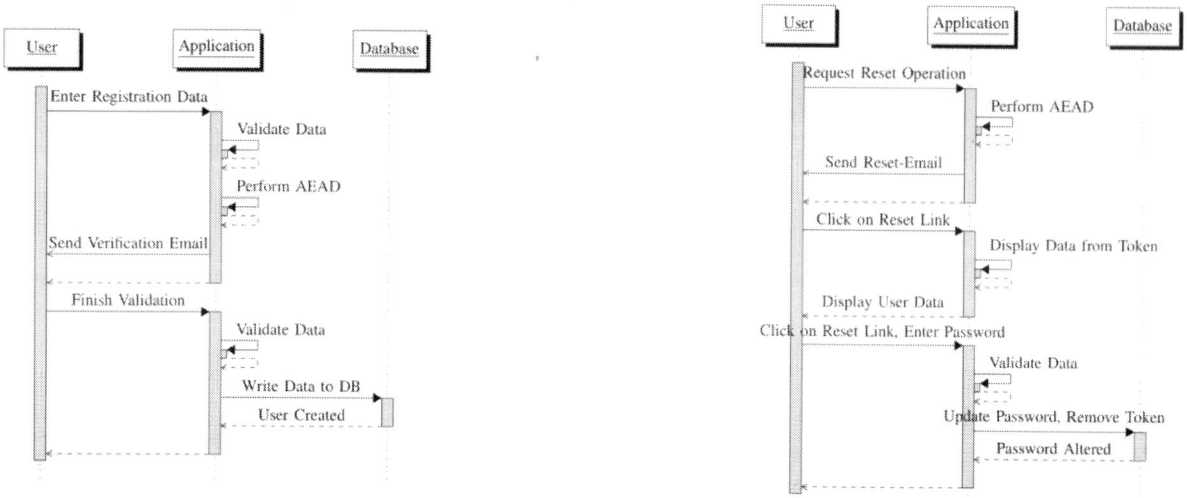

(a) User Registration. The encrypted data includes an operation identifier, expiry as well as all data needed for the user registration.

(b) Resend Password Functionality. The encrypted data includes an operation identifier, user, expiry, hash of the stored password hash.

Fig. 3. Sequence Diagrams for cryptographic-based work flows. Note the reduced amount of database operations.

database transaction is performed. This also removes metadata fields, as well as "verification"-states from user records.

A. Data-Field Selection

Proper selection of fields used as input for the HMAC/AEAD-function prevents replay attacks. This selection should be sufficient to uniquely identify the executed operation and its context.

An unique *operation identifier* is mandatory. Otherwise given $operation_1$ and $operation_2$, the encoded data from $operation_1$ could be used during verification of $operation_2$.

A *stable user identified* is needed to associate the encoded data with an user account.

Once the server has authenticated a data block, it is valid until the server's private key is changed. A real-world implementation would include a *creation or expiry date* to limit the lifetime of the verification token.

An *anchor element* is needed to differentiate between subsequent states. For example, a "reset password"-function should include a hash of the current password. The hash will be compared to the currently stored hash during operation execution and thus limit's the operation's validity to changing the "current" password. Otherwise, the same verification token could be maliciously used to repeatedly change the user's password.

All *user-supplied data* that would otherwise be stored as temporary data within the server-side database must be included within the data block.

In our "user registration" case, we could select the following parameters: *[operation-id: "registration", expiry: "2016-1-30", user-id: "andreas.happe@ait.ac.at", user-data: "..."]* as input for the AEAD/HMAC function. For a potential "password reset" function, we would chose *[operation-id: "reset", expiry: "2016-1-30", user-id: "andreas.happe@ait.ac.at", old-password-hash: "hash of my currently stored password"]* as verification token.

IV. Related Work

To the best of our knowledge, the first and only study—and thus inspiration for this paper— of using HMACs for *Request-Verification-Execution* workflows was published within a blog post by Mahmoud Al-Qudsi[2]. In contrast, our paper details potential replay attack vectors and introduces data confidentiality through usage of AEAD schemes.

A comparable mechanism lies at the heart of HTTP session management: here, the session is managed on either server- or client-side. With client-side management the session's data is signed on the server with a secret key, transmitted and stored at the client. On subsequent requests the cookie is transmitted to the server and validated with the server's secret key. When using a server-side scheme all session-data is stored at the server and only a session identifier is stored at the client. The overall scheme is similar to our proposed approach but it's applicability differs: HTTP cookies are limited to the client's browser and thus allow for identification of a browser-based session. We see usage for our scheme within persisted mails. As mails can be stored and forwarded between clients our approach is more akin to token passing.

As an concrete example, the Ruby on Rails' *CookieStore* stores session information within a client-side cookie and verifies the validity of the cookie through a server-side computed HMAC utilizing a secret server-side key. An alternative session-store is database-backed. The Ruby on Rails Security Guide[3] describes implications of the different session stores that are similar to the those of using AEAD/HMAC-based temporary state storage.

In August 2008, AEAD schemes were made mandatory for TLSv1.2[4], [5]. The ambiguity of encrypted HTTPS communication lead hardware vendors to the inclusion of dedicated encryption co-processors and/or inclusion of encryption-specific instructions within their microcode thus making hardware-supported high-performance AEAD functions commonly available on server-grade hardware. The situation will further improve in the future as the current TLSv1.3 draft mandates the usage of AEAD ciphers.

V. Implications and Limitations

Usage of the cryptography-centric approach has several implications:

No server-side state. As no temporal data is stored, the server has no opportunity to detect operations waiting for user confirmation. This functionality is sometimes used to implement an "reminder" email to improve user response rate.

A *stable ID and anchor element are needed to prevent playback attacks*. For example, if user-changeable email addresses are used as stable identifiers, an attacker can create a new "user deletion token", change his email account, wait until a victim creates an account using the same email address, and then delete this account until the token expires. To solve this, an additional anchor element has to be included, in this case the initial creation time could be used. For another example of an anchor element, consider the mentioned "reset password"-function: request should include a hash of the current password. This anchors the update to the current database state and prevents the replay attack. Without an unique anchor element, race conditions can occur. For example, if two users sign-up with the same email address the first user that confirms (through his link) will be created. A similar race condition is present at the traditional scheme, but in this case the critical section is the initial data entry form.

The *wrong HTTP Verb is used.* Confirmation will commonly happen through a HTTP GET link. Data alteration operations should be performed through a HTTP PUT, POST or DELETE operation. The same discrepancy is true for traditional schemes.

The *Privacy of the secret key is paramount.* If an attacker retrieves the secret key (used for encryption or HMAC-operation) from the server he can forge any operation request. We think this attack vector to be non-critical, as an attacker with this capability can already access the database directly.

Size limit for transmitted messages. While the HTTP/1.1 protocol initially did not limit the transmission size for GET request[6], a later revision did place a limit of 8000 octets[7]. Real-world web browsers and servers enforce different limits, especially older Internet Explorer Versions (2048 bytes). Current browsers and servers should be able to cope with 8192 bytes of data while 2048 bytes should be reasonable safe.

Aesthetic Considerations. With AEAD all information is encoded within the passed parameter. This parameter can get large and leads to an unaesthetic URL – this can be a problem for usage within text-based emails while it is acceptable within HTML-based emails.

Usage before confirmation is not possible. Sometimes web-applications offer limited functionality between user-sign-up and user-verification. This is not possible with our alternative scheme as the server-side user-account is only created upon user-verification.

Also please note that the integrity and confidentiality of the transport layer needs to be provided by additional means. With a captured token the attacker has all needed means for an Man-in-the-Middle attack. This implies mandatory usage of TLS.

VI. Conclusion

This paper initially introduced common problems that arise with server-side state management. Cryptographic means allow alternative schemes that do not share those issues, but in turn, their applicability highly depends upon the surrounding use-case. We have shown how two common use-cases, "user registration" and "password reset" can be implemented using our new scheme.

As shown with those examples, we believe that our alternative solution has real-world merits and can improve existing software solutions. In addition, we hope, that this paper shines more light upon the generic technique and increases it's visibility among software engineers.

VII. Acknowledgements

The authors would like to thank Mahmoud Al-Qudsi for his detailed comments.

References

[1] H. Krawczyk, M. Bellare, and R. Canetti, "Rfc 2104: Hmac: Keyed-hashing for message authentication," *URL http://www.rfc.net/html/rfc2104*, 1997.

[2] M. Al-Qudsi. (2015) Life in a post-database world: using crypto to avoid db writes. [Online]. Available: https://neosmart.net/blog/2015/using-hmac-signatures-to-avoid-database-writes/

[3] Ruby on rails security. [Online]. Available: http://guides.rubyonrails.org/security.html#session-storage

[4] T. Dierks and E. Rescorla, "Rfc 5246: The transport layer security (tls) protocol version 1.2," *URL http://www.rfc.net/html/rfc5246*, 2008.

[5] J. Salowey, A. Choudhury, and D. McGrew, "Rfc 5288: Aes galois mode (gcm) cipher suites for tls," *URL http://www.rfc.net/html/rfc5288*, 2008.

[6] R. Fielding, J. Gettys, J. Mogul, H. Frystyk, L. Masinter, P. Leach, and T. Berners-Lee, "Rfc 2616: Hypertext transfer protocol–http/1.1, 1999," *URL http://www.rfc.net/rfc2616.html*, 2009.

[7] R. Fielding and J. Reschke, "Rfc 7230: Hypertext transfer protocol (http/1.1): Message syntax and routing," *URL http://www.rfc.net/rfc7230.html*, 2014.

Experiment of Sensor Fault Tolerance Algorithm combined with Cyber System for Coil Tilter on the Smart Hybrid Powerpack

Jaegwang Lee
Department of Mechanical Engineering
Sungkyunkwan University
Suwon, Korea
email: leejkcool@gmail.com

Janggeol Nam, Buchun Song, Hyeonwoo Kim, Iksu Choi and Hunmo Kim
Department of Mechanical Engineering
Sungkyunkwan University
Suwon, Korea
email: mystic777@skku.edu, theme7749@gmail.com, 88jamesk88@gmail.com, cis326@naver.com, kimhm@me.skku.ac.kr

Abstract — This paper presents a Smart Hybrid Powerpack (SHP) for the sensor failure recovery algorithm for coil tilter and cyber system for control and monitoring. The SHP is combined with all advanced technologies: an Electro Hydraulic Actuator (EHA), fault tolerant control, intelligent control, and Graphic User Interface (GUI) based remote control and monitoring. The proposed algorithm for the sensor failure recovery uses a Kalman filter for noise caused by electric currents and temporary failures caused by a disturbance. In addition, sensor hardware that becomes damaged due to external impact, fails due to aging, or permanently fails due to damage, uses the Sliding Mode Observer (SMO) for normal waveform estimation and recovery. The proposed algorithm for the sensor failure recovery was implemented using an experiment. The performance of the proposed algorithm is verified through an alarm and monitoring of the cyber system in the event of failure of the coil tilter system.

Keywords — Coil tilter; Smart Hybrid Powerpack (SHP); Electro Hydraulic Actuator (EHA); fault tolerance; Machine GUI; Office GUI; Mobile GUI.

I. INTRODUCTION

Hydraulic actuators are widely used in various industries where high actuating forces are required. In order to enhance the performance of the hydraulic system, disturbances due to the external environment and effects of interference should be minimized [1]. In addition, Electro Hydraulic Actuator (EHA) systems were developed to compensate for the disadvantages of the conventional hydraulic actuator, such as low energy efficiency, limited installation spaces, heavy weight of components, and fluid leakage [2]. The EHA system has high energy efficiency due to a two-way fluid pump and an electric motor directly connected to each pump. The existing remote system was only possible for fault diagnosis through system monitoring [3][4]. The newly proposed Smart Hybrid Powerpack (SHP) combined with the cyber system are shown in Fig.1. Unlike the existing remote system, the EHA system is applied to the control and monitoring through a ECU control board and Graphic User Interface (GUI) by wireless communication and wire network. The cyber system includes an intelligent fault tolerance control, such as real time feedback of sensor signals, software filter, and sensor observer detecting and recovering from sensor faults. [5][6].

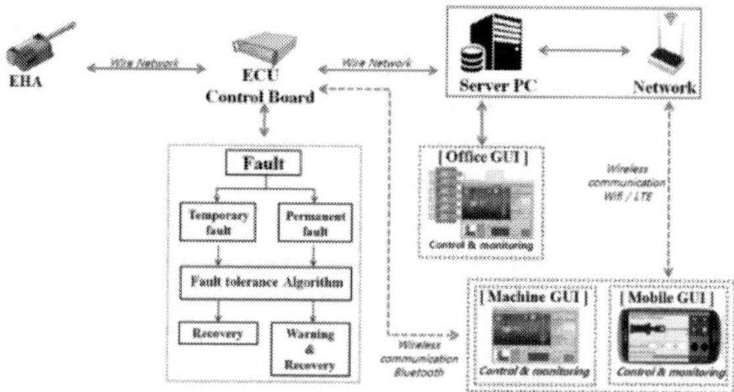

Figure 1. The SHP structure combined with cyber system

The various sensors in the SHP are applied by intelligent control systems for its safety and reliability, for the remote control system with monitoring, and for precision and accuracy of control. The sensors applied to the SHP are the LVDT (Linear Variable Differential Transformer) for tracking the change of the position of the cylinder, pressure for controlling the thrust, and encoder for motor speed. The LVDT sensor is mounted onto the cylinder rod, and the pressure sensors are attached to the cylinder head and rod. When a fault occurs in the SHP sensors, it is difficult to control the cylinder due to inaccurate sensor values. If a transient noise occurs due to an electrical malfunction, the noise can be recovered by using hardware methods, such as a coil filter. Also, the noise can be recovered by using software methods, such as a Kalman filter. If a permanent failure occurs in sensors attached to the SHP, such as disturbances, vibration, internal hardware problem in the sensors, or aging equipment, a rapid recovery is required because it can cause serious problems with the control. When a permanent failure occurs in the SHP, the original sensor signal is estimated and recovered by the Sliding Mode Observer (SMO). The prototype is operated through the (Office/Machine/Mobile) GUI, and the failure recovery algorithm is performed through a MATLAB Simulink [5].

The rest of the paper is structured as follows. In Section 2, two types of faults (temporary and permanent) are presented, and the design and analysis of the SMO algorithm for failure recovery are discussed. In Section 3, the experimental results of fault recovery are shown. We conclude in Section 4.

II. Design of Fault Tolerance Algorithm

A. Classification of fault types

Sensor fault modes are classified in two categories, as shown in TABLE I. Once electronic noises are generated due to external factors, there is a possibility that normal signal accompany sensor errors or failure can occur. If the normal sensor signal is blended with a temporary fault caused by an electric current or outer high-voltage surge, it can generate instantaneous errors on account of high frequency noise. Permanent fault (Failure) can be caused by a sensor hardware problem, such as physical force, heat, deterioration of equipment, or being a defective product. It can generate permanent failure of the sensor [6].

TABLE I. THE CLASSIFICATION

Faults	Cause	Effects
Temporary fault (Error)	Noise	Error value by transient noise
Permanent fault (Failure)	Breaking of wire, Short circuit	Output Voltage 0V
	Fixation	Fixed voltage output
	Zero drift	Offset change

Fig 2. shows the characteristics of the sensor waveform in the event of the two types of sensor faults (temporary and permanent) [6].

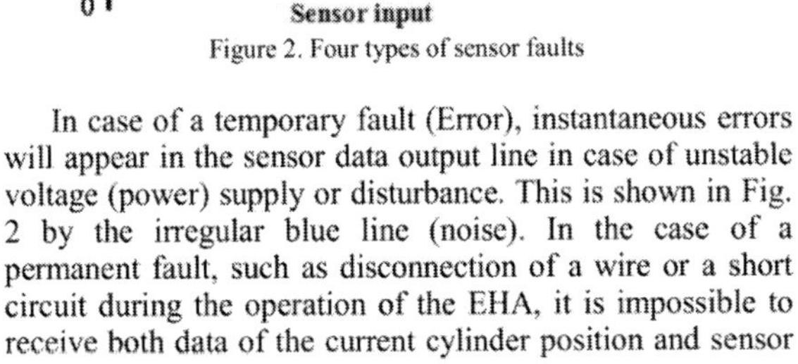

Figure 2. Four types of sensor faults

In case of a temporary fault (Error), instantaneous errors will appear in the sensor data output line in case of unstable voltage (power) supply or disturbance. This is shown in Fig. 2 by the irregular blue line (noise). In the case of a permanent fault, such as disconnection of a wire or a short circuit during the operation of the EHA, it is impossible to receive both data of the current cylinder position and sensor status due to the physical breakdown of the data line. This is shown in Fig. 2 by the wide dashed green line. Eventually, the output signal goes to zero voltage. When the output signal is constant (see middle dashed red line in Fig. 2), it is defined as fixation. When fixation occurs, the SHP will not recognize the stop command and will operate the EHA continuously; the EHA may cause a malfunction of over output exceeding the reference input. Also, the pump continues to rotate due to wrong information coming from the sensors. Eventually, pressure inside of the pump increases and it can become a serious threat to the safety of the system. In the case of zero-drift, an offset occurs because of the addition of an initial signal and jumping voltage signal (see the short dashed purple line in Fig. 2). Offset signal occurs with a permanent fault.

B. Analysis of fault tolerance algorithm

Sensor errors caused by noise are recovered by the Kalman filter. The Kalman filter estimates the current sensor signal value from past sensor signal values based on the system model [7].

$$K_{t+1} = C^{-}_{t+1} H^{T} (H C^{-}_{t+1} H^{T} + R)^{-1} \quad (1)$$

$$C_{t+1} = C^{-}_{t+1} - K_{t+1} H C^{-}_{t+1} \quad (2)$$

$$\hat{x}_{t+1} = \hat{x}^{-}_{t+1} + K_{t+1} z_{t+1} - K_{t+1} H \hat{x}^{-}_{t+1} \quad (3)$$

Equation (1) calculates the Kalman gain K_{t+1} by using system model H , R , prediction error covariance C^{-}_{t+1} . Kalman acts as a scale for the calculation of estimated value $\hat{x}_{t+1}$ which is the final output in the Kalman filter algorithm. In (2), the error covariance C_{t+1} is calculated by using the Kalman gain, system model H , and prediction error covariance C^{-}_{t+1}. Error covariance is used to determine how accurate is the estimated value in the prediction equation. The error covariance is larger than the largest error. Equation (3) calculates the estimated value of current time by using predicted estimated value $\hat{x}^{-}_{t+1}$, input z_{t+1} , K_{t+1} as the weighting and system model variable H . According to previous situations and system model, Kalman filter tunes a Kalman gain each time by repeating equation. So, it can correct the estimated value within the normal margin of error in the face of rapid waveform variations due to noise [7].

In order to control the output of the cylinder, we have to know the position of the rod and the internal pressure of the cylinder. If the position sensor has a permanent fault, ECU cannot control the cylinder because the exact position of the cylinder rod cannot be detected. If the pressure sensor has a permanent fault, ECU cannot obtain the information for the precise axial control because ECU cannot detect the internal pressure of the system. In order to estimate the output of the sensors, we should be aware of the change of discharge flow rate in the pump to be input to the system and system dynamics model of the EHA [8][9].

Through dynamic cylinder models, SMO estimates a signal of the position sensor or pressure sensor, which requires a repair by using the input flow rate variation. The SMO model for estimating the position sensor is expressed as follows [10].

$$\dot{\hat{y}} = g_1 \operatorname{sgn}(\hat{y} - y) - y + \left\{ \frac{\beta_e Q}{(V_H + S_H y)} \right\} \quad (4)$$

where, Q is the discharge flow rate of the pump, S_H is the cross section of the cylinder head, y is the location of the cylinder rod, V_H is the volume of the cylinder head, and β_e is the effective bulk modulus of the hydraulic fluid. In the (4), $\dot{\hat{y}}$ is the estimated output speed of the cylinder rod, $\hat{y}$ is the estimated location of cylinder rod, and g_1 is an arbitrary constant of the signum function (sgn). The SMO algorithm has characteristics that estimate the original sensor signals and vibration with signum function of difference between the output value of the sensor and the estimated value. The signum function compares the difference between the location of the cylinder rod and the estimated location of the cylinder rod based on the system model and reduces their error range. The SMO can quickly recover the permanent fault of the sensor because it has a robust characteristic for the disturbance and a succinct model equation [10].

III. EXPERIMENT OF THE FAULT TOLERANCE ALGORITHM COMBINED WITH CYBER SYSTEM

The coil tilter SHP is composed of three main parts that include the EHA system, the fault tolerance in ECU, and the cyber system.

The cyber system consists of the Office GUI, the Machine GUI, and the Mobile GUI. The Mobile GUI of the cyber system is connected to the ECU and exerts its control over the SHP by wireless network communication. The Machine GUI and the Office GUI are connected to the ECU by a wire network. The GUI sends the reference input signal to the ECU and the ECU sends command signals to the EHA.

In this experiment, we consider a fault that may occur while operating the SHP through the cyber system shown in Fig. 3. The sensor fault occurs through a function generator and relay. The object of this experiment is to determine whether the fault tolerance algorithm can make the cyber system detect the fault, send an alarm for the fault, and recover from the fault by using the fault tolerance algorithm.

Fig. 4 shows the SMO algorithm of the LVDT sensor by using the function blocks from MATLAB Simulink.

Figure 3. The experiment equipment

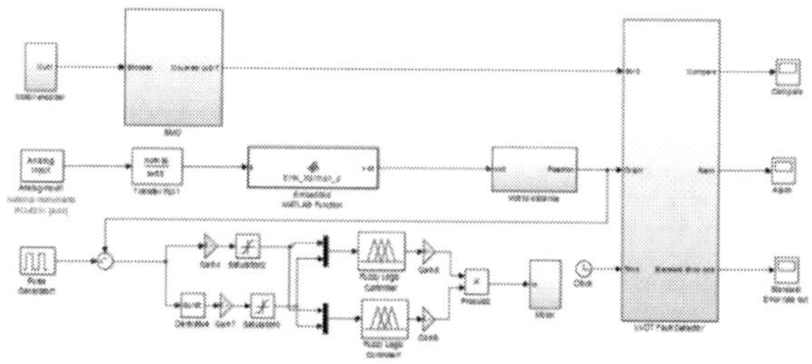

Figure 4. Fault tolerance algorithm of LVDT

The fault tolerance algorithm indicates that the SMO algorithm used as an input of the flow rate change by using speed of the motor is combined with the dynamic equation of the SHP model. When the temporary fault happens, a Kalman gain changes in real time in the Kalman filter and it calculates estimated value of the sensor. So, the ECU can correct the estimated value within the normal margin of error. When a fault occurs (temporary or permanent), a comparison is done between the reference input signals and the SMO signal calculated by the SMO formula, and the fault input signal is replaced with the recovered sensor input signal through a fault detector in the fault tolerance algorithm.

IV. RESULTS

When a fault does not happen, the normal position value of the cylinder rod is shown in Fig.5.

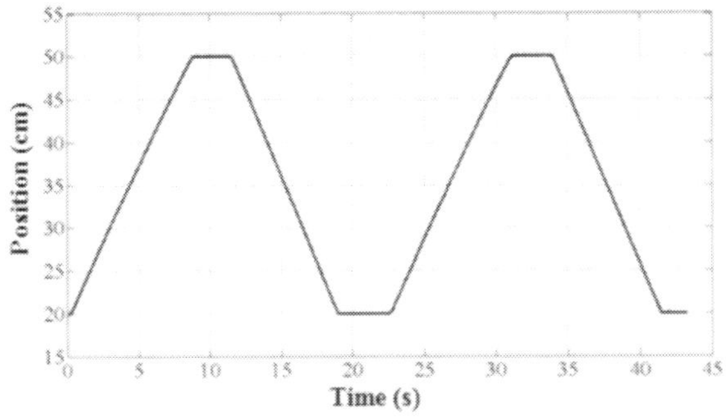

Figure 5. Normal signal of LVDT

To get the temporary fault, a function generator was used to give random noise signals. Fig. 6 shows the estimation of the LVDT sensor output using the Kalman filter and the threshold predictor. Mixed noise signals (see the dashed line in Fig. 6) were recovered through the Kalman filter.

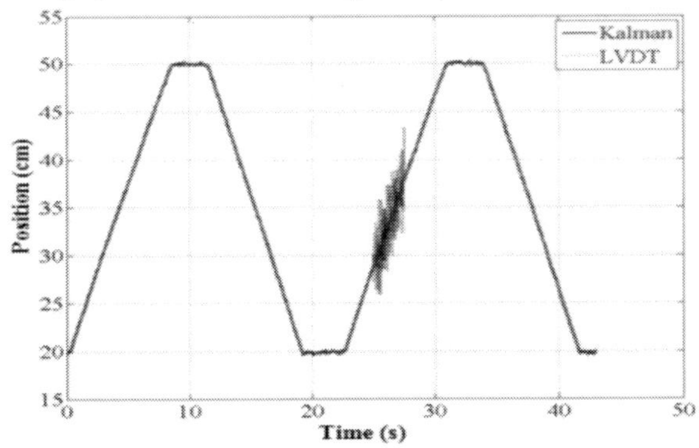

Figure 6. Noise signal and recovered signal by using Kalman filter

To generate the LVDT sensor signal with a permanent sensor fault, the experiment used a relay which is an electromagnetic switch to generate the sudden permanent fault (breaking of the wire and short circuit). After a fault occurs (relay operated), the voltage of the LVDT goes to 0V. When the relay is electrically switched at time 27 seconds, the LVDT signal goes to 0V due to breaking of the wire and short circuit. When the signal is over the allowable error range, the LVDT signal is replaced to threshold predictor signal from encoder related to motor rpm. Estimates of the LVDT sensor outputs by using the SMO model and recovered signal are shown in Fig. 7.

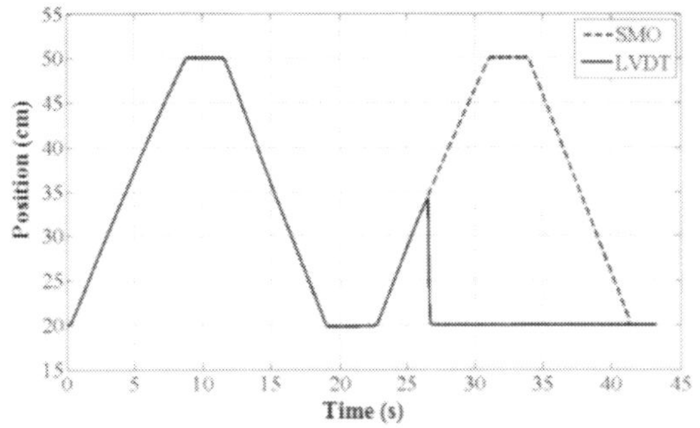

Figure 7. Short circuit / Disconnection of wire fault signal and recovered signal by using SMO

The position of the cylinder rod follows the recovered signal into the reference error based on the SMO model. After that, the alarm output is switching from 0 to 1 as shown in Fig. 8. Also, the cyber system alarm is warning on the display and the (Office/Machine/Mobile) GUIs show that LVDT is under recovery while the alarm goes on.

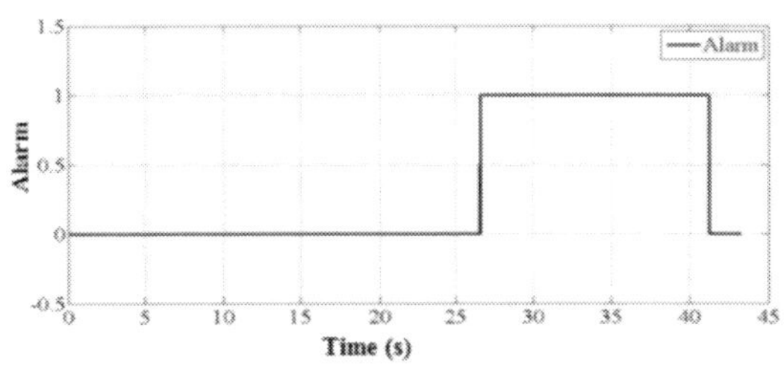

Figure 8. Fault detection alarm of Short circuit / Disconnection of wire

To find out the error rate of the SMO, by comparing the LVDT signal with the SMO threshold predictor signal, it shows that the recovered signal is well operated because the maximum of the reference error is under an allowable range. If the LVDT signal exceeds the allowable signal, the fault detector gives an alarm during recovery. Also, the LVDT sensor signal is replaced by the SMO signal in parallel. If the fault persists, the signal may be considered as a permanent fault, as indicated in the fault classification shown in TABLE I. Following the previous experiments, two sudden permanent fault experiments (fixation, zero-drift) will be applied.

To generate the LVDT sensor signal with a permanent fault, we use a relay for sudden operation and power supply to engender fixation. After the fault occurs, the voltage of the LVDT goes to a fixed voltage (3V). When the signal exceeds the allowable error range, the LVDT signal is replaced by a threshold predictor signal from encoder related to motor rpm. Estimates of the LVDT sensor outputs by using the SMO model and recovered signal are shown in Fig. 9.

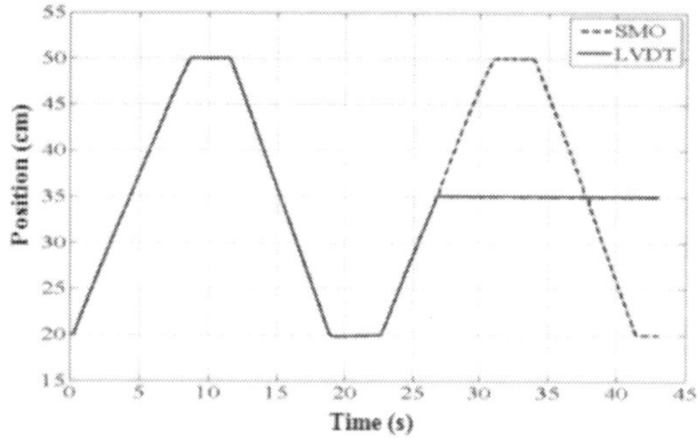

Figure 9. Fixation fault signal and recovered signal by using SMO

After that, the alarm output is switching from 0 to 1, as shown in Fig. 10. We see a fault where chattering occurred near time 27 seconds during the alarm, but the duration of the alarm is too short to determine the presence of the permanent fault. Also, the cyber system alarm is warning in display and the (Office/Machine/Mobile) GUI shows that the LVDT is under recovery while the alarm operates.

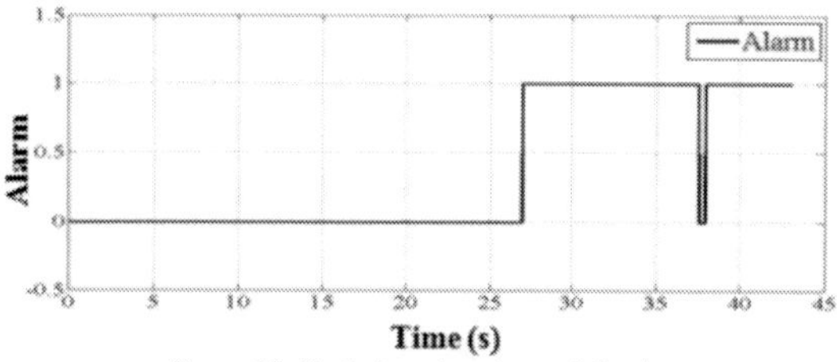

Figure 10. Fault detection alarm of fixation

To generate the LVDT sensor signal with a permanent fault, we use a relay for sudden operation and power supply to make zero-drift. After the fault occurs, the voltage of LVDT will be lower offset. When the signal exceeds the allowable error range, the LVDT signal is replaced by a threshold predictor signal from encoder related to motor rpm. Estimates of the LVDT sensor outputs by using the SMO model and the recovered signal are shown in Fig. 11.

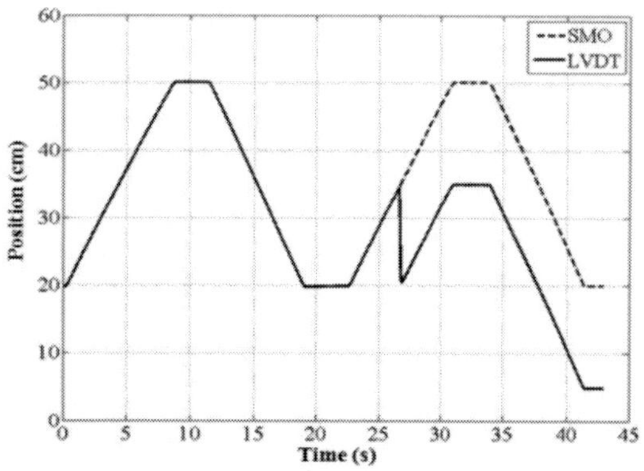

Figure 11. Lower zero-drift fault signal and recovered signal by using SMO

After that, the alarm output is switching from 0 to 1 as shown in Fig.12.

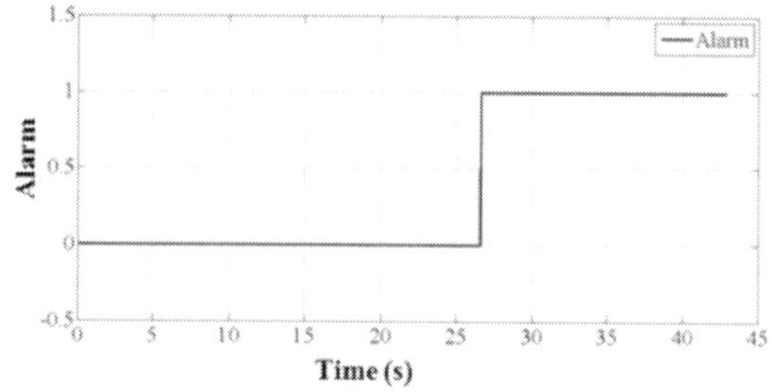

Figure 12. Fault detection alarm of lower zero-drift

After a fault occurs, the voltage of LVDT will be upper offset. Estimates of the LVDT sensor outputs by using the SMO model and the recovered signal are shown in Fig. 13.

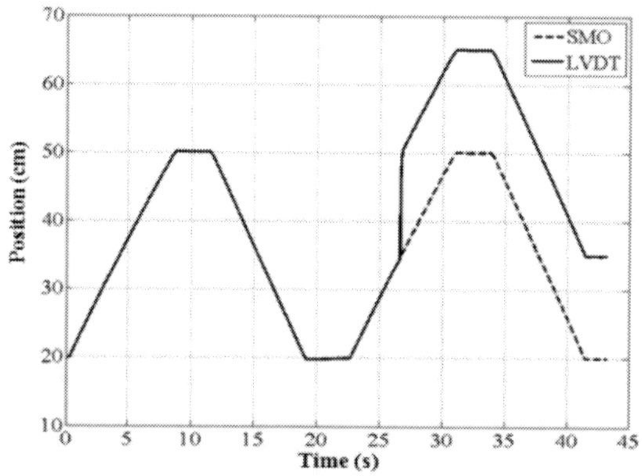

Figure 13. Upper zero-drift fault signal and recovered signal by using SMO

After the permanent fault occurs, the alarm output is switching from 0 to 1, as shown in Fig. 14.

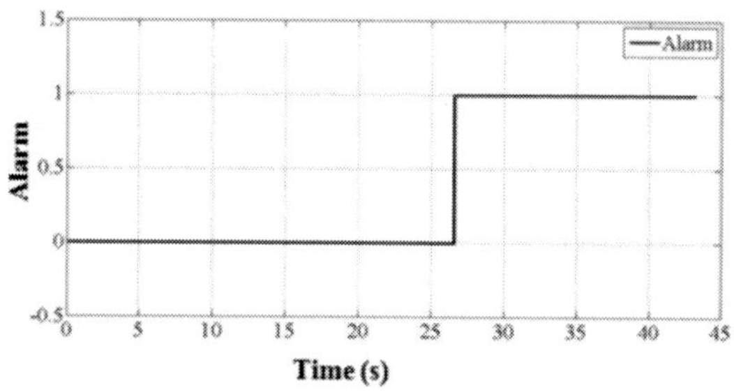

Figure 14. Fault detection alarm of upper zero-drift

During the whole process of permanent fault experiment, the cyber system alarm is warning in the display and the (Office/Machine/Mobile) GUI shows that the LVDT is under recovery while the alarm operates, as shown in Fig. 15.

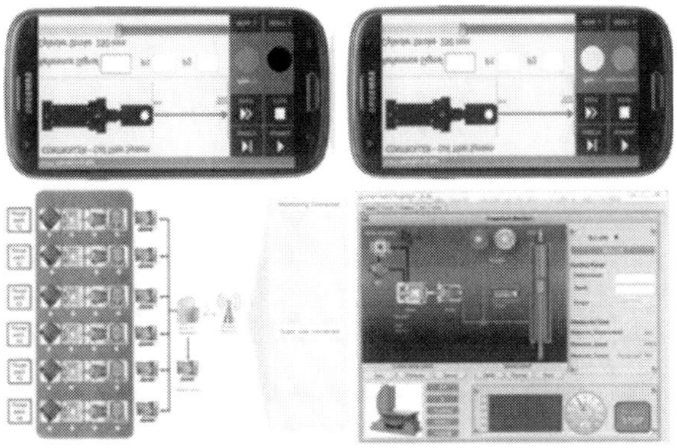

Figure 15. Fault detection alarm of cyber system

Fig.16 shows the overall configuration of the coil tilter system.

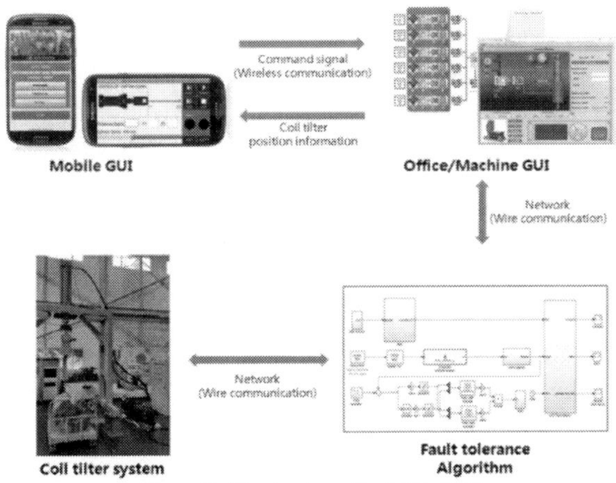

Figure 16. The structure of coil tilter SHP

When operating without a fault, the command signal is given to the coil tilter SHP through (Office/Machine/Mobile) GUI. If the coil tilter SHP in not the normal operation due to the fault, the fault tolerance algorithm will be operated and (Office/Machine/Mobile) GUI are verified through an alarm to users and recover the fault. After the fault is returned to normal waveform, the alarm will turn off and the coil tilter SHP will operate normally.

V. CONCLUSION

In this paper, SHP system uses the sensor fault tolerance algorithm combined with the cyber system for the coil tilter. When a fault happens in the coil tilter SHP, a proposed fault tolerance algorithm verifies the fault type and recovers the (temporary or permanent) fault and the (Office/Machine/Mobile) GUI observes the recovering procedure through a monitoring display. In consideration of the fault that may occur during control through the cyber system, the importance of a sensor fault tolerance technology is emphasized. When sensors do not detect the fault properly, the fault tolerance algorithm automatically and simultaneously operates with the prototype. If one sensor does not operate properly, the fault tolerance algorithm replaces a broken signal to estimate signal from Kalman filter or SMO related to other sensor signals. The proposed fault tolerant algorithm is designed and performed for temporary or permanent faults with the LVDT sensor as an experiment. Also, monitoring and alarming in the cyber system confirms the performance. As a result, a sensor fault tolerance technology with the cyber system is suitable for coil tilter SHP. In the future, all experiments will be applied to new prototypes.

ACKNOWLEDGMENT

This research is supported by the SW Fusion Component Development of the KEIT grant funded by Korea government Ministry of Trade, industry & Energy.

REFERENCES

[1] E. Sampson, S. R. Habibi, Y. Chinniah, R. Burton, "Model identification of the electrohydraulic actuator for small signal inputs", In 18th Bath workshop on power transmission and motion control (PTMC 2005), pp. 7-9, Sep. 2005.

[2] S. R. Habibi, and A. Goldenberg, "A Mechatronics Approach for the Design of a New High Performance Electro Hydraulic Actuator", SAE transactions, vol. 108, pp. 353-360, Sep. 1999, doi:10.4271/1999-01-2853.

[3] D. Kim, K. W. Oh, D. Hong, Y. K. Kim, S. H. Hong, "Motion Control of Excavator with Tele-OperatedSystem," In 26th International Symposium on Automation and Robotics in Construction (ISARC 2009), pp. 341-347, June. 2009.

[4] J. H. Kim, and Y. H. Yu, "Development of electro hydraulic ballast remote valve control system with diagnostic function using redundant modbus communication," Journal of the Korean Society of Marine Engineering, vol.38, pp.292-301, Mar. 2014, doi: 10.5916/jkosme.2014.38.3.292.

[5] B. Song, et al. , "Application of an advanced graphic user interface for the coil tilter smart hybrid powerpack system," In International conference Electrical, Electronic & Computer Engineering Technologies (ICEECET 2016), pp. 1-13, Apr. 2016, in press.

[6] S. Jo, H. Kim, I. Choi, H. Kim, "Design of Permanent Sensor Fault Tolerance Algorithms by Sliding Mode Observer for Smart Hybrid Powerpack," World Academy of Science, Engineering and Technology, International Journal of Mechanical, Aerospace, Industrial, Mechatronic and Manufacturing Engineering, vol. 8(9), pp. 1664-1671, Sep. 2014, PISSN:2010-376X, EISSN:2010-3778.

[7] G. Welch, and G. Bishop, "An introduction to the kalman filter Department of Computer Science, University of North Carolina," July. 2006.

[8] C. Guan, and S. Pan, (2008). "Adaptive sliding mode control of electro-hydraulic system with nonlinear unknown parameters," Control Engineering Practice, vol. 16(11), pp. 1275-1284, Nov. 2008,doi:10.1016/j.conengprac.2008.02.002.

[9] S. Habibi, and A. Goldenberg, "Design of a new high performance electrohydraulic actuator," In Advanced Intelligent Mechatronics, Proc. 1999 IEEE/ASME International Conference on. IEEE, pp. 227-232, Sep. 1999, doi: 10.1109/AIM.1999.803171.

[10] J. J. E. Slotine, J. K. Hedrick, E. A. Misawa,"On sliding observers for nonlinear systems," Control vol. 109(3), pp.245-252, Sep. 1987, doi:10.1115/1.3143852.

An Approach for Protecting Privacy in the IoT

George O. M. Yee
Computer Research Lab
Aptusinnova Inc.
Ottawa, Canada
email: george@aptusinnova.com

Dept. of Systems and Computer Engineering
Carleton University
Ottawa, Canada
email: gmyee@sce.carleton.ca

Abstract—**The Internet of Things (IoT) is attracting great interest within the research community. Yet, there is little research on how data generated by the "things" can be shared while respecting the privacy wishes of the data's owners. Consider a smart refrigerator as one of the "things". It keeps track of which food items are consumed, in order that the consumer can know when and what foods need to be replenished. Suppose the smart refrigerator sends this consumption information to online grocers that can automatically schedule deliveries to replenish the food. The consumption information may contain personal information (e.g., foods identifying a particular medical condition) leading to privacy concerns. This paper proposes an approach that utilizes personal privacy policies and policy compliance checking to protect privacy in the IoT, using the smart refrigerator as an example to illustrate the approach.**

Keywords-privacy; protection; IoT; policy; compliance.

I. INTRODUCTION

The objective of this paper is to present an approach that makes use of privacy policies and policy compliance checking to protect privacy in the IoT. Privacy protection is in the context of smart devices (defined below) that supply data to e-services (defined below). The smart devices themselves may also be providing e-services. The objective of this paper is achieved by focusing on a smart device as sending data that needs privacy protection.

A "smart" device is any physical device endowed with computing and communication capabilities. Some smart devices may have more computing and communication capabilities (e.g., smartphones) than others (e.g., sensors). An e-service is a grouping of computation that optionally takes input and produces output (the service). For example, the connected smart refrigerator would access the food replenish e-service from the online grocer and transmit its food consumption information (the input) to the food replenish e-service. In response, the food replenish e-service would schedule food deliveries (the output). As another example, a sensor would provide an e-service of transmitting data to another e-service that requested the data. In this case, the sensor e-service would not require any input (except for the request to transmit data).

This work addresses an Internet of things environment (see Fig. 1) with the following characteristics:

- Smart devices (e.g., laptops, Personal Digital Assistants (PDAs), smartphones, workstations, smart sensors, smart appliances) are optionally locally networked (e.g., Ethernet, Wi-Fi, IrDA, Bluetooth) or standalone (i.e., not locally networked). The locally networked or standalone smart devices are connected to the Internet via an Internet Service Provider (ISP).
- The locally networked or standalone smart devices are owned by a human or an organization.
- Human users employ these devices to make use of e-services, to offer e-services, or both. A user who makes use of an e-service sends information to that e-service and is called a *data sender*. One who offers an e-service receives information needed by that e-service and is called a *data receiver*. A user who both makes use of e-services and offers e-services is both a data sender and a data receiver.

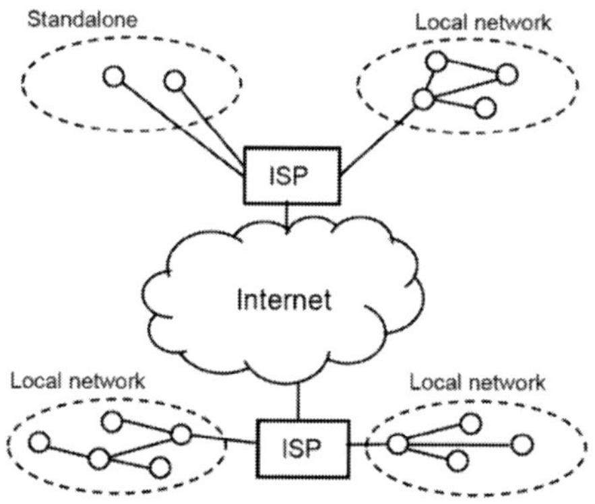

Figure 1. IoT network environment (ISP = Internet Service Provider, circles are smart devices)

The remainder of this paper is organized as follows. Section II looks at privacy and the use of privacy policies. Section III presents the proposed approach. Section IV gives an example of applying the approach. Section V evaluates the approach by discussing some strengths and weaknesses. Section VI examines related work. Section VII concludes the paper and lists some ideas for future research.

II. PRIVACY POLICIES

A. Privacy

As defined by Goldberg et al. in 1997 [1], privacy refers to the ability of individuals to *control* the collection, retention, and distribution of information about themselves. This is the definition of privacy used for this work. Protecting an individual's privacy then involves endowing the individual with the ability to control the collection, retention, and distribution of her personal information.

B. Use of Privacy Policies

In this work, a data sender is given control over her private information as follows. The data sender specifies in her sender privacy policy how she wants her personal information handled by the data receiver; the data receiver, on the other hand, specifies in her receiver privacy policy what personal information her service requires from the data sender and how she plans to handle the data sender's information. The data sender's policy has to be compatible or match the data receiver's policy before information sending can begin. If the policies do not match, the data sender can either negotiate with the data receiver to try to resolve the disagreement or choose a different data receiver. Once the information is sent, the data receiver has to comply with her receiver privacy policy (which is compatible with the data sender's privacy policy). Foolproof mechanisms must be in place to ensure compliance. The mechanics of privacy policy matching [2] and negotiation [3] are outside the scope of this work.

Fig. 2 shows example sender and receiver privacy policies for a smart refrigerator.

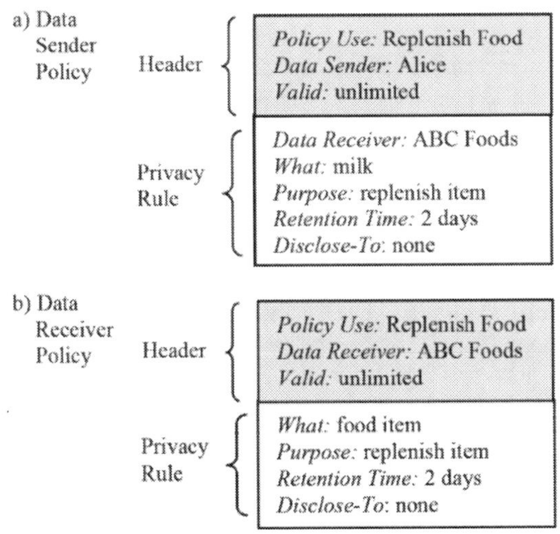

Figure 2. Example data sender / data receiver privacy policies. Each policy can have as many privacy rules as are needed.

Referring to Fig. 2, a privacy policy for sending personal information consists of a header section (shaded) followed by one or more privacy rules, where there is one rule for each item of personal information. The fields within the header have the following meaning: *Policy Use* identifies the e-service (e.g., replenish food), *Data Sender / Data Receiver* gives the name of the party that owns the policy, and *Valid* indicates the period of time during which the policy is valid. The fields in each privacy rule have the following meaning: *Data Receiver* identifies the party that receives the information, *What* describes the nature of the information, *Purpose* identifies the purpose for which the information is being sent or received, *Retention Time* specifies the amount of time the data receiver can keep the information, and *Disclose-To* identifies any parties who will receive the information from the data receiver. The above privacy rules and fields conform to Canadian privacy legislation, which is representative of privacy legislation in many parts of the world including the European Union and the United States. Thus, a data receiver who complies with such privacy policies also complies with a data sender's legislated privacy rights.

III. APPROACH

For each smart device, the approach consists of two phases: a privacy policy agreement (PPA) phase and a privacy policy compliance (PPC) phase. These phases apply to both data senders and data receivers.

A. PPA Phase and Design of Policy Controller

The PPA phase consists of the composition and exchange of privacy policies between data sender and data receiver, using a Policy Controller (PC), which runs on a desktop, laptop, or mobile device such as a smart phone or tablet. The components and functionality of the PC are given in Table 1.

TABLE 1. POLICY CONTROLLER (PC)

PC Component	Functionality
Policy Module (PM) - Data Sender	Partially composes the data sender policy; searches for e-services (data receivers) and obtains their receiver policies; determines if data receiver policies match the sender policy; selects a data receiver with a matching policy and completes the data sender policy by filling in the name of the data receiver; sends the sender privacy policy to the selected data receiver; sends the sender policy to the smart device; optionally sets up a privacy policy negotiation between the data sender and a data receiver for a particular policy pair that does not match
PM - Data Receiver	Composes the data receiver privacy policy; sends the data receiver privacy policy to the PM of the data sender when requested; receives the data sender privacy policy and verifies that the sender policy matches its own policy; optionally cooperates to set up a privacy policy negotiation with the owner of a data sender
Policy Store (PS) – Data Sender	Holds the data sender privacy policy; holds the privacy policies received from data receivers
PS – Data Receiver	Holds the data receiver privacy policy; holds the privacy policies received from data senders

Fig. 3 presents a message sequence chart showing the interactions between the PMs of a data sender and a data receiver (only one receiver shown and policy composition excluded for simplicity). A first time successful privacy policies match is assumed.

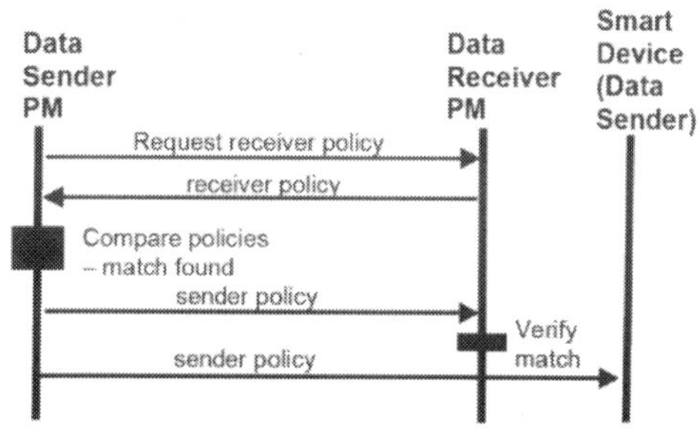

Figure 3. Message sequence chart showing the interactions for a first time successful policy match.

Fig. 4 shows the same scenario as Fig. 3 except that the first time policy match is unsuccessful, resulting in the need for policy negotiation, assumed to be successful. If the negotiation was unsuccessful, the sender would not be able to proceed any further with the receiver and would have to select a new receiver or find some way to satisfy the receiver's policy.

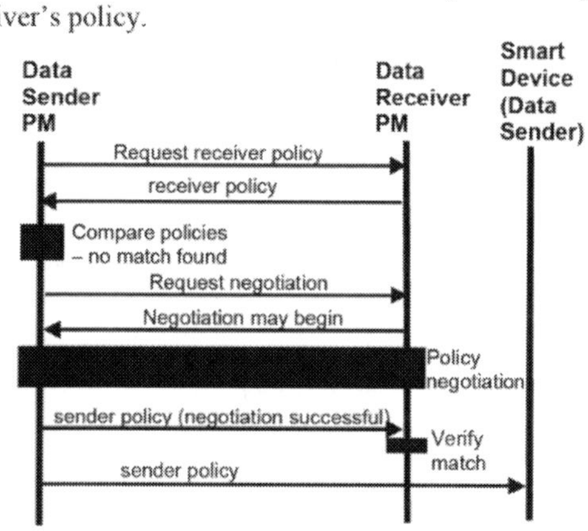

Figure 4. Message sequence chart showing the interactions for a first time unsuccessful policy match and the ensuing negotiation (assumed successful).

B. PPC Phase and Design of Compliance Controller

In the PPC phase, the data sender sends its data to the data receiver, while ensuring that both sender and receiver privacy policies are respected. This phase is carried out using software called a Compliance Controller (CC), which runs on the smart device or on a computing platform (e.g., tablet) that is "attached" to the device. The components and functionality of the CC are given in Table 2. In Table 2, for a particular smart device, Compliance Module (CM) functionality depends on whether the device sends data, receives data, or both sends and receives data. In the latter case, each component would have the functionalities prescribed for a data sender and data receiver combined.

TABLE 2. COMPLIANCE CONTROLLER (CC)

CC Component	Functionality
Compliance Module (CM) – Data Sender	Requests the LM to set up a connection with the data receiver; periodically requests the secure log (SL) from the data receiver to verify policy compliance; automatically verifies compliance and warns the user if the verification fails
CM – Data Receiver	Ensures that a data receiver complies with the privacy policy of a data sender; maintains a SL of all transactions involving the sender's private data; sends the SL to the sender when requested
Link Module (LM) – Data Sender	Sets up a connection for sending data to the selected data receiver with a matching privacy policy; tears down the connection once the associated data sending session is finished
LM – Data Receiver	Cooperates with the LM of the data sender to set up the connection for data reception, e.g., provides the port number to use in case there is a need to bypass a firewall
Data Store (DS) – Data Sender	Holds the sender's private information that is to be sent to the data receiver; holds the sender privacy policy received from the sender's PC
DS – Data Receiver	Holds the private information received from the data sender; holds the data receiver privacy policy

In addition to the CC itself, the following are also required: a) local and global networking as shown in Fig. 1, and b) interfaces to connect the CC to the smart device. Local and global networking are assumed to be what is most commonly available, i.e., Ethernet, Wi-Fi, IrDA, or Bluetooth for local, and the Internet for global. Smart devices need to have appropriate interfaces that inter-work with the Compliance Controller to carry out policy compliance management (e.g., checking a secure log to verify compliance), connection setup for sending data, and the storage and retrieval of private data.

Fig. 5 presents a message sequence chart showing the interactions between the LMs and CMs of a data sender and a data receiver (only one receiver is shown for simplicity) for a data sending session.

The non-privacy preserving IoT network of Fig. 1 is converted to a privacy-preserving IoT network by adding a CC to each smart device or node (Fig. 6). In Fig. 6, the double arrows in the CC blow-up represent expected communication directions based on the functionalities described in Table 2. However, the actual communications will depend on how the CC is implemented.

Prior to using a smart device to send or receive data, the user accesses the device using some secure form of authentication, such as 2-factor authentication requiring a password and a fingerprint scan. This is needed to protect the user's personal data that is stored in the device and can be satisfied by authentication software within the user's device (e.g., part of operating system). As well, any additional security needed to secure the data sender's personal information and privacy policies from attack must be in place. This is satisfied by additional security measures such as certificates and encryption (discussed in Section III C below).

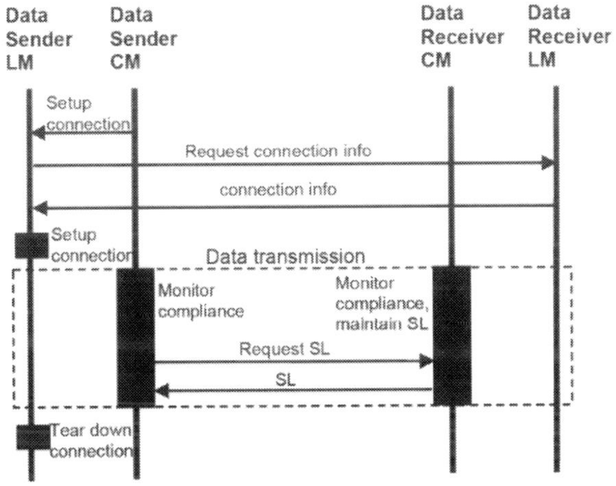

Figure 5. Message sequence chart showing the interactions for a connection setup, data transmission, policy compliance monitoring, and connection teardown.

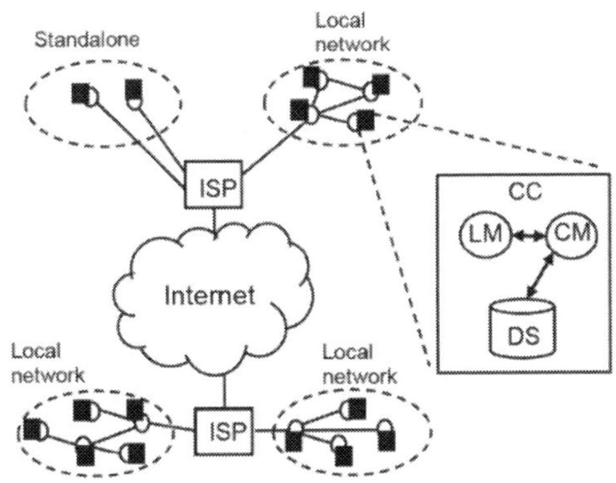

Figure 6. Proposed privacy preserving IoT network; each smart device (small circle) has a CC (black rectangle); a blow up of a CC is also shown (all acronyms defined above).

C. *Implementation Notes*

Some implementation aspects of the approach are considered here.

How does the owner of a data sender come up with her sender privacy policy? It is proposed that data receivers (e-services) routinely advertise their data requirements on the Internet. Note that this is in a way being done today by service websites (e.g., when the user is asked to fill out an online form). Data sender owners can then use the PM to compose the sender policy based on these data requirements. The owners of data receivers also use the PM to compose receiver privacy policies based on how they would like to handle the private information that they receive.

The heterogeneous nature of today's smart devices may present some implementation problems for the proposed approach. Some devices may not have sufficient computing power to host the CC in addition to the required software for the device. However, this may depend on how the CC is implemented. If the CC is implemented as a stand-alone module running on a tablet or smartphone "attached" to the device (as mentioned above), and only needs to communicate with the smart device to operate, then the device can be less powerful.

The search for data receivers in the PM may return a reputation value for each receiver. This would help the owner of a data sender to choose which receiver to include in her sender privacy policy. The reputation value may be calculated based on the receiver's history of past transactions, as is done on eBay.com for buyers and sellers. Gupta et al. [4] investigate the design of a reputation system for P2P networks like Gnutella. These authors believe that having reliable reputation information about peers can guide decision making such as whom to trust for a file, similar to this work.

What does matching of policies mean between data sender and data receiver? There needs to be a way of comparing two policies using some measure of compatibility such as levels of privacy [2].

Privacy policies need to be amenable to machine processing. Policy languages such as APPEL [5] that are XML-based are good choices.

Any additional security needed to secure the data sender owner's private information and her privacy policies from attack must be installed. Suitable authentication mechanisms, such as the use of certificates, will be needed for data sender / data receiver authentication. Other security mechanisms such as the use of encryption to encrypt the private information will need to be applied or developed and applied. Table 3 suggests some security mechanisms that may be employed.

TABLE 3. ADDITIONAL SECURITY MECHANISMS

System Component Requiring Protection	Security Protection Mechanism
data sender / data receiver authentication	SSL with 2-way authentication
Internet communication channels	SSL with 2-way authentication
privacy policies stored in PS and DS	encryption (e.g., 3DES)
personal information stored in DS	encryption (e.g., 3DES)
smart device software, CC software	anti-malware tools (e.g., Kaspersky)

In addition, the CC and in particular, the CM, need to be protected from malicious tampering. Since the CM plays the important role of checking for compliance, critical elements of the CM may be implemented in hardware to resist tampering (e.g., by using the Trusted Platform Module [6]). In fact, to further resist tampering, the entire CC may be implemented as a stand-alone hardware module that plugs into the smart device to operate (e.g., via a USB port). It can then be standardized and certified by a trusted authority such as a privacy commissioner to increase user trust.

IV. APPLICATION EXAMPLE

Suppose Alice has a smart refrigerator, which is running low on a number of food items. Alice's refrigerator is connected to the Internet through WI-FI as a node in the privacy-preserving IoT network proposed in this work. Before ordering these food items replenished, Alice's refrigerator compares their prices at three online grocers and orders the items from the grocers with the lowest price for each item. The following steps are performed:

1) Alice accesses her laptop (after entering her password), gets on the Internet, and launches her PC. Using network software that was packaged with her PC, she requests to see all grocers located within 10 kilometers of her home who are online. Alice receives a listing of online grocers along with their reputations. (Note: The details of grocer lookup and online messaging are assumed to go on in the background).

2) Alice uses her PC to retrieve her pre-specified privacy policy from her laptop's local storage (PS) and completes it by choosing and including three online grocers (e-services), based on their reputations.

3) Alice's PC requests the privacy policy of each online grocer that Alice specified in her privacy policy after mutual authentication with each grocer. With the arrival of each grocer's policy, Alice's PC compares Alice's policy with the grocer's policy to see if the policies match up. All grocers' policies match except for one. Alice is asked if she wants to negotiate with the non-matching grocer to try to resolve the non-match. Alice agrees to negotiate and is able to negotiate to a successful conclusion. Now all policies match. Alice's PC sends her sender policy to the PC of each grocer whose policy matches Alice's policy. For added safety, the PC of each grocer receiving Alice's policy does a quick verification of the policy match. If a non-match is found here (unlikely since already checked by Alice's PC) the grocer's PC could terminate the interaction with Alice. Alice's PC sends the sender policy to the CC of the smart refrigerator.

4) The CC in Alice's refrigerator sets up connections between Alice's refrigerator and the three online grocers with the cooperation of the grocers' CCs. Alice's refrigerator then starts sending data to the grocers.

Alice's refrigerator sends personal consumption information to the grocers, such as Alice's favorite brand of food item, her consumption rate for each food item, and the prices that she expects to pay. In return, the online grocers provide Alice's refrigerator with the food items' prices. Alice's refrigerator completes the data transmission, ordering food items from the grocers with the lowest prices. In addition, during and after the transmission, the CM modules of the grocers' respective CCs, continuously checks the grocers' handling of Alice's personal information to ensure compliance with Alice's sender privacy policy. These CM modules log all private data activities to secure logs and sends them to Alice's CC when requested. Alice's CC verifies these secure logs for policy compliance and notifies Alice upon detection of any discrepancy, so that Alice can challenge the grocers' handling of her data when warranted.

V. EVALUATION

Some strengths of the proposed approach are: a) upholds personally specified privacy preferences, b) can theoretically be used for all smart devices and all types of receivers or e-services, c) highly scalable due to the use of CCs, and d) easy to retrofit an existing non-privacy preserving IoT into a privacy preserving one. One weakness may be that the CM is not trusted to enforce privacy policy compliance. These points are elaborated below.

In terms of the strengths, the proposed approach allows each user to specify her privacy preferences in a privacy policy and for this policy to be upheld. Further, disagreements in privacy policies may be negotiated. Next, the approach allows a privacy preserving "session" to be set-up in which a data sender sends data to a data receiver. It leaves open what computing can be done in the session. Therefore, the session can be an e-commerce session where the data sender is a buyer and the data receiver is a seller, as in the above example, or a health monitoring session where the data sender is a smart body worn sensor and the data receiver is a medical monitoring service for the aged, or any other type of data transmission session that requires privacy protection. Another strength is the fact that the proposed approach is highly scalable. The privacy preserving IoT can be easily expanded by adding CCs to devices that do not yet possess them. Each additional device so equipped would also require a privacy policy exchange session. However, the increase cost per additional device is linear. The addition of CCs does increase network traffic, e.g., requests for the receiver's SL. However, the increased traffic can be accommodated by increasing network capacity, which is consistent with network growth and is not a limiting factor on scalability.

In terms of the weakness of trusting the CM, it must be made clear that malicious attacks on the CC and CM are always possible and could result in violation of privacy. One defense is to make it as hard as possible for those attacks to succeed, by protecting the CM. Ways to protect the CM and build trust for it have already been suggested above.

Reviewers of this work have pointed out additional weaknesses, as follows: a) enforcement using SLs is not foolproof, i.e., the receiver can still leak personal information using channels not captured by SLs, b) people would need help in defining privacy policies, c) the approach may not apply to less powerful IoT devices, d) the CC may have performance issues in all that it is asked to do, and e) continuous checking of the vendor's handling of private information (Section IV above) could violate the vendor's privacy. These weaknesses are acknowledged, attenuated, or removed as follows. While enforcement using SLs is not foolproof, there is probably no method that is foolproof. As well, there would be tradeoffs to consider between using a more complex enforcement scheme, which is potentially more effective, and the complexity involved in the enforcement. For example, Mont and Thyne [11] (see next Section) propose a potentially more effective enforcement scheme but which is more complex and thereby more error prone. Nevertheless, replacing SLs with a potentially more effective enforcement method is part of future work. People do need help defining privacy policies, usually through automation. Yee and Korba [10] address this issue (see next Section) by proposing two semi-automated methods of privacy policy derivation. The approach can be applied to less powerful devices by implementing the CC as a software module running on a smartphone or tablet which is connected to the device, as mentioned above. In this scenario, the smart device merely has to forward its data to the smartphone or tablet running the CC, a change that should be implementable on even the least compute capable smart device. In terms of the CC potentially having performance issues, this is a possibility, especially if the smart device is not very powerful. This potential problem would be mitigated to some extent if the CC were to run on a smartphone or a tablet. In any case, this potential issue will be addressed through prototyping the CC, a part of future work. Finally, with regard to the possible violation of the vendor's privacy by the continuous checking of the vendor's handling of private information, note that this continuous checking is performed by the vendor's CC running on the vendor's platform for the benefit of the vendor so that the vendor can be assured that it is complying with the sender's privacy policy. Since there is no data associated with this checking that is forwarded back to the sender (only the SL is forwarded back to the sender – see Table 2) there can be no violation of the vendor's privacy. It should also be noted here that the SL would not violate the vendor's privacy either, as it only refers to the sender's private information and how the receiver processed it in terms of the sender's privacy policy. In other words, the SL should not contain any vendor private information.

VI. RELATED WORK

This work shares the notion of using controllers to monitor privacy policy compliance with an earlier work [7] in which we applied "privacy controllers" to protect privacy in web services. In this work, we have updated and re-designed the components in [7] to apply to the IoT.

Works that are related in terms of the application of personal privacy policies to implement privacy preferences are as follows. Yee [8] proposed a hybrid centralized / P2P architecture for ubiquitous computing that also protects privacy using privacy policies. Yee and Korba [9] examine privacy policy compliance for web services, and Yee and Korba [10] discuss privacy policy derivation. Another related work in this area, as suggested by a reviewer, is Mont and Thyne [11], which gives an approach for automatic privacy policy enforcement within an enterprise, by making data access control privacy-aware. Their approach incorporates a "Privacy Policy Decision Point" which makes decisions for allowing access based on privacy policies, and a "Data Enforcer" which intercepts attempts to access personal data and enforces the decisions made at the Privacy Policy Decision Point.

In the privacy literature for IoT, Kanuparthi et al. [12] describe privacy protection through the use of security measures such as encryption. Alquassem [13] presents a privacy and security requirements framework for developing IoT, taking account of these requirements from the beginning of development. Zhang et al. [14] describe the security challenges in the IoT and examine conventional security mechanisms (e.g., authentication) to look for countermeasures. Davies et al. [15] state that unease over data privacy will retard consumer acceptance of IoT deployments. They consider this to be primarily due to lack of user control over raw data that is streamed directly from sensors to the cloud and propose the use of privacy mediators on every data stream. Savola et al. [16] consider e-health applications in the IoT, such as biomedical sensor networks, as holding great promise but security and privacy are major concerns. They propose a high-level adaptive security management mechanism based on security metrics to cope with these concerns. A reviewer has suggested Appavoo et al. [17] as another related work. These authors address privacy-preserving access to sensor data for IoT based services such as health monitoring services. Appavoo et al. observed that a large class of applications can function based on simple threshold detection, e.g., blood pressure above a pre-determined threshold. They propose a privacy-preserving approach based on this observation, their goal being to minimize privacy loss in the presence of untrusted service providers. The main algorithm in their proposed approach is an anonymization scheme that uses a combination of sensor aliases to hide the identity of the sensor data source, together with initialization vectors (or filters) to reveal information only to relevant service providers. Appavoo et al.'s work differs from this work in at least two ways. First, their work addresses a particular segment of services (monitoring services) whereas this work is applicable to all types of services. Second, they protect privacy through anonymizing the source of private information and restricting the private information to service providers that need to know. This work protects privacy through privacy policies and ensuring that the service provider complies with the policies.

VII. CONCLUSIONS AND FUTURE WORK

This work has proposed a straightforward effective approach to protect privacy in the IoT, making use of compliance controllers together with sender and receiver privacy policies. In this approach, privacy is protected through compliance with privacy preferences, expressed as sender privacy policies.

Once privacy is protected, the smart devices in the IoT can engage in many applications, such as e-commerce (smart refrigerator using replenish food services) and e-health (smart body worn sensors using a health monitoring service).

The approach presented here is only theoretical. The effectiveness of the approach remains to be proven through prototyping and experimentation.

Future work includes the construction of a prototype to fine-tune the proposed approach, determine its effectiveness, and investigate some of the ideas discussed in the implementation notes, such as the use of reputation to help data senders decide which data receivers to select. We also plan to investigate other means of enforcing compliance with privacy policy that do not involve verifying SLs, as well as applying the approach to the transmission of private data from e-health smart devices in the wearable world (e.g., Apple watch).

REFERENCES

[1] I. Goldberg, D. Wagner, and E. Brewer, "Privacy-Enhancing Technologies for the Internet," Proc. IEEE COMPCON'97, pp. 103-109, Feb. 23-26, 1997.

[2] G. Yee and L. Korba, "Comparing and Matching Privacy Policies Using Community Consensus," Proc. 16th IRMA International Conference, in Managing Modern Organizations with Information Technology, edited by Mehdi Khosrow-Pour, pp. 208-211, 2005. Available Aug. 23, 2016: http://www.irma-international.org/proceeding-paper/comparing-matching-privacy-policies-using/32576/

[3] G. Yee and L. Korba, "The Negotiation of Privacy Policies in Distance Education," Proc. 14th IRMA International Conference, pp. 702-705, May 18-21, 2003. Available Aug. 23, 2016: http://www.irma-international.org/proceeding-paper/negotiation-privacy-policies-distance-education/32116/

[4] M. Gupta, P. Judge, and M. Ammar, "A Reputation System for Peer-to-Peer Networks," Proc. 13th International Workshop on Network and Operating Systems Support for Digital Audio and Video, pp. 144-152, 2003.

[5] W3C, "A P3P Preference Exchange Language 1.0 (APPEL1.0)," available as of May 14, 2016 at: http://www.w3.org/TR/P3P-preferences/

[6] Trusted Computing Group, "Trusted Platform Module (TPM)," available as of May 14, 2016 at: http://www.trustedcomputinggroup.org/work-groups/trusted-platform-module/

[7] G. Yee, "A Privacy Controller Approach for Privacy Protection in Web Services," Proc. ACM Workshop on Secure Web Services (SWS '07), pp. 44-51, Oct. 29 – Nov. 2, 2007.

[8] G. Yee, "A Privacy-Preserving UBICOMP Architecture," Proc. Privacy, Security, Trust 2006 (PST 2006), pp. 224-232, 2006.

[9] G. Yee and L. Korba, "Privacy Policy Compliance for Web Services," Proc. 2004 IEEE International Conference on Web Services (ICWS 2004), pp. 158-165, July 6-9, 2004.

[10] G. Yee and L. Korba, "Semi-Automatic Derivation and Use of Personal Privacy Policies in E-Business," International Journal of E-Business Research, Vol. 1, Issue 1, pp. 54-69, 2005.

[11] M. C. Mont and R. Thyne, "A Systemic Approach to Automate Privacy Policy Enforcement in Enterprises," Proc. 6th Annual International Workshop on Privacy Enhancing Technologies (PET 2006), pp. 118-134, June 28-30, 2006.

[12] A. Kanuparthi, R. Karri, and S. Addepalli, "Hardware and Embedded Security in the Context of Internet of Things," Proc. 2013 ACM Workshop on Security, Privacy & Dependability for Cyber Vehicles (CyCAR'13), pp. 61-65, Nov. 4, 2013.

[13] I. Alqassem, "Privacy and Security Requirements Framework for the Internet of Things (IoT)," Proc. ICSE Companion'14, pp. 739-741, May 31-June 7, 2014.

[14] K. L. Zhang, M. C. Y. Cho, and S. Shieh, "Emerging Security Threats and Countermeasures in IoT," Proc. 10th ACM Symposium on Information, Computer and Communications Security (Asia CCS '15), pp. 1-6, 2015.

[15] N. Davies, N. Taft, M. Satyanarayanan, S. Clinch, and B. Amos, "Privacy Mediators: Helping IoT Cross the Chasm," Proc. 17th International Workshop on Mobile Computing Systems and Applications (HotMobile '16), pp. 39-44, 2016.

[16] R. M. Savola, H. Abie, and M. Sihvonen, "Towards Metrics-Driven Adaptive Security Management in e-health IoT Applications," Proc. 7th International Conference on Body Area Networks (BodyNets '12), pp. 276-281, 2012.

[17] P. Appavoo, M. C. Chan, A. Bhojan, and E.-C. Chang, "Efficient and Privacy-Preserving Access to Sensor Data for Internet of Things (IoT) Based Services," Proc. 8th International Conference on Communication Systems and Networks (COMSNETS), pp. 1-8, 2016.

Consideration of Security Threats for Identification System in Internet of Things

Daewon Kim, Jeongnyeo Kim, and Yongsung Jeon
Information Security Research Department
Electronics and Telecommunications Research Institute
Daejeon, Korea
emails: {dwkim77, jnkim, ysjeon}@etri.re.kr

Abstract—**During the last years, people have expressed and increased interest towards Internet of Things (IoT) technology. Among various systems in the IoT environment, the identification system has an important role to recognize IoT things. However, current IoT identification systems do not consider security aspects carefully. This paper presents the security threats related to the IoT identification systems.**

Keywords-internet of things; identification; object identifier; security threats.

I. Introduction

Things, which are constructing the Internet of Things (IoT) environment, can have various physical communication modules, such as ZigBee, Bluetooth, and so on [1]. The IoT environment needs higher level identification systems than physical module-level to recognize things and to communicate with each other. This is the role of the IoT identification system.

Current IoT identification systems are primarily focusing on interworking, interoperability, scalability, distributability, and performance, and they do not consider security aspects carefully [2], [4]. Therefore, researches related to IoT identification security are required to mitigate security threats due to vulnerable identification management.

The nature of security problems related to the IoT identification is that it can be applied to authentication and authorization. As the purpose of our paper, we describes the details related to the security threats of IoT identification, and our challenge is to classify and analyze the sufficient contents of predictable threats for the secure implementation of identification system.

The rest of the paper is organized as follows. In Section 2, we describe the IoT environment, the necessity and role of IoT identification system, and the features of IoT identification. In Section 3, for the IoT identification system, we present the security threat, vulnerability, threat action, threat purpose, and threat result. Finally, we conclude the paper in Section 4.

II. IoT Identification System

In this section, as the background to list the security threats of IoT identification system, we will describe the IoT environment, the necessity and role of the IoT identification system, and the features of IoT identification.

A. IoT Environment

IoT environment is the environment in which Internet-connected physical and logical devices are interworked and interoperated. The interworking means that various devices can exchange information among them, and the interoperating means that various devices can use services mutually. The interoperating devices are in a common IoT platform, and if many IoT platforms can exchange information among them, a huge IoT environment is constructed.

B. The Necessity and Role of IoT Identification System

Even in a common IoT platform, there are various physical communication modules, and it is sure that a huge IoT environment includes even more, and more diverse, physical modules. Therefore, some identification methods, which are independent on physical layer communication, are required to recognize various IoT things and to communicate with each other. It is the reason for the necessity of IoT identification system.

The normal role of identification systems is to control identification information to identify physical and logical objects. Therefore, the identification information of IoT identification system has a role to identify physical and logical objects in the IoT environment.

C. Features of IoT Identification

In the communication environment including various physical modules, for the exact and smooth communication, the IoT identification system and information needs to have the following features.

- From top-level things to bottom, unique identifiers are allocated to identify all things. In the sub-areas under the things with unique identifiers, independent identifiers can be allocated only for the sub-areas.
- Identification system and information are independent on various physical communication methods.
- IoT identification system manages naming information to identify each thing.
- IoT identification system manages addressing information to find routes for things.
- IoT identification system manages discovery information to find the naming and addressing information that traces the mobility of things.

- IoT identification system has a life cycle including generation, registration, searching, deletion, and so on.

III. Security Threats of IoT Identification System

In this section, based on the background of Section 2, for IoT identification system and information we will present security threat (ST), identification threat (IT), and the threat description (TD) including vulnerability, threat action, threat purpose, and threat result. Among various identification pieces of information, in this paper, we focus on device identification such as Object IDentifier (OID) [3].

- **ST: Device Malfunction, IT: Damaged Identification Information**

TD: It can occur when identification system and information are vulnerable to the unauthenticated and unauthorized accesses. It is possible to miswrite and delete identification information. The threat purpose is to cause internal service troubles to vulnerable devices and systems.

- **ST: Out of Service Request, IT: Tampered Identification Information**

TD: It can occur when identification system and information are vulnerable to the unauthenticated and unauthorized accesses, and cache poisoning. It is possible to change the identification information to that of the attacker. The threat purpose is to cause external service request troubles to vulnerable devices and systems. Since this is tampering with the identification information for connection to remote servers, service requests may fail due to wrong destination.

- **ST: Denial of Service Attack, IT: Tampered Identification Information**

TD: It can occur when identification system and information are vulnerable to the unauthenticated and unauthorized accesses, and cache poisoning. It is possible to change the identification information to that of the attacker. Similar to tampering with the information for identifying destination devices, this may cause denial of service attacks to the tampered destination devices.

- **ST: Information Leakage, IT: Tampered Identification Information**

TD: It can occur when identification system and information are vulnerable to the unauthenticated and unauthorized accesses and cache poisoning. It is possible to change the identification information to that of the attacker. Similar to tampering with the information for identifying destination devices, critical information can be leaked to the devices compromised by attackers.

- **ST: Illegal Service Access, IT: Counterfeited Identification Information**

TD: It can occur when identification system and information are vulnerable to the unauthenticated and unauthorized accesses, and sniffing. After the device identification information is exposed to attackers, they can use the counterfeited identification information. As illegally gaining the identification information from vulnerable devices and systems, attackers can illegally access critical services granted to legal users and devices.

- **ST: Illegal High Authority Access, IT: Counterfeited Identification Information**

TD: It can occur when identification system and information are vulnerable to the unauthenticated and unauthorized accesses, and sniffing. After the device identification information is exposed to attackers, they can use the counterfeited identification information. As illegally gaining the identification information from vulnerable devices and systems, attackers can illegally access critical resources through high authority, such as the administrator.

- **ST: Information Eavesdropping, IT: Counterfeited Identification Information**

TD: It can occur when identification system and information are vulnerable to the unauthenticated and unauthorized accesses, and sniffing. After the device identification information is exposed to attackers, they can use the counterfeit identification information. As illegally gaining the identification information from vulnerable devices and systems, attackers can eavesdrop messages in the communication area of the attacker device disguised through the counterfeit identification information.

IV. Conclusions

Identification is a very important component in IoT environment. However, current IoT researches do not consider security aspects related to the identification carefully. In this paper, we described IoT environment, the necessity and role of IoT identification system, and the features of IoT identification. Based on the background information, we presented security threat, identification threat, and the threat description including vulnerability, threat action, threat purpose, and threat result.

Acknowledgment

This work was supported by Institute for Information & communications Technology Promotion (IITP) grant funded by the Korea government (MSIP) (B0190-16-2032, Development of Operating System Security Core Technology for the Smart Lightweight IoT Devices).

References

[1] D. Katusic, et al., "Universal Identification Scheme in Machine-to-Machine Systems," Proc. of 12th International Conference on Telecommunications (ConTEL), pp. 71-78, 2013.

[2] European Research Cluster on The Internet of Things, "EU-China Joint White Paper on Internet-of-Things Identification," European Commission-Information Society and Media, Nov. 2014. [Online]. Available from: http://www.internet-of-things-research.eu/pdf/IERC_Position_Paper_EU-China_IoT_Identification_Final.pdf 2016.05.18.

[3] International Telecommunication Union, "Information technology - Procedures for the operation of object identifier registration authorities: General procedures and top arcs of the international object identifier tree," ITU-T X.660, July 2011.

[4] oneM2M-TS-0003, "oneM2M Security Solutions Technical Specification," V1.4.2, Mar 2016.

Advanced Device Authentication: Bringing Multi-Factor Authentication and Continuous Authentication to the Internet of Things

Rainer Falk and Steffen Fries
Corporate Technology
Siemens AG
Munich, Germany
e-mail: {rainer.falk|steffen.fries}@siemens.com

Abstract—**Robust and practical device authentication is an essential security feature for cyber physical systems and the Internet of Things. After giving an overview on device authentication options, several proposals for advanced device authentication means are presented to increase the attack robustness of device authentication. A well-known cryptographic device authentication using a symmetric cryptographic key or a digital certificate for device authentication can be extended with additional validations to check the device identity. Ideas from advanced human user authentication means like multi-factor authentication and continuous authentication are applied to enhance device authentication.**

Keywords–device authentication; Internet of Things, embedded security, cyber security.

I. Introduction

The need for technical information technology (IT) security measures increases rapidly to protect products and solutions from manipulation and reverse engineering [1]. This scope is further broadened to also include operational technology (OT). Cryptographic IT security mechanisms have been known for many years, and are applied in smart devices (Internet of Things, Cyber Physical Systems, industrial and energy automation systems, operation technology) [2]. Such mechanisms target authentication, system and communication integrity and confidentiality of data in transit or at rest.

A central security mechanism is authentication: By authentication, a claimed identity is proven. Authentication of a person can be performed by verifying something the person knows (e.g., a password), something the person has (e.g., a physical authentication token, smart card, or a passport), or something the person is (biometric property, e.g., a fingerprint, voice, iris, or behavior).

Advanced authentication techniques make use of multiple authentication factors, and performing authentication continuously during a session. With multi-factor authentication, several independent authentication factors are verified, e.g., a password and an authentication token. With continuous authentication, also called active authentication, the behavior of a user during an authenticated session is monitored to determine if the authenticated user is still the one using the session.

While advanced authentication techniques like multi-factor authentication and continuous authentication are known for human users, it seems that these technologies have not yet been applied for device authentication.

With ubiquitous machine-oriented communication, e.g., the Internet of Things and interconnected cyber physical systems, devices have to be authenticated in a secure way. This paper presents and investigates approaches for advanced device authentication.

After describing single device authentication means in Section II, the combination of authentications is covered in Section III. The advantages of enhanced device authentication factors to increase the security level of Internet of Things systems and Cyber Physical Systems is investigated in Section IV. Section V summarizes related work. Section VI concludes with a summary and an outlook. Note that the paper investigates different options for providing enhance authentication from a conceptual point of view. The options are discussed in the context of system design and require an implementation as the consequent next step.

II. Device Authentication Means

As for users, authentication of a device can be based on different authentication factors, similar to user authentication means [8]:

- Something the device knows: credential (device key, e.g., a secret key or a private key)
- Something the device has (integrated authentication IC, authentication dongle)
- Something the device is (logical properties, e.g., the device type, configuration data, firmware version; physical properties: physical unclonable function (PUF), radio fingerprint)

Besides these well-established authentication factors, more unconventional authentication factors can also be used:

- Something the device does (behavior, functionality, e.g., automation control protocol)
- Something the device knows about its environment (sensors)
- Something the device can (functional capability, actuators)

- The context of the device (neighbors, location, connected periphery)

Different usages in IoT systems apply device authentication:

- Identity Authentication toward a remote system (access control, communication security). May be a supervisory system, or a peer device.
- Network access security (IEEE 802.1X [3], mobile network access authentication [4]).
- Original device authentication
- Attestation of device integrity
- Attestation of device configuration

The remainder of this section provides an overview about device authentication means. The authentication would typically be performed by an authentication server that, after successful authentication, may allow access to further system specific data directly or issues a temporal token (e.g., SAML assertion [5], OAUTH token [6], short-term X.509 certificate [7]).

A. *Cryptographic Device Authentication*

The authentication of a device allows a reliable identification. For authentication, a challenge value is sent to the object to be authenticated. This object calculates a corresponding response value, which is returned to the requestor and verified. The response can be calculated using a cryptographic authentication mechanism, or by using a PUF [1].

For cryptographic authentication, different mechanisms may be used. Examples are keyed hash functions like HMAC-SHA256 or symmetric ciphers in cipher block chaining (CBC-MAC) mode, or symmetric ciphers in Galois counter mode (GMAC) up to digital signatures. For the symmetric ciphers, AES would be a suitable candidate. Common to keyed hashes or symmetric key based cryptographic authentication approaches is the existence of a specific secret or private key, which is only available to the object to be authenticated and the verifier. One resulting requirement from this fact is obviously the need for robust protection of the applied secret key. Also, asymmetric cryptography can be used for component authentication. A suitable procedure based on elliptic curves has been described in [24]. Also in this use case, the secret key has to be protected on the authenticating component.

The device is authenticated as only an original device can determine the correct response value corresponding to a given challenge. The verifier sends a random challenge to the component that determines and sends back the corresponding response. The verifier checks the response. Depending on the result, the component is accepted as genuine/authenticated or it is rejected.

Various approaches are available to realize a cryptographic device authentication:

- Software credential: Credentials are hidden in software, configuration information, or the system registry. Be aware that practices of storing cryptographic credentials in firmware or cleartext configurations are weak [11][12]. However, techniques for whitebox cryptography are available that hide keys in software [13].
- Central processing unit (CPU) and microcontroller integrated circuits (IC) with internal key store: Some modern CPUs resp. microcontrollers include battery-backed SRAM or non-volatile memory, e.g., security fuses, that can be used to store cryptographic keys on the IC [14]. Also, an internal hardware security module (HSM) or secure execution environment can be included (e.g., Infineon Aurix with integrated HSM [15], or ARM TrustZone [16]).
- Separate authentication ICs can be integrated (e.g., Atmel CryptoAuthentication ECC508A [17] , Infineon Optiga Trust E [18]).
- Crypto controller (e.g., Infineon SLE97 [19]).
- Trusted platform module (TPM 1.2 [20], TPM 2.0 [21], TPM automotive thin profile [34]).

B. *Device Authentication based on Device Properties*

Physical and logical properties of a device can be verified as part of a device authentication. For this purpose, information about the device properties can be provided in a cryptographically protected way. In particular, an attestation, a digitally signed information confirming properties of a device, can be created by a protected component of the device.

Properties of the device can be logical information (software version, device configuration, serial number of components of the device) or physical properties of the device that can be determined by sensors or a PUF [9].

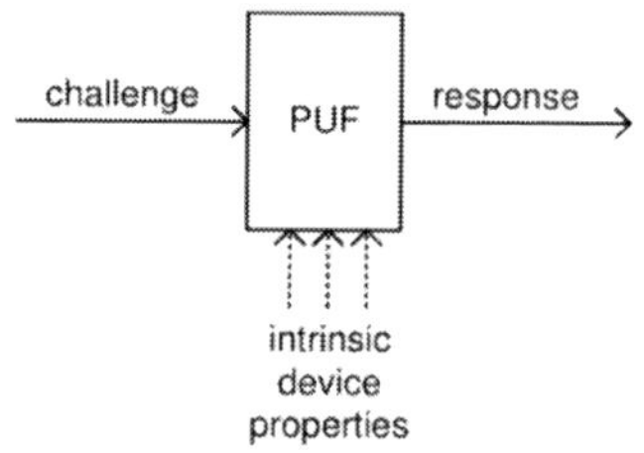

Figure 1. Challenge-Response-PUF

Fig. 1 shows the basic concept of a PUF [1]. A PUF performs a computation to determine a response value depending on a given challenge value. Intrinsic device properties influence the PUF calculation so that the calculation of the response is different on different devices, but reproducible – with some bit errors – on the same device.

A PUF is used here for device authentication in a different way: It is by itself not a strong authentication. Instead, a cryptographically protected attestation can be used to attest physical properties of a device that are measured using a PUF. So, a PUF is not used directly for authentication, but indirectly as integrated device sensor to measure physical properties of the device. It can be considered as a "two-factor device authentication" where the PUF is used as second authentication factor.

C. Authentication based on Device Context and Monitoring Information

Information about the context of a device can be used, e.g., the device location, or information about the environment of neighbor devices, the network reachability under a certain network address, or over a certain communication path.

The device context is determined and checked. The context information can be provided by the device itself, or the device's context information can be requested from a context server. One example from industrial environments is the system and device engineering, which basically provides information about the type and functionality of connected devices. Hence, it can be used to retrieve information about the devices deployment environment. The device location can be obtained using known localization technologies, e.g., global navigation satellite systems (GNSS) as GPS, GALILEO, BEIDOU, GLONASS, or localization using base stations (WLAN, cellular, broadcast) and beacons [22].

Furthermore, the device operation can be monitored: The behavior of the main, regular functionality of the device can be monitored and checked for plausibility.

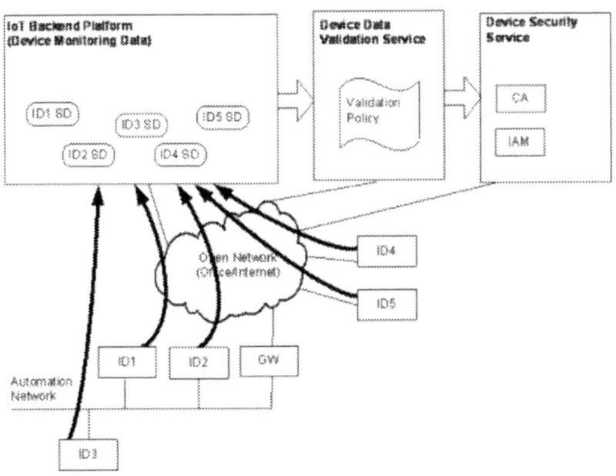

Figure 2. Validation of Device Monitoring Data

Fig. 2 shows an example for an IoT system with IoT devices (ID1, ID2, etc.) that communicate with an IoT backend platform. The devices provide current monitoring information about their status, measurements, etc. to the backend platform (e.g., for predictive maintenance). The backend platform maintains the data for the IoT devices (ID1 SD, ID2 SD, etc.) as IoT device supervisory data ("digital twin"). Furthermore, context information about the environment of a device can be provided by the device itself using its sensors, or by neighboring devices.

The devices authenticate, e.g., using a device certificate, towards a device security service that maintains information about registered devices and their permissions. Furthermore, the device security service can issue and revoke device credentials (e.g., device certificate, authentication tokens).

In addition, a device data validation service can ensure that the device operation can be monitored, supporting also a continuous verification of the devices purpose. The validation service requests information about the IoT device supervisory data of supervised devices and checks it for validity using a configurable validation policy. Hence, the behavior of the main, regular functionality of the device can be monitored and checked for plausibility. Additionally, some arbitrary dummy functionality can be realized for monitoring purposes (e.g., predictable, pseudo-random virtual sensor measurement).

If a policy violation is detected, a corrective action is triggered: provide alarm message for display on a dash board (the alarm message can be injected in the device supervisory data set of the affected device maintained by the IoT backend platform). Furthermore, an alarm message can be sent to the IoT backend platform to terminate the communication session of the affected IoT device. Moreover, the device security service can be informed so that it can revoke the devices access permissions, or revoke the device authentication credential.

D. Authentication based on Device Capability

The authenticity of a control device can be verified by checking that a device can in fact perform a certain operation. The device is given an instruction to perform a certain test operation. It is checked that the device can perform a certain computation on provided test data: The device is given a set of input parameters (test data) and has to provide the correct result that is a valid result of the computation. The computational function could be a cryptographic puzzle involving a secret. The functionality can be realized by software/firmware on the control device, by a programmable hardware (FPGA), or by a periphery device (e.g., separate signal processor or IO device). Furthermore, it can be verified that a device can act on the expected physical environment (proofing that it has control on a certain effect in the physical world). The effect is observed by a separate sensor device. In an embodiment, the separate sensor device may provide an assertion.

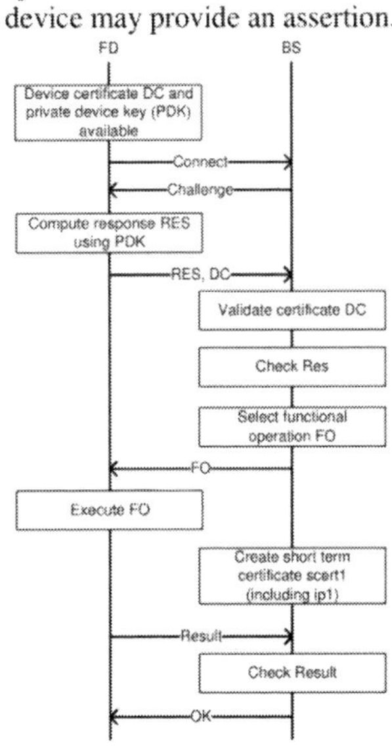

Figure 3. Verification of Device Capability

Fig. 3 shows a possible message exchange. The functional capability check is performed over a cryptographically authenticated communication link (e.g., transport layer security (TLS) protocol [25]). A device passes the authentication if both its cryptographic authentication is valid and its functional operation (FO) is verified successfully. For a successful attack, where a fake device is to be accepted, it is not sufficient that the attacker has access to the used cryptographic key. In addition, the attacker has to realize the expected functionality of the real device.

An example for combining authentication and the property to control a specific environment can be given by the recently established letsencrypt [38] infrastructure. Here, a (web)server applies for an X.509 certificate to be used for authentication in the context of https connections made to the web server. The certificate will be issued once the server can prove that it controls the domain it is requesting a certificate for. The proof is provided by putting dedicated information onto a random address in the applying servers address space. If this information can be retrieved externally, the proof of control is provided.

III. Combined Device Authentications

This section describes various advanced options for device authentication where multiple device authentications are combined.

A. *Multi-Factor Device Authentication*

A device can support multiple independent authentications. These authentication options may be performed iteratively.

In particular, an initial cryptographic device authentication can be used to setup an authenticated communication session with an authentication server. Additional checks can be performed to complete the device authentication, e.g., in the scope of a specific application.

B. *Separate Re-authentication Connection*

In communication security, a secure session is established by an authentication and key agreement protocol (e.g., IKEv2, TLS authentication and key agreement). The authentication is typically performed for each communication session.

It is proposed that a single device has to set-up multiple authenticated communication sessions. The device has to re-authenticate regularly towards a backend system respectively a separate authentication server using a first communication session. If this is not done, the second communication session is terminated or blocked by the backend system. This realizes a form of continuous device authentication where a device is continuously re-authenticated during a communication session, but without degrading the main communication link for which delays and interruptions shall be avoided.

The second communication session can be used for real-time / delay sensitive control traffic. The communication session will often be established for a long time (e.g., months). The re-authentication of the device can be performed independently using a second communication session without interfering with the second communication session (interruptions, delays during re-authentication). Note that the different communication sessions may terminate at different points in the backend systems. Hence, besides the multiple authentication sessions from the device, there needs to by a synchronization of the authentication sessions in the backend.

Also, the re-authentication of the first connection may be used to create a dynamic cryptographic binding with a further (separate) security session. This property can be used, to ensure that the entities involved in a separate security session know, that there is a persistent first session with either the same entity or a different entity. This approach may be used for instance in publish/subscribe use cases to ensure, that there is a persistent connection with the publish/subscribe server, while actually having an end-to-end communication session between the clients.

C. *System Authentication*

In industrial control systems and the Internet of Things, often a set of field devices will be used to realize a system. It is proposed to check the authentication of a set of devices (system authentication) that have to authenticate towards a backend system. A single device is accepted as authenticated only as long as a defined set of associated devices, forming the system, authenticates as well (with plausible context of the devices, e.g., network connectivity, location). The devices may have a different criticality assigned to enable a distinction between necessary and optional devices.

The communication link of a device (as member of a group) is set to an active state (permission to send/receive data) only if all required devices of the group have authenticated successfully. Thereby, an attacker cannot perform a successful attack by setting up only a single fake device. A single device is accepted as authenticated only as long as a defined set of associated devices authenticates as well (with plausible context, e.g., network connectivity, location).

IV. Evaluation

The security of a cyber system can be evaluated in practice in various approaches and stages of the system's lifecycle:

- Threat and risk analysis (TRA) of cyber system
- Checks during operation to determine key performance indicators (e.g., check for compliance of device configurations).
- Security testing (penetration testing)

During the design phase of a cyber system, the security demand is determined, and the appropriateness of a security design is validated using a threat and risk analysis. Assets to be protected and possible threats are identified, and the risk is evaluated in a qualitative way depending on probability and impact of threats. The effectiveness of the proposed enhanced device authentication means can be reflected in a system TRA. The proposed enhancements to simple cryptographic device authentication can lead to a reduction of the probability and/or the impact of a threat, so that the overall risk for successful attacks is reduced.

Two exemplary threats affecting a device are given (using for this example a simple qualitative assessment metric of low/medium/high):

- An attacker obtains device authentication credential by attacking the authentication protocol (probability: medium, impact: high; risk: high).
- An attacker succeeds in exploiting an implementation vulnerability of a device to get root access to the device and manipulate the device functionality (probability: high, impact: high; risk: high).

With selected additional protection measures, the risk can be reduced to an acceptable level: A device authentication credential cannot be used by an attacker for a successful attack as the device credential alone does not allow for a successful device authentication. With functional verification of device capability, a manipulated device can be detected. For a successful attack, the attacker would have to ensure continuously the correct operation of the device as verified by the capability check, which increases the effort for the attacker. While in real-world attack models, it is never possible to prevent all attacks, the presented countermeasures help to increase the required effort for a successful, undetected attack.

V. Related Work

Authentication within the Internet of Things is an active area of research and development. Gupta described multi-factor authentication of users towards IoT devices [29]. The Cloud Security Alliance published recommendations on identity and access management within the IoT [30]. Ajit and Sunil describe challenged to IoT security and solution options. Authentication systems for IoT where analyzed by Borgohain, Borgohain, Kumar and Sanyal [32].

Al Ibrahim and Nair have combined multiple PUF elements into a combined system PUF [33].

An "automotive thin profile" of the Trusted Platform Module TPM 2.0 has been specified [34]. A vehicle is composed of multiple control units that are equipped with TPMs. A rich TPM manages a set of thin TPMs, so that the vehicle can be represented by a vehicle TPM to the external world.

For electric vehicle charging, a vehicle authentication scheme has been described by Chan and Zhou that involves two authentication challenges, sent over different communication links (wireless link, charging cable) to the electric vehicle.

Host-based intrusion detection systems (HIDS) as SAMHAIN [36] and OSSEC [37] analyze the integrity of hosts and report the results to a backend security monitoring system.

Continuous user authentication, i.e., the checking during a session whether the user is still the same as the authenticated one, has been described by [26] and [27].

VI. Conclusion

Robust and practical device authentication is an essential security feature for cyber physical systems and the Internet of Things. The security design principle of "defense in depth" basically means that multiple layers of defenses are designed. This design principle can not only be applied at the system level, but also at the level of a single security mechanism.

This paper proposed advanced device authentication means to increase the attack robustness of device authentication. A well-known cryptographic device authentication can be extended with additional validations to check the device identity. The paper described how ideas from advanced human user authentication like multi-factor authentication and continuous authentication can be applied to device authentication.

The consequent next step addresses the integration of a selection of enhanced authentication means as proof of concept to verify the concept as such and also the supremacy in comparison with single authentication schemes.

References

[1] R. Falk and S. Fries, "New Directions in Applying Physical Unclonable Functions", The Ninth International Conference on Emerging Security Information, Systems and Technologies (SECURWARE), pp. 31-36, 23-28 August 2015, Venice, Italy, Thinkmind, available from: https://www.thinkmind.org/index.php?view=article&articleid=securware_2015_2_20_30028, last access: January 2016

[2] IEC 62443, "Industrial Automation and Control System Security" (formerly ISA99), available from: http://isa99.isa.org/Documents/Forms/AllItems.aspx , last access: April 2016

[3] "IEEE Standard for Local and metropolitan area networks--Port-Based Network Access Control", IEEE standard, 802.1X-2010, available from https://standards.ieee.org/findstds/standard/802.1X-2010.html , last access April 2016

[4] G. Horn and P. Schneider, "Towards 5G Security", 14th IEEE International Conference on Trust, Security and Privacy in Computing and Communications (IEEE TrustCom-15), Helsinki, Finland, 20-22 August, 2015, available from http://networks.nokia.com/sites/default/files/document/conference_paper__towards_5g_security_.pdf , last access April 2016

[5] Wikipedia, "Security Assertion Markup Language", available from https://en.wikipedia.org/wiki/Security_Assertion_Markup_Language , last access April 2016

[6] J. Richer, "User Authentication with OAuth 2.0", available from http://oauth.net/articles/authentication/ , last access April 2016

[7] E. Gerck, "Overview of Certification Systems: X.509, CA, PGP and SKIP", MCG, 1998, available from http://mcwg.org/mcg-mirror/certover.pdf , last access April 2016

[8] L. O'Gorman, "Comparing passwords, tokens, and biometrics for user authentication", Proceedings of the IEEE, vol. 91, issue 12, pp. 2021 – 2040, 2003

[9] C. Herder, Y. Meng-Day, F. Koushanfar, and S. Devadas, "Physical Unclonable Functions and Applications: A Tutorial", Proceedings of the IEEE, vol. 102, nr. 8, pp. 1126-1141, Aug. 2014, available from:

http://ieeexplore.ieee.org/stamp/stamp.jsp?arnumber=6823677, last access: January 2015

[10] R. Falk and S. Fries, "Advances in Protecting Remote Component Authentication", International Journal on Advances in Security, vol 5, nr. 1-2, pp. 28-35, 2012, Available online: http://www.iariajournals.org/security/ , last access: April 2016

[11] A. Costin, J. Zaddach, A. Francillon, and D. Balzarotti, "A Large-Scale Analysis of the Security of Embedded Firmwares", 23rd USENIX Security Symposium, August 20–22, 2014, San Diego, CA, available from https://www.usenix.org/system/files/conference/usenixsecurity14/sec14-paper-costin.pdf , last access April 2016

[12] R. Santamarta, Identify Backdoors in Firmware By Using Automatic String Analysis, 2013, available from http://blog.ioactive.com/2013/05/identify-back-doors-in-firmware-by.html , last access April 2016

[13] J. A. Muir, "A Tutorial on White-box AES", Cryptology ePrint Archive, Report 2013/104, available from https://eprint.iacr.org/2013/104.pdf , last access: April 2016

[14] M. Balakrishnan, "Freescale Trust Computing and Security in the Smart Grid", Freescale white paper, document number: TRCMPSCSMRTGRDWP REV 1, 2013, available from http://cache.nxp.com/files/32bit/doc/white_paper/TRCMPSCSMRTGRDWP.pdf , last access April 2016

[15] Infineon, "Highly integrated and performance optimized 32-bit microcontrollers for automotive and industrial applications",2016, available from http://www.infineon.com/dgdl/TriCore_Family_BR-2016_web.pdf?fileId=5546d46152e4636f0152e59a1581001d

[16] ARM: "Building a Secure System using TrustZone Technology", ARM whitepaper PRD29-GENC-009492C, 2005 - 2009, available from http://infocenter.arm.com/help/topic/com.arm.doc.prd29-genc-009492c/PRD29-GENC-009492C_trustzone_security_whitepaper.pdf , last access April 2016

[17] Atmel, "ATECC508 Atmel CryptoAuthentication Device", summary datasheet, 2015, available from http://www.atmel.com/images/atmel-8923s-cryptoauth-atecc508a-datasheet-summary.pdf , last access April 2016

[18] Infineon, "Optiga Trust E SLS32AIA", product brief, 2016 available from http://www.infineon.com/dgdl/Infineon-OPTIGA%E2%84%A2+Trust+E+SLS+32AIA-PB-v02_16-EN.pdf?fileId=5546d4624e765da5014eaabac63f5a38

[19] Infineon, "SOLID FLASH™ SLE 97 Family", product brief, 2012, available from http://www.infineon.com/dgdl/Infineon-SOLID_FLASH_SLE_97_Family_32-bit_High_Performance-PB-v08_12-EN.pdf?fileId=db3a30433917ea3301392ec288fc4ff0 , last access April 2016

[20] Trusted Computing Group: "TPM Main Specification", Version 1.2, , available from http://www.trustedcomputinggroup.org/resources/tpm_main_specification , last access April 2016

[21] Trusted Computing Group, "Trusted Platform Module Library Specification, Family 2.0", 2014, available from http://www.trustedcomputinggroup.org/resources/tpm_library_specification , last access April 2016

[22] K. Pahlavan, et al., "Taking Positioning Indoors, Wi-Fi Localization and GNSS", InsideGNSS, pp. 40-47, May 2010, available from http://www.insidegnss.com/auto/may10-Pahlavan.pdf , last access April 2016

[23] B. Parno, " Bootstrapping Trust in a Trusted Platform", 3rd USENIX Workshop on Hot Topics in Security, July 2008, available from http://www.usenix.org/event/hotsec08/tech/full_papers/parno/parno_html/ , last access: April 2016

[24] M. Braun, E. Hess, and B. Meyer, "Using Elliptic Curves on RFID Tags," International Journal of Computer Science and Network Security, vol. 2, pp. 1-9, February 2008

[25] T. Dierks and E. Rescorla, "The Transport Layer Security (TLS) Protocol Version 1.2", RFC 5246, Aug. 2008, available from http://tools.ietf.org/html/rfc5246 , last access: April 2016

[26] H. Xu, Y. Zhou, and M. R. Lyu: Towards Continuous and Passive Authentication via Touch Biometrics: An Experimental Study on Smartphones, Symposium on Usable Privacy and Security (SOUPS) 2014, July 9–11, 2014, Menlo Park, CA, available from: https://www.usenix.org/system/files/conference/soups2014/soups14-paper-xu.pdf , last access: April 2016

[27] K. Niinuma and A. K. Jain, "Continuous User Authentication Using Temporal Information", available from http://biometrics.cse.msu.edu/Publications/Face/NiinumaJain_ContinuousAuth_SPIE10.pdf , last access: April 2016

[28] N. Costigan and I. Deutschmann, DARPA's Active Authentication program, RSA Conference Asia Pacific 2013 available from https://www.rsaconference.com/writable/presentations/file_upload/sec-t05_final.pdf , last access: April 2016

[29] U. Gupta, "Application of Multi factor authentication in Internet of Things domain: multi-factor authentication of users towards IoT devices, Cornell university arXiv:1506.03753, 2015, available from: http://arxiv.org/ftp/arxiv/papers/1506/1506.03753.pdf , last access: April 2016

[30] A. Mordeno and B. Russel, "Identity and Access Management for the Internet of Things - Summary Guidance", Cloud Security Alliance, 2015, available from: https://downloads.cloudsecurityalliance.org/assets/research/internet-of-things/identity-and-access-management-for-the-iot.pdf , last access: April 2016

[31] J. Ajit and M.C. Suni, "Security considerations for Internet of Things", L&T Technology Services, 2014, http://www.lnttechservices.com/media/30090/whitepaper_security-considerations-for-internet-of-things.pdf

[32] T. Borgohain, A. Borgohain, U. Kumar, and S. Sanyal, "Authentication Systems in Internet of Things", Int. J. Advanced Networking and Applications, vol. 6, issue 4, pp. 2422-2426, 2015, available from http://www.ijana.in/papers/V6I4-11.pdf , last access: April 2016

[33] O. Al Ibrahim and S. Nair, "Cyber-Physical Security Using System-Level PUFs", 7th International Wireless Communications and Mobile Computing Conference (IWCMC), 2011, available from http://lyle.smu.edu/~nair/ftp/research_papers_nair/CyPhy11.pdf , last access: April 2016

[34] Trusted Computing Group, "TCG TPM 2.0 Automotive Thin Profile", level 00, version 1.0, 2015, available from http://www.trustedcomputinggroup.org/resources/tcg_tpm_20_library_profile_for_automotivethin , last access: April 2016

[35] A. C-F. Chan and J. Zhou, "Cyber-Physical Device Authentication for Smart Grid Electric Vehicle Ecosystem", IEEE Journal on Selected Areas in Communications, vol. 32, issue 7, pp. 1509 – 1517, 2014

[36] R. Wichmann, "The Samhain HIDS", fact sheet, 2011, available from http://la-samhna.de/samhain/samhain_leaf.pdf, last access April 2016

[37] OSSEC, "Open Source HIDS SECurity", web site, 2010 - 2015, available from http://ossec.github.io/ , last access April 2016

[38] Letsencrypt, letsencrypt.org, last access April 2016

AUTHOR INDEX

Azhar, M A Hannan Bin 35
Barton, Thomas Edward Allen 35
Choi, Iksu 54
Costeira, Ricardo 17
Duncan, Martin L 7
Falk, Rainer 69
Fries, Steffen 69
Gimler, Greg 11
Happe, Andreas 50
Jeon, Yongsung 67
Kim, Daewon 67
Kim, Hunmo 54
Kim, Hyeonwoo 54
Kim, Hyunki 27
Kim, Jeongnyeo 67
Klemas, Thomas 1, 11
Klemas, Thomas J. 7
Kübler, Sandra 29
Lee, Jaegwang 54
Loruenser, Thomas 50
Massoth, Michael 29
Nam, Janggeol 54
Nelson, John 11
Rinjes, Christian 29
Rossey, Lee 1
Santos, Henrique 17
Song, Buchun 54
Tebekaemi, Eniye 41
Weil, Paul D. 7
Wiens, Anton 29
Wijesekera, Duminda 41
Yee, George O. M. 60
Yi, Jeong Hyun 27
Yoo, Joonsang 27

International Academy, Research,
and Industry Association (IARIA)
412 Derby Way
Wilmington, DE 19810

ISBN 978-1-5108-3092-9

CURRAN ASSOCIATES INC.
proceedings.com